101 Internet Businesses You Can Start From Home

Second Edition

Other Titles of Interest From Maximum Press

Top e-business Books

- *101 Ways to Promote Your Web Site*

- *3G Marketing on the Internet*

- *Protecting Your Great Ideas for FREE*

- and many more...

For more information go to *www.maxpress.com/ibmpromo1*
or e-mail us at *moreinfo@maxpress.com*

101 Internet Businesses You Can Start From Home

Second Edition

How to Choose and Build Your Own Successful e-Business

Susan Sweeney

MAXIMUM PRESS
605 Silverthorn Road
Gulf Breeze, FL 32561
(850) 934-0819
www.maxpress.com

Publisher: Jim Hoskins

Manager of Finance/Administration: Joyce Reedy

Production Manager: Gina Cooke

Cover Designer: Lauren Smith

Copyeditor: Ellen Falk

Proofreader: Jacquie Wallace

Indexer: Susan Olason

Printer: P.A. Hutchison

This publication is designed to provide accurate and authoritative information in regard to the subject matter covered. It is sold with the understanding that the publisher is not engaged in rendering professional services. If legal, accounting, medical, psychological, or any other expert assistance is required, the services of a competent professional person should be sought. ADAPTED FROM A DECLARATION OF PRINCIPLES OF A JOINT COMMITTEE OF THE AMERICAN BAR ASSOCIATION AND PUBLISHERS.

Library of Congress Cataloging-in-Publication Data

Sweeney, Susan, 1956-
101 Internet businesses you can start from home : how to choose and build your own successful e-business / Susan Sweeney. — 2nd ed.
    p. cm.
ISBN 1-931644-48-9 (pbk.)
1. Home-based businesses. 2. New business enterprises. 3. Internet. 4. Electronic commerce. I. Title. II. Title: One hundred one Internet businesses you can start from home. III. Title: One hundred and one Internet businesses you can start from home.
HD62.38.S94 2007
658.8'72—dc22
                    2006021704

Acknowledgements

Many, many, many thanks to my great team at Verb Interactive (*http://www.verbinteractive.com*)—Ed Dorey and Andy MacLellan, who have been with me since their university days, and our whole team of Internet marketing experts.

Thanks to Maureen Welsman for all the help with this edition of *101 Internet Businesses You Can Start From Home*.

The Internet is a fascinating, vast, and publicly accessible resource from which we can learn a great deal. I'd like to thank all those people who share their information so freely on the Net through such sites as Wilson Web (*www.wilsonweb.com*) by Dr. Ralph Wilson, SearchEngineWatch by Danny Sullivan, and newsletters such as I-Search by Detlev Johnson.

Many thanks to my large network of experts whom I know I can always call to get the latest scoop on what's really happening. Joe Mauro of inBox360.com and Ken Teeter of nTarget.com are always extremely knowledgeable and helpful in terms of the ever-changing world of private mail list marketing.

Thanks to Jim Hoskins, Gina Cooke, and Joyce Reedy at Maximum Press. This is our eleventh book together. It's always a pleasure to work with you. One of these days we're going to have to meet face to face!

Special thanks to my absolutely wonderful husband, Miles, who makes all things possible. I wouldn't be able to do what I do if not for you. Also thanks to our three amazing children—Kaitlyn, Kara, and Andrew—for their love, encouragement, and support. Love you more than the last number!

Special thanks to mom and dad, Olga and Leonard Dooley, for always being there and for instilling in me the confidence to know that I can do anything to which I set my mind. It's amazing what can be done when you "know you can."

Disclaimer

This book is not intended to replace the manufacturer's product documentation or personnel in determining the specifications and capabilities of the products mentioned in this book. The manufacturer's product documentation should always be consulted, as the specifications and capabilities of computer hardware and software products are subject to frequent modification. The reader is solely responsible for the choice of computer hardware and software. All configurations and applications of computer hardware and software should be reviewed with the manufacturer's representatives prior to choosing or using any computer hardware and software.

Trademarks

The words contained in this text which are believed to be trademarked, service marked, or otherwise to hold proprietary rights have been designated as such by use of initial capitalization. No attempt has been made to designate as trademarked or service marked any personal computer words or terms in which proprietary rights might exist. Inclusion, exclusion, or definition of a word or term is not intended to affect, or to express judgment upon, the validity of legal status of any proprietary right which may be claimed for a specific word or term.

Your "Members Only" Web Site

The Internet world changes every day. That's why there is a companion Web site associated with this book. On this site you will find updates to the book and other Web site promotion resources of interest. However, you have to be a member of the "101 Internet Businesses Insiders' Club" to gain access to this site.

When you purchased this book, you automatically became a member (in fact, that's the only way to join), so you now have full privileges. To get into the "Members Only" section of the companion Web site, go to the Maximum Press Web site located at *www.maxpress.com* and follow the links to the "101 Internet Businesses" area. From there you will see a link to the "101 Internet Businesses Insiders' Club" section. When you try to enter, you will be asked for a user ID and password. Type in the following:

- For your user ID, enter: *101Inte2e*

- For your password, enter: *space*

You will then be granted full access to the "Members Only" area. Visit the site often and enjoy the updates and resources with our compliments—and thanks again for buying the book. We ask that you not share the user ID and password for this site with anyone else.

Susan Sweeney's Internet Marketing Mail List

You are also invited to join Susan Sweeney's Internet Marketing Bi-weekly Internet Marketing Tips, Tools, Techniques, and Resources Newsletter at *www.susansweeney.com.*

Table of Contents

Part 2
101 Profiles of Top Internet Business Concepts   18

Introduction

Internet Business—The Opportunity of Our Lifetime

Communicating with customers and other businesses has changed dramatically over the past century. It started with print, then radio, television, phone, and fax, and now all of us are operating in the fastest medium yet—the Internet. The future is bright for businesses that utilize the Net as a primary medium of communication and sales.

The number of Internet users and the amount of business done online around the world is growing at a staggering rate. The world's population currently holds well over 1 billion Internet users, and the majority of these web-savvy humans have online access at home. They research, study, e-mail, chat, download podcasts, and shop online.

Why question the amazing rate at which the average business is moving onto the Net? It makes too much sense to deny the obvious answer. Having a business online is the opportunity of our lifetime. Besides the greatly expanded market reach afforded by the Net, there is also the reduced cost of doing business online. Look at all the time, money, trees, and travel costs that are spared from the average business's operating budget due to this new medium. The collective business world realizes the bounty of opportunity to be seized in cyberspace.

All businesses that have a Web presence are seeing the advantages of selling online. They are committing more and more of their marketing dollars to online activities, where they are seeing a greater return on investment.

Expansion of the Internet into all business and personal communications is inevitable. What was once considered a trend is becoming the norm. Overall familiarity and trust in online transactions and consumer relationships improve each month as new security-based technologies are developed. New media support groups hasten the learning curve of the average Internet user, a factor that earlier had hindered the speed at which consumers feel confident enough in their own understanding of the Web to make money-related decisions based on their own online research. The time is now for everyone to get online. In our lifetime, "newbies" will cease to exist.

The future is really bright, so put on your shades and a thinking cap! Hot items are software, music, books, electronics, and travel. Broadening the gamut of goods sold online will happen quickly.

The opportunity is there for you to create a dynamite business online if you do it right. It's not a matter of throwing a Web site together, putting it online, and having the world beat a path to your door. You have to choose the right business, develop the right Web site for your target market, and build substantial traffic to your Web site. The online customer is extremely demanding, with expectations that exceed those of the offline buyer in many ways. Online buyers want what they want, how they want it, when they want it, at the right price. The product and service must be exactly what they ordered, delivered immediately to the correct place and for the lowest price they can find. Competition is fierce, so you have to create a professional and secure online presence for your business, target the demographic of Internet users with an affinity for your product or service, and work diligently to attract traffic. Serious marketing research is required to successfully access and captivate these eyeballs.

It's a challenge, but the opportunity is substantial. Many who have gone before you are reaping the benefits today. This book will provide you with a myriad of online business ideas for your consideration.

Defining What's Important to You

"What are the benefits of this new age?" you ask. Today and in the future, personal lifestyle plays a significant part in career choice. Perhaps you have no inclination to commute in traffic each working day. Maybe you want more time with your family. If your dream is to be self-employed, this is your era!

Run a successful global business from an island in the Caribbean or from the comfort of your living room. Hours are flexible, and the business is operational 24 hours a day, all year round. No matter how small your business is, if you set it up correctly, you can compete with the big boys.

Before embarking on an e-business venture, it is very important that you very clearly define your objectives. Take your time—brainstorm with family and friends. Find out what's really important to you, and then find a business that you can build that will help you achieve those objectives. Starting a business, online or offline, is serious business. Without adequate preparation in defining your objectives, researching for the best business for you, and then developing an adequate business plan, you are asking for problems.

When you are defining your objectives, you will have to ask yourself a series of pertinent questions. What type of time commitment do you foresee?

Do you want this to be a full-time or a part-time endeavor? The options are wide open. Many online businesses are ideal for extra income to leverage your regular salary and make the budget of daily life easier to manage. The beauty of working online is that it's sustainable without having to quit your regular job if you don't want to. The point is that you should allocate in your business plan how much time you are willing to spend on the venture, and then you can decide which online businesses fit with the time you are willing to invest.

Would you prefer to work out of your home or have an outside office? Where you work is important too. For many, a major benefit of having an online business is the luxury of working from home. Another advantage is to work while you travel or from remote areas. Not all online businesses guarantee complete mobility and staying home, but you can decide on these critical lifestyle options before choosing which specific online avenue to pursue. It's all up to you—for a change.

If you already have a physical "bricks-and-mortar" business location, do you want to use the Web as a marketing outlet? There are many ways to run a successful online business. Traditional storefronts and catalogues can be mirrored on the Web site, which expands the sales capacity significantly, *but* you must make sure that there is enough inventory and internal organization to accept, fill, and deliver incoming orders. The other option if you have an existing bricks-and-mortar setup is to use the Web site as a responsive marketing force and information source for your business. The design and content should urge customers to come to your location and return to your site.

What kind of start-up costs are you considering? Budget is everything. Research the investment you will have to put into the Web site. Ask around to see how much people are spending on their online presence, and remember that you can grow gradually as funds and profits permit with an online business. There is no rule saying you have to spend everything you've got in the beginning to succeed in the long term.

Would you like to develop an idea and sell it, or sustain the management and grow the business in the future?

Want to run your business from home but not have to be there 24/7 to answer the phone? No problem! For every challenge there is an opportunity. There are companies that will answer and screen your calls based on scripts you provide, provide information to your callers, take your orders and messages, and offer a whole myriad of professional and personal services; they can even screen and respond to your e-mail and fax messages, do research for you, and provide a ton of administrative services. One such company that I am affiliated with is PatLive. I have arranged a special deal for any of my readers who are interested in this service—go to *http://www.patlive.com/signup/ssc* for this special offer if this is something you might be interested in.

What is your risk comfort level? Trying anything new is slightly nervy. Just remember that if you embark on the online journey now, you share a common technology learning curve with those who remember what it was like before the Internet existed. Soon this group will be extinct, so this is the time to go for it!

What are your revenue and profit expectations? (Fun question, isn't it?) How rich do you want to be? Seriously, there is huge potential for major profit in online business. While picking the right virtual business for you, make sure to factor in the start-up costs and continuing operating costs. Begin with a modest revenue projection (to stay on the safe side), and if the result pleases you, stick with it.

Do you want employees, or are you looking for a business you can start and maintain on your own? If you are planning to have a staff to run your business, how many are you comfortable with? Employees are an added responsibility. If the online business you choose to enter requires employees, make sure you are prepared. What do you know? What are you comfortable with? What do you enjoy? If you are going to be spending lots of hours in your new e-business, it might as well be doing something you enjoy.

Once these questions have been answered and you have done a lot of soul-searching with regard to defining your objectives, it is time to take a closer look at all the e-business opportunities that are available to you. The next chapter offers this closer look.

Part 1

Doing Business Online

The term *e-business* means different things to different people. To some, e-business is simply having a Web site and e-mail capability through which customers can place an order, request a quote, or make a reservation. For other people, e-business is having a Web site that enables customers to order and submit their credit card information online, even though their orders may then be processed manually just like a fax or telephone order. For others still, e-business means being able to place a secure online order, having immediate credit card verification, and having fully integrated back-end systems that are dynamically updated and inform the customer of the latest prices and whether or not an item is in stock. The point is, the appropriate e-business solution for you will depend on the type of business you operate, the products and services you intend to sell, your budget, your target market, what your competition is doing, and so on.

For instance, a software development company that sells a downloadable software application (i.e., has no physical boxed version) has no inventory per se. Therefore, they would not require a back-end inventory database to be integrated with their e-business system. All they might need is an e-business system that includes payment processing capability. On the other hand, if you have an online business that intends to sell books and you want to become the next Amazon.com, you will require a full-blown, full-featured e-business system to compete with the Amazon.coms of the world. Otherwise, potential customers will shop at Amazon.com because their e-business system is more convenient and easier to use. In this chapter we discuss the features of e-business sites, online storefront options, taking online payments, and selecting the right e-business model for your online business.

Getting the Point Across

The consumer is king. This statement is especially true in the e-business realm. For instance, if you were to visit an offline bookstore to do your holiday shopping, you might browse through the aisles for a few hours, pick out a few books you wanted to buy, and take them to the cashier to pay for them. If you asked the cashier whether the bookstore offered gift-wrapping or shipping services, the response from the vendor would probably be "no, we don't provide those services." You would be satisfied with this and make the purchase anyway. You would then take the gifts home, wrap them, and ship them to their various destinations.

If you are making the same gift purchases in an online bookstore, you expect to be able to have them gift-wrapped and delivered to any address you desire. It defeats the purpose somewhat if you have to pay to have the books delivered to your address, only to turn around and pay to ship them someplace else. If you are purchasing the books as gifts, you want to have them gift-wrapped. Again, it defeats the purpose if you have to have the books sent to your address so that you can gift-wrap them and then reship.

Online it's a whole different world. Consumers have higher expectations. Often they shop online for the convenience and expect the online merchant to meet all their needs. Consumers expect the online merchant to deliver what they want, when they want it, and how they want it. If you don't provide what they want the way they want it, another vendor is just a click away.

Not all possible features of an e-business site are applicable to every business, but if you intend to be competitive online, you must give your consumers what they are looking for. You might have something they want, but if they cannot conduct transactions easily on your site and competitors offer more point-of-sale service, people will leave your site and shop at another site that is easier to buy from. This section focuses on some possible e-business features that you might want to include on your site. Decide which features are most applicable to your business and implement them into your e-business system.

Storefront Development Options

Depending on your online objectives, your products and services, and your budget, you might have to develop an electronic storefront for your business.

An electronic storefront is the interface that a customer sees when purchasing goods on a Web site. The need for an electronic storefront varies with the level of e-business that your company chooses to implement. The various levels of e-business are discussed in more detail later in this chapter.

When developing a storefront for your business, you have three options available. You can

- Use the ASP (Application Service Provider) model

- Purchase storefront development software

- Program and develop your own storefront.

Each option has its strengths and weaknesses, and some are more appropriate than others, depending on your business's budget and online marketing objectives. In determining how to develop an electronic storefront for your business, you should evaluate the following options and select the one that is most appropriate for your business.

ASP Storefront Model

ASP stands for Application Service Provider. The ASP owns the storefront software and operates its own e-commerce server. An ASP licenses out the use of its software and e-commerce hosting services to clients that desire to sell products and services online. The software is hosted on the ASP's server, and as the client you pay the ASP to use its software and server. This option is often much cheaper than purchasing your own storefront software package.

When using the ASP's storefront solution, a client can be quite confident in the fact that the system will always be up to date. The ASP's server handles all system updates, back-ups, and technical support on a regular basis. There is no need for a business to purchase any extra on-site equipment or software, and the installation process is fast, straightforward, and affordable.

The ASP's storefront solution can be integrated with your existing Web site. The portion of the storefront that is hosted on the ASP's server can be customized to duplicate the appearance of your site. This adds to the level of professionalism and maintains a sense of consistency across all pages of your site and the purchase process.

The ASP's storefront model is known for its high reliability, as well as an unfailing online selling security system. A great benefit of using an ASP's server is that business owners are able to access their data from any place, at any time. The only equipment needed is an Internet connection as well as your ASP server ID and password.

Each client is given a unique user name and password to allow for easy management of its account. The information hosted on the ASP's server can be modified at any time—you can add or remove products at your convenience, alter the layout, and so on.

This solution is ideal for those businesses that are looking to maintain their own site but do not want to be responsible for configuring and maintaining the technical aspects of the e-commerce system. The ASP model is easy to configure for those individuals with limited HTML knowledge and can be set up and running in a very short timeframe. For more information on a few great examples of ASP storefront applications, go to the Internet Marketing Resources section of my site at *http://www.susansweeney.com/resources.html*.

Storefront Software Packages

There are a variety of storefront software development packages available that enable you to develop your online storefront for your business. If you choose to use this approach, more technical knowledge of computers will be required and you will have to find an Internet service provider to host your electronic storefront.

Storefront software is commonly installed on the same server as your site. This can be a more involved process, and in some cases it may be necessary to hire a person with the appropriate technical knowledge to set up and maintain your storefront. Many medium-sized to large businesses have their own in-house team to manage their e-business operations, so this is not an issue for them. Do some research on features needed and select the storefront option that best fits your business requirements.

Program and Develop Your Own Storefront

If you have a broad product line, a complex system with different prices for different customers, or volume discount levels, or if you want a high level of integration with your accounting, inventory, and sales systems, you may want to consider developing your own storefront. This requires in-depth technical knowledge and programming capabilities. If you don't have the technical capability in-house, you can outsource this activity to a firm capable of developing such a program for your business or hire an employee or team to handle the storefront development.

If you decide to develop your own storefront software, you should ensure that everything is running smoothly before you launch the storefront into cyberspace. Every aspect of the storefront selection and purchasing procedure should be tested and retested to ensure that there are no bugs, miscalculations, or errors in the process. Once you are sure that everything is working correctly and smoothly, you then have to find a place to host the storefront, whether it be on your own server or on an ISP's server. From that point on, your only recurring expense is that of hosting your storefront and payment processing and authorization charges from a payment processing company.

Storefront Features

There are many different features available with different electronic storefronts. Features vary depending on the storefront option that you have selected. Typically, higher-end software has more advanced features than that of a template service; however, some of these features may not be essential to running your particular online business. The following is a list of features that you should consider when selecting your storefront development option for your online business:

- Shopping cart

- Purchase notification

- Inventory management integration

- Client database management

- Integrated mail list

- Searchable product database

- Thumbnail image capability

- Customer e-mail notification

- Unlimited autoresponders

- Shipping and delivery options

- Coupons, discounts, and special offers

- Technical support

- Affiliate programs.

Shopping Cart

An electronic shopping cart is an excellent feature for sites selling multiple products or services. The online shopping cart system operates much like an actual shopping cart. Buyers can add items to their cart as they please, and they can remove items just as easily. As the customers add and subtract items from their shopping cart, a running total of their purchase choices is dynamically updated. This is a great feature that shouldn't be overlooked when you choose your storefront software.

Purchase Notification

This software feature enables merchants to be notified via e-mail whenever a purchase is made on their Web site. The e-mail typically states the product purchased, the purchaser's contact information, and the credit card information. This feature is terrific if you use offline methods (e.g., the telephone) to authorize credit card purchases. You can simply pull up the e-mail message on your screen and call in to receive an authorization number.

Inventory Management Integration

Does the software enable you to integrate the storefront with your back-end system? Back-end systems refer to the company's internal accounting, inventory, contact management, customer service, and other supporting software systems. This is a fantastic feature for companies selling multiple products online. By integrating the back end with your storefront, you can track inventory levels to (1) ensure that you don't run out of a certain product or (2) notify customers that you are out of stock before they make a purchase. More information on integrating your back-end systems with your storefront is explained later in this chapter.

Client Database Management

A client database is essential to any business that would like to keep track of the people utilizing its site. This includes all users who interact in some way with your site, either by filling out one of your forms, becoming an affiliate of yours, or purchasing something through the shopping cart. All users will have a record of their actions in your client database. You can find out information such as who bought a particular product, who is subscribed to a particular newsletter, the time a client has been added to your database, and so on. Once a search is conducted, you will get a list of all clients and their online actions on your site. With this list, you are able to create a customized mailing list.

Integrated Mail List

Many ASP storefront solutions integrate private mail list software with their application. It just makes sense that when someone makes a purchase, they might like to give permission for you to send them your e-zine or newsletter, your e-specials, or coupons. The mail list application should be able to be fully integrated with your Web site and should provide good tracking and management reports. Today it is essential that mail list software have an integrated spam checker so that your mail can have the best chance of getting through to the intended recipients.

Searchable Product Database

Practically a necessity for companies selling hundreds of products online, this feature enables a consumer to visit your site and search through your database of product listings. Normally consumers will know what they want when they visit your site, so offering this feature will enable them to go directly to the product SKU (stock keeping unit) they want, rather than searching through multiple pages trying to find the product. An SKU is similar to the ISBN number you find on the back of books—it is a numerical value that identifies an individual product.

Thumbnail Image Capability

Your storefront software should enable you to place small thumbnail images of the products next to their listing. The user can then click on the image to enlarge it and see a better view of the product. This enhances the overall listing for each of your products in your storefront. Thumbnails also assist in optimizing your site's download time. It takes much less time to download several thumbnail 2K images as opposed to several full-sized 50K images.

Customer E-mail Notification

This feature enables you to automatically send your clients an e-mail directly after they purchase an item on your Web site. The message will confirm that you have received their order, and you can also take the time to thank them for doing business with your company. This is a great way to provide quality customer service to your clients.

Unlimited Autoresponders

An autoresponder is a customized e-mail notification with a few added features. Autoresponders can be used for different purposes, and you can send an unlimited number of sequential messages. For example, you might have one general autoresponder for all your customers and a few more-detailed autoresponders for customers who purchase a particular product. This way you can ensure a great follow-up for future repeat sales. By using this method you can offer classes with the lessons delivered by autoresponder e-mails once per week, as well as train your affiliates on up-and-coming news with your business. An autoresponder can be set to go out over a period of time and be composed of one or more messages. Autoresponders are becoming a very powerful Internet marketing tool.

Shipping and Delivery Options

Another way to provide excellent customer service is by offering different shipment options to your clients. This feature enables your customers to select a shipping option that best suits their needs during the checkout period, when they are finalizing their order on your Web site. Some people like to receive their purchases in the mail sooner than others. By offering a variety of shipping and delivery options, you have an opportunity to up-sell, utilizing different price points for different delivery periods. You could set a specific price point for each of your delivery options, which may include "next day," "two or three days," "surface, one to two weeks," and so on. In addition, some customers may prefer to send individual items to separate locations—perhaps they are doing their Christmas shopping. Giving the user the option to send each item to a different location is a great feature to include.

Coupons, Discounts, and Special Offers

Many storefront solutions provide the ability to offer discounts, accept coupons, and provide for special deals to generate urgency to drive up your sales.

Technical Support

Above all, whether you purchase storefront development software or choose to use a template service, you should always ensure that the service provider has excellent customer support. If you have any problems with your storefront, you should be able to call and receive immediate assistance to remedy your problem. Downtime or malfunctions in your storefront can hinder your business's professionalism, so you should have the best technical support available to help you solve any problem you may encounter.

Affiliate Programs

A major challenge for new Internet businesses is how to drive traffic to their site. Some possible shoppers come to your site; they look around and really like what they are seeing. On your Web site you have a "Join Our Affiliates Program" link. They click on it, fill out a quick form, and choose a user name and password. They then will receive an e-mail with instructions and access to referral URLs. Once they have the URLs, they must send their prospects to your site either through outbound e-mail or via links from their own Web site. Along the way, your new site viewers will get tagged as having been referred by the affiliate. If they become customers and make a purchase, the affiliate will be credited with the sale. Both you and your affiliate can see this in the order record, using a login page with a full history of all their commissions. Affiliates are wonderful because they send traffic your way, and you pay them only for paid customers.

Payment Processing Methods

One of the key components of doing business online is the ability to take payment for goods and services online. Essentially, taking payment online involves the ability to successfully transfer payment from the buyer to your bank account. There are a number of factors you need to be aware of before venturing out and developing your online business. The main form of payment online is the credit card, which is the focus of this section. Currently 95 percent of all purchases online are made using credit cards.

The Advantages of Taking Online Payments

The ability to take payment for goods and services online presents several significant advantages to you as a business owner. Many Internet users expect speed and convenience. They want what they want, when they want it. By offering Internet shoppers the ability to make a purchase and pay for it online, you're helping to facilitate their needs and desires. You're enabling them to make their purchase at any time of day or night. Basically, your online storefront is open for business 24 hours a day, 7 days a week, 365 days a year. By allowing users to purchase goods and services online, you're allowing them to pay for items on their own terms as well. Independence and freedom play a role. Users are able to make purchases on their own without any reliance on another individual. They do not need to wait for the assistance of a sales associate to make their purchase, they do not need to wait an extensive period of time for approval of their purchase because everything is automated, and they do not need to write down a phone number or other information to contact someone to make their purchase. It's on their terms, and they like that.

Automated online payment processing can benefit your business in the form of reduced costs. You do not need to pay someone to process your transactions, and you do not need to pay to produce paper invoices and statements. Think of the additional time automated online payment processing can save you as well. You or an employee will not have to spend time processing payments yourself. Your time will be free to be better used on more important business matters.

Having your site set up to take online payments portrays a professional image and boosts the credibility of your operation in the eyes of the consumer. It shows that you have taken the time and have invested the money to develop a well-run operation.

You may experience increased sales. Why? Many of the purchases made online are impulse buys. Living up to consumer expectations is key to your success!

Acquire an Internet Merchant Account

Before you can accept credit card payments online, you need to acquire an appropriate Internet merchant account. (Your other option is to utilize that of third parties, which we discuss later.) A merchant account allows you to accept payment for goods and services. You may be saying to yourself, "I already have a merchant account" if you currently operate a business; however, you will need a merchant account that allows you to take payment over the Internet, and you will need a merchant account for each credit card you plan to accept. To get an Internet merchant account or to change your merchant account to the correct type, you must contact your financial institution or bank.

When you approach your financial institution for a merchant account, you will have to prove to them that you deserve it and that you are a safe investment. They will want to know a significant amount of detail about your online business, but the most important issue is your credit history. Your type of business (products and services you offer), the length of time you have been in business, and your existing relationship with the financial institution will influence their decision on whether or not to issue you an Internet merchant account. They will likely also want to know how you plan to process transactions, what your payment processing company of choice is, and so on. They may ask you to provide details of how an actual transaction on your Web site will work.

Doing business on the Internet is significantly different from doing business at a traditional bricks-and-mortar storefront location because the credit card and the cardholder are not present at the point of sale. Some banks have no problems issuing an Internet merchant account because as far as they are concerned, it's just like any other sale where the transaction does not take place at the point of sale (e.g., a mail-order catalogue). On the other hand, some banks are a little uneasy when it comes to doing business online and will be hesitant to issue you a merchant account for such transactions. In fact, they may not be willing to work with you at all, in which case you will have to approach another financial institution for assistance.

Because there is a higher perceived risk with doing business over the Internet, the issuing financial institution may present you with a higher discount rate. Feel free to talk to other banks and find out their feelings on online business—you may be able to get a lower discount rate. Those banks that are accepting of home and mail-order businesses generally tend to be more accepting of online businesses and will likely offer a better discount rate. A discount rate is simply a percentage fee of each transaction charged to the merchant, based on the perceived risk. The higher the risk, the higher the discount rate.

In addition to the discount rate, you will be responsible for various other fees. There may be an account application or setup fee, a per-transaction fee, a monthly fee, a statement fee, support fees, and possibly other related fees. Make sure you cover these details with your financial institution! One financial institution may require a security deposit of up to 20 percent of annual sales before it is willing to issue you an Internet merchant account; another may have you set up and operational in 24 hours.

You can opt to use a third-party alternative, also known as an Internet payment service. One such company is PayPal (*http://www.paypal.com*). PayPal is a quick alternative to having your own merchant account. The main advantage of using another company's Internet merchant account is that you avoid a lot of the hassle of getting and setting up your own Internet merchant account. The third party will let you use theirs for a fee. Like the bank, there will be various fees such as setup fees and transaction fees. These fees are sometimes more than those of having your own merchant account because you're paying for the privilege of using someone else's account. The choice is yours as to whether you use a third-party company or acquire your own Internet merchant account, but base your decision on your needs and objectives.

What Level of E-business Is Appropriate for You?

E-business involves having the right e-business model, the right Web site, and the right volume of targeted traffic to your site. When developing your e-business strategy, you have to take into account your online objectives, your budget or financial position, and the size and type of operation you run. The extent of your e-business strategy relates directly to these criteria. For some businesses it is not necessary to develop a fully integrated e-business strategy because it is not required in day-to-day business. Nonetheless, it is important to understand your e-business needs before you implement your e-business strategy. Additional costs not discussed within each level of e-business include the design and hosting of your Web site as well as any costs associated with the promotion of your products or services.

E-business Level 1—Interactive Order Taking

The introductory level is the most basic form of conducting e-business. It consists of the ability to take orders or reservations through e-mail or via an online form on your Web site. You will find this level of e-business used by newcomers to the online business realm who have a low budget and little to worry about with respect to inventory, as well as by businesses that cannot put a specific price on a product or service. For example, an engineering or marketing firm often cannot put a standard price on their services, as this is decided on a case-by-case situation, but they do encourage the site visitor to request a proposal or to contact the firm about their services. These businesses must communicate extensively with their target market about their needs and objectives in order to determine the extent of work required before agreeing to do a project for a certain value.

The primary advantage of this level of e-business is that it allows the business to conduct business online with minimal effort. The business does not need to worry about selecting and setting up an e-commerce software package, finding and paying to use a payment-processing company, or ensuring that all of its online and offline systems are integrated and working properly. A bed-and-breakfast operation may choose to provide a reservation form on its Web site to encourage bookings. An online form certainly makes booking a room simple for site visitors and allows them to take care of it while they're online without having to write down information in order to make a reservation at a later time. You're providing visitors with the convenience they look for.

If you are a business looking to sell a variety of products with set prices online, this level of e-business will not be adequate for you. One of the other levels described here will fit your online strategy more appropriately.

E-business Level 2—Taking Electronic Payment

The next level of e-business incorporates the ability to accept payment for goods and services online. This level of e-business is appropriate if you are selling products or services with a fixed price and inventory is not an issue.

Your online business consists of two core functional areas—the front end and the back end. The front end of your online business is essentially everything that your target market interacts with. It is your Web site, your online storefront. The back end refers to all supporting operations that take place behind the scenes, such as inventory management, accounting systems, and processing special offers or discounts. This level of e-business does not involve integrating the front end of your business with back-end operations. Each operates as a separate entity, but in such a way that the business runs efficiently. Businesses using this level of e-business often do not have the budget to integrate systems or have a business setup that makes integration inappropriate or unnecessary. Some examples of business types that would follow this strategy include businesses that sell:

- Downloadable software

- Accommodations where a deposit is required

- Seminar or course registration

- Theme park admittance

- Memberships

- Ski hill lift tickets

- Magazine subscriptions

- Gift certificates

- Products where supply is not a big issue.

You can tackle processing online payment for goods and services two ways on your site. Some businesses operating at this level of e-business will choose to process payment information manually. Quite often you will notice that sites using this type of payment strategy will require the user to fill out some kind of form that requests the customer's personal information, purchase information, and credit card information. When users submit their information through the form, it is transferred to the site owner's e-mail account. The site owner then manually verifies the user's credit card information and processes the sale. Once the sale is authorized, the site owner or whoever takes care of ensuring that sales are processed should notify customers that their transaction was approved and their item or items are on their way.

Using the services of a payment processing company is the other alternative to managing credit card transactions on your Web site—we covered this in depth earlier in this chapter. You must select the most appropriate method for your business. Processing payment manually may be more time-consuming than having your transactions processed automatically in real time by a payment processing company, but it may be more cost-effective for smaller businesses. Also, if the company is doing low volumes of business, the additional time required to process transactions may cause no interference in daily operations.

This level of e-business is very simple to implement and is quite affordable. A good example of a business that would use this level of e-business would be a software company that allows clients to download the software directly from its Web site. There is no inventory issue for this type of company. The company can simply design a generic payment form that takes all contact and payment information. The form may have a couple of additional fields asking users about their hardware configuration or marketing research questions, but other than that the form would be straightforward. This e-business strategy has low cost and low overhead, and is easy to implement.

E-business Level 3—Storefront Selection and Payment Automation

This level of e-business takes the previous level of e-business up a notch. It is similar to operating a catalogue sales business, but does so online. Companies that operate solely online as well as companies that have an offline presence use this model, but it is more common among online-only businesses. The key is that inventory does not pose much of a problem in day-to-day operations.

This e-business solution encompasses the use of an online stand-alone storefront, but the back end is not integrated with other systems in the business. A company could have a number of reasons for not integrating supporting systems. For example, current business systems may not support back-end integration, it may not be necessary for the business to integrate the back end, or the company may not have the available funds at its disposal to make integration worthwhile.

There are many storefront options available to the user. More information on storefront options can be found in the Internet Marketing Resources section of my Web site at *http://www.susansweeney.com/resources.html*. It is up to the company, its needs, and what its budget allows for when deciding whether to develop its own storefront solution or to purchase a package solution.

As with the previous model, you are responsible for setting up your payment processing system and acquiring a merchant account. Once this has been established, you will receive payment for your products automatically when a consumer makes a purchase. At this level of e-business, the ability to process transactions over a secure connection and in real time is extremely important.

Because company systems are not integrated, businesses that choose to use this e-business strategy have to constantly monitor inventory levels and ensure there is adequate supply, must remove the out-of-stock items from the site, or need to see that an appropriate "item temporarily out of stock" message is displayed to the consumer. The business may consider creating an opt-in mail list to automatically notify individuals when out-of-stock merchandise is replenished, as this will encourage the potential customer to revisit the site.

E-business Level 4—Total Integration

Total integration is the final and most complex level of e-business. It encompasses all details of the previous e-business levels as well as much, much more. Total integration is exactly what it sounds like—the integration of your online business with all or some of your back-end systems. This means that your inventory, accounts receivable, accounting systems, special offers and discounts, consumer database, and so on, are completely integrated with one another, enabling your business to operate like a well-oiled machine.

Companies that are committed to selling online are common users of this level of e-business, and you will usually find that the investment required is fully supported by management. The costs associated with operating a fully integrated Web site can be significant. Integration costs are higher than most small businesses can afford, and as such, it is usually medium-size to large businesses that opt to use this level of e-business. Companies that sell large volumes will also find this model more convenient. Sometimes competition will force the implementation of this model if you wish to remain competitive and meet your target market's needs and expectations. Often the consumer demand requires this level of integration; if you are booking a hotel room and require a non-smoking room with a king-size bed and an ocean view, the hotel's storefront or reservation system has to be fully integrated with its inventory system to be able to book the specific type of room for you.

Integrating your consumer database with your online business provides a number of significant advantages. For one, it facilitates the consumer. The first time that users buy from your site they will be required to fill out a personal profile. Once the profile is filled out, users are assigned a user name and password so that when they return to your site they simply log in using their user name and password—they do not need to fill out their personal and credit card information each time they return. Your customers will certainly appreciate this. Integrating your consumer database facilitates easy referencing of customer information for: Selective ship-to addresses, credit card details, user preferences and personalization features, new-product notification, order history, order tracking and status.

Knowing a consumer's personal information and product preferences can be very important when you are announcing new products that you are offering from your site. If you know that certain customers enjoy a particular product brand, you can use this information to notify them when you carry a new product from that brand. This retention strategy is a great way to encourage repeat traffic and repeat sales.

Integrating your inventory management system with the rest of your online business is terrific for providing optimal customer service. If you're out of stock on a particular item, it is good customer service to place a "temporarily out of stock" message near the product in consideration. If you can provide an estimated-availability message, that's even better. You could ask users if they would like to be notified via e-mail when the item does become available. Integrating your inventory management system and your online storefront allows you to automatically update your virtual storefront and keep your customers informed. This frees up your time, and it is of great assistance to the consumer.

Integrating your accounting systems with your online business can also be quite beneficial. This enables you to easily track your accounts receivable and customer purchase history. Having a fully integrated and automated accounting system can also cut down on the amount of time and effort your staff will have to allocate to accounting details, since the system will run self-sufficiently.

The most prominent example one can give of an online business that currently uses this level of e-business is Amazon.com (*http://www.amazon.com*). Amazon.com's fully integrated e-business approach enables them to provide customers with past purchase history, customer discounts, and purchase tracking. Amazon.com also allows customers to set up a user account so that upon return they simply log in using their user name and password—this makes using the site more efficient and convenient for the consumer. Each time the customer logs on to Amazon.com's Web site, he or she is presented with "recommendations" based on past history and information Amazon.com has acquired. Amazon.com's inventory management system is tied in with its storefront software, which automatically updates product listings whenever inventory is out of stock. Amazon.com also gives the user the option of requesting to order the out-of-stock item and have it shipped automatically once stock has been replenished. This high level of integration and organization enables Amazon.com to provide its customers with the ultimate online shopping experience.

Closing E-business Comments

There are a lot of steps to the e-business process and many decisions to be made. Unless you are a coding genius yourself, you will likely require e-commerce software, a Web development firm, or your ISP to customize an e-business system that works for your business. The methods used to reach an effective e-business solution will vary depending on your business, your products and services, and the expertise of the particular contractor you are working with.

Please keep in mind that customized e-business solutions can be rather expensive to have designed and maintained. If your business is a small start-up operation, if you develop and manage your own Web site, or if you have a limited budget for this project, you may want to start small and add e-business components as your business or your budget grows. Companies such as Amazon.com (*http://www.amazon.com*) and CDNow (*http://www.cdnow.com*) have had years to design and refine their e-business presence. These enterprises are also well capitalized and can afford their own in-house e-business team. However, if you have a product or service that a lot of people want, the e-business system will pay for itself.

Part 2

101 Profiles of Top Internet Business Concepts

1. Ad Network

OVERVIEW OF BUSINESS MODEL

Ad networks are among the top methods of online advertising. The "network" component is organizing the sale of ads and finding high-traffic sites on which to place the banner ads or hyperlinks for your clients. Ad networks are just like other ad agencies. They research Web sites that attract the target demographic of their clients. The revenue comes from the percentage of advertising dollars that you retain during each campaign.

SKILLS NEEDED

Knowledge of online advertising techniques is an asset to run this type of business. If you decide to offer banner ad design services, knowledge of graphic design would benefit your business by eliminating the costs associated with outsourcing to a graphic designer.

COST TO START THIS BUSINESS

You will have to pay for the development, design, and hosting of your Web site. Computer hardware and software will be the main start-up expense. You will need a software program that delivers the appropriate ads to the sites in your network every time it has a visitor. The software should also be able to provide reports of results for your clients. Estimated cost is a minimum of $3,000 to $10,000 to start. Some of the sophisticated software, if your clients want extremely targeted banner ad placement, could run you over $100,000.

NUMBER OF EMPLOYEES NEEDED TO START

The minimum number of employees needed to start and run this type of business is one dedicated individual.

INTERNATIONAL POTENTIAL

This business has strong international potential. Online advertising is an important part of the marketing strategy for many businesses, in all countries.

E-BUSINESS MODEL/PAYMENT PROCESSING METHOD

As the advertising campaign needs to be developed with the client and decisions must be made about where and when the ads will be appropriately placed, e-business level 1 or 2 would be appropriate for this type of business. For more information, see Part 1.

IMPORTANT BUSINESS ISSUES TO BE ADDRESSED

The software you develop or purchase to administer the ad network should be researched and be suitable to your level of operation. You should be available by phone for prospective and current clients to contact you. You should plan what you are going to do with the excess capacity ad space—for example, you may want to offer last-minute volume discounts. Concentrate on associating yourself and including in your network those Web sites that have sustained high traffic levels. Always get paid up front for an advertising campaign.

You will need to address the sophistication levels you want to get into with the site advertising. Are you offering static ads, or are you going to provide keyword advertising, geo-targeted advertising, behavioral advertising, and the like? The level of sophistication will impact the software and the cost of that software.

ONLINE MARKETING TECHNIQUES

- Developing a comprehensive affiliate/associate program would not only increase the awareness of your ad network, it would also send referral business to your site.

- Get linked from online advertising directories.

- Develop a sponsored listings campaign to bid on appropriate keyword phrases with the popular search engines.

- Participate in newsgroups and discussion forums related to online advertising or the industries that your ad network targets.

- Launch your own strategic banner advertising campaign on Web sites frequented by your target market.

For a more detailed description of these techniques, along with many other effective online marketing methods, I recommend the companion book *101 Ways to Promote Your Web Site*. You can also find tons of free resources at *http://www.susansweeney.com/resources.html*.

ADDITIONAL INCOME

You could generate additional income for your ad network by providing graphic design services to businesses. You could design banner advertisements for businesses that are not capable of handling this task in-house. This additional service would add value to your online business.

ONLINE EXAMPLES

AdForce
http://www.adforce.com
AdForce is an independent centralized ad servicing and management solution on the Web. Focusing on pay-per-click marketing, they offer expertise in the management of online advertising.

.Com Marketing
http://www.commarketing.com
Having managed thousands of online operations, .Com Marketing's strength has focused on maximizing online media placements. .Com Marketing assesses

each component of our clients' campaigns prior to, during, and post-launch. Consideration to detail is what sets .Com Marketing ahead of the rest.

2. Apartment Locator

OVERVIEW OF BUSINESS MODEL

Moving to a new city is never easy. Everyone needs a place to live, but not everybody has the time to look. This is a problem that is being solved by many businesses in major cities across the world. Many savvy individuals are launching their own apartment locator Web sites and are turning quite a profit from doing so.

Your main source of income will be referral fees from rental offices of apartments, condominiums, and other real estate structures. You could also charge a fee for sublets, apartment sharing, and private rental listings. Requests are sent via e-mail from those seeking an apartment to you, the site administrator, with a description of the desired apartment location, size, necessities, and so on, that the individual is looking for. You then take the request and find the best possible location to suit the person's needs. Once you have found a match, you set up a time for your client to view the apartment. You collect a referral fee if the client signs a lease.

Another way to run this type of business would be to set up a searchable database. Those with apartments to rent or sublet would pay a fee to add their listing. People looking for an apartment would search based on specific criteria such as location, maximum rent, number of bedrooms, etc.

SKILLS NEEDED

This business is great for someone with a thorough grasp of the available living space in the local area and basic Web publishing skills. You should be a clear communicator via e-mail and phone with your clients and the owners of rental buildings so they take you seriously.

COST TO START THIS BUSINESS

Costs associated with starting this business range from $1,000 to $5,000. Initially you will have to pay to design and develop your Web site along with all costs associated with this (e.g., hosting service). If you want to develop the database, there will be additional costs involved—the amount will be determined by the level of sophistication, the number of fields, and the number of searchable fields. Additional costs associated with opening this business include online advertising costs and any offline promotion that you may implement.

NUMBER OF EMPLOYEES NEEDED TO START
Typically this business can be run by one individual to start and will increase depending on the volume of referrals.

INTERNATIONAL POTENTIAL
Although people from other countries may use this service if they are moving to the country, city, or state that you represent, this business generally has national and regional potential.

E-BUSINESS MODEL/PAYMENT PROCESSING METHOD
E-business level 1 or 2 would be most appropriate for this type of business—level 1 if you are providing hands-on services and level 2 if you want to go the database route and have the site run itself. For more information, see Part 1.

IMPORTANT BUSINESS ISSUES TO BE ADDRESSED
Although you want to receive as many referrals as possible, it is important not to let the apartments that you represent take advantage of your site as a free advertising opportunity. To avoid this problem, don't list the specific names or addresses of the apartment complexes that you represent. You can provide pictures, and general location information. If you give the specific address of the suggested match, your client may go directly to the apartment without even using your service. Of course, if you run this Web site as a database, this will not be an issue as you will be paid up front for all listings.

Collection of referral fees is an important issue. Ensure that you have contracts in place with the apartment owners and safeguard procedures that help you to keep your incoming fees organized.

Your Web site *has to be* constantly updated and maintained. When an apartment is rented through you, make sure to show this on your site. When an apartment is no longer available, remove it immediately from your site.

ONLINE MARKETING TECHNIQUES

- Develop links from as many Web sites and meta-indexes as possible that target your geographic audiences.

- Purchase banner ads on geographically targeted Web sites (e.g., if you represent apartments in New York, purchase a banner ad on a Web site about living in New York).

- Participate in sponsored listings with the search engines by bidding on appropriate keyword phrases.

- List your site in the classified ad section of nearby online newspapers.

- Participate in real estate or geographically specific mailing lists with a cleverly designed signature file.

For a more detailed description of these techniques, along with many other effective online marketing methods, I recommend the companion book *101 Ways to Promote Your Web Site.* You can also find tons of free resources at *http://www.susansweeney.com/resources.html.*

ADDITIONAL INCOME

You should consider partnering with businesses that could benefit from your referrals. For example, local moving companies or furniture rental businesses could benefit from your referrals, since you target the same market. This could prove to be quite profitable for your business. An alternative to this would be selling advertising to these businesses on your site.

ONLINE EXAMPLES

Sami-Apts.com
http://www.sami-apts.com
This is a great student apartment locator service.

AOK Apartment Locators
http://www.aokapartmentlocators.com
A dynamite apartment location service in the Dallas-Fort Worth, Texas, area.

3. Art Supply Store

OVERVIEW OF BUSINESS MODEL

Today everyone is buying products and services online, even artists. The number of potential customers for an art supply store is tremendous. Many artists frequent the Internet to buy supplies such as paint, canvas, brushes, carving tools, and more. The Internet makes it easy for artists to buy products, especially uncommon supplies that are not carried by your local art supply store.

Offering uncommon supplies also enables you to practice niche marketing and can produce high returns for your business.

Here's how it works. With the click of a button artists can easily browse through your selection of art products, adding what they like to their shopping cart. When they are finished they can simply check out, pay for the products online with a credit card, and wait to receive the products in the mail. It's as easy as that.

SKILLS NEEDED

Knowledge of different art supplies and techniques is an asset, as you want to provide the best customer service to your clients. You can't do that without understanding their needs.

COST TO START THIS BUSINESS

The cost to set up and run this type of business ranges from $2,500 to $5,000. Initially you will have to pay for the design, development, and hosting of your Web site along with your storefront solution and merchant account setup. All additional costs are associated with promoting your business online and offline, and purchasing and holding inventory.

NUMBER OF EMPLOYEES NEEDED TO START

To start this operation all you will need is one person. This operation is ideal if you are looking to start a business part-time.

INTERNATIONAL POTENTIAL

This online business has strong international potential, as its products are of interest to artists around the globe.

E-BUSINESS MODEL/PAYMENT PROCESSING METHOD

E-business level 3 is most appropriate for this type of business. For more information, see Part 1.

IMPORTANT BUSINESS ISSUES TO BE ADDRESSED

The site must be kept current. When items are discontinued or out of stock, the Web site and storefront should be updated. The shipping operation of your business should be timely. The prices have to be competitive with the same products available off the Web. Keep in mind that shipping and handling charges have to be added for products bought in your online store.

ONLINE MARKETING TECHNIQUES

- Develop as many links as possible from art-related Web sites and directories.

- Participate in newsgroups and discussion forums related to art with a cleverly designed signature file.

- Host your own art advice column or daily art tips that will feature your products and current promotions. You could leverage your exposure through an RSS feed.

- Participate in sponsored listings by bidding on appropriate keywords with the popular search engines.

- Develop a permission-based mailing list of potential customers and send weekly e-specials or a newsletter with Art Tips and Resources.

For a more detailed description of these techniques, along with many other effective online marketing methods, I recommend the companion book *101 Ways to Promote Your Web Site*. You can also find tons of free resources at *http://www.susansweeney.com/resources.html*.

ADDITIONAL INCOME

In addition to selling art supplies on your site, you could also help artists sell their artwork. You could auction other artists' work from your site and then take a percentage of the sale for your services. This would be a great way to earn additional income and would also help to generate repeat traffic to your Web site.

ONLINE EXAMPLES

MisterArt.com
http://www.misterart.com
MisterArt.com is a large discount art supply store that uses a fully integrated e-business strategy to provide art supplies to consumers.

Island Blue Art Supplies Catalogue
http://shopping.islandblue.com

This is a great site (Figure 2.1) with a huge catalogue of art supplies that can easily be purchased directly from their site.

4. Association Management

OVERVIEW OF BUSINESS MODEL

The number of associations related to different industries and interests is phenomenal. Many of these associations cannot afford to hire (or do not have the volume to warrant hiring) one or more full-time employees to handle the day-to-day administrative duties involved with running the association. Associations are now outsourcing all of these administrative duties to an association management firm.

Here's how it works. The duties that associations want taken care of are administrative. Common tasks include billing, bookkeeping, and accounting, taking minutes at meetings, collection of annual dues, association event promotion, Web site maintenance, and distribution of weekly or monthly newsletters. Since these tasks will be repetitive and not very time-consuming, you are able to handle the association management for multiple associations, and because the tasks will remain similar between associations, you will be able to work much more efficiently.

Figure 2.1.   IslandBlue.com offers a wide range of art supplies from its site.

The key to success in this business is organization. Make sure that you are always on time with your work. If you don't keep yourself organized or you take on too much work, you increase the chance that you might not perform up to the associations' expectations of your firm. This could result in the termination of a management contract and ultimately will affect the professionalism and overall appeal of your organization's services.

SKILLS NEEDED

Excellent organization and communication skills are necessary for starting this type of business. Other skills that would be an asset include knowledge of accounting, creative writing capabilities, and other basic administrative skills.

COST TO START THIS BUSINESS

Since you are providing a service that has no inventory, your initial costs will be minimal. The cost to start this type of business ranges from $1,000 to $10,000. This type of business typically can be run out of your home, which eliminates overhead costs of setting up an office for your management firm.

NUMBER OF EMPLOYEES NEEDED TO START

One person can run this business part-time to begin. This is a perfect idea for someone working from home.

INTERNATIONAL POTENTIAL

This business does not have strong international potential due to the nature of the service provided. Common tasks include taking minutes at weekly or monthly meetings or attending other functions held by the association. This will require your business to be located in the surrounding area of the association, so this business has a more regional appeal. Of course, if this is a national association, most meetings may be online, with one or two a year being face-to-face with everyone flying to a common location. If this is the case, the business could have national or international appeal.

E-BUSINESS MODEL/PAYMENT PROCESSING METHOD

E-business level 1 is most appropriate for this type of business. For more information, see Part 1.

IMPORTANT BUSINESS ISSUES TO BE ADDRESSED

With all your clients, make sure to have a detailed contract that clearly outlines all the services and duties you will be providing. The contract should indicate important dates and contact lists, and someone within the association should be appointed to provide you with all the necessary information and approvals to run the association efficiently.

ONLINE MARKETING TECHNIQUES

- Participating in newsgroups and discussion forums related to your target audience would be a great way to increase the traffic to your Web site.

- Launch a strategic banner advertising campaign on Web sites frequented by your target market.

- Develop links from as many Web sites, directories, and meta-indexes related to your target audience as possible.

- Participating in mail lists and discussion groups related to different industries and associations with a cleverly designed signature file would be a great way to generate awareness for your services.

For a more detailed description of these techniques, along with many other effective online marketing methods, I recommend the companion book *101 Ways to Promote Your Web Site*. You can also find tons of free resources at *http://www.susansweeney.com/resources.html*.

ADDITIONAL INCOME

In addition to handling the daily administrative tasks for associations, you could also provide your clients with promotional services. This would help to promote the association's membership benefits to prospective members and would also increase the awareness of the association. Providing a newsletter circulated to association members where you may feature paying advertisers is a chance for additional income.

ONLINE EXAMPLES

Maguire/Maguire, Inc.
http://www.maguireinc.com
Maguire/Maguire, Inc. is a dynamite business that provides not-for-profit association management and marketing services.

Smith, Bucklin & Associates, Inc.
http://www.smithbucklin.com

Smith, Bucklin & Associates provides unparalleled association management and professional services through strong client relationships.

5. Auction Site

OVERVIEW OF BUSINESS MODEL

Online auction sites are one of the fastest growing businesses on the Internet today. Almost everyone knows at least one person who has either bought or sold a product through an online auction service such as eBay or Yahoo!

Setting up an auction Web site may seem easy at first glance. However, the popularity and success of online auctions has led to an explosion of these sites. This has resulted in stiff competition among auction sites. You must find a niche market—for example, rare collectibles, baseball cards, celebrity memorabilia, or autographed items—to set yourself apart from the competition.

If you decide to open an online auction site, you will be using a special computer program that places items up for auction on your Web site. People interested in the auctioned item place bids. If you are using a good auction program, then your computer will keep track of these bids and will finally close the auction and notify the seller and the successful bidder. The bidder and seller must arrange for the shipping of the item privately. Your sources of income will be the commission earned from the sale of each item on your site or the fee charged to submit an article and banner advertising revenue. Some auction sites also include a membership fee for access to selling on the site.

SKILLS NEEDED

What you'll need to embark on this opportunity is basic Web publishing and digital imaging know-how, and an in-depth knowledge of the auction software program you are going to use. You will also want a robust list of contacts with items available for auction on your site or knowledge of Internet marketing to spread the word about your business online.

COST TO START THIS BUSINESS

The cost to set up and run this type of business ranges from as low as $10,000 into the millions for a presence like eBay. The most expensive elements of the startup will be the auction software and the extensive marketing needed to launch this type of business. You will also have to pay for the design, development, and hosting of your Web site.

NUMBER OF EMPLOYEES NEEDED TO START

The number of employees needed may change as the business grows. It will depend on the volume of business you handle and the degree of automation of your online presence. To start, one competent person can handle operations.

INTERNATIONAL POTENTIAL

Online auctions have strong international potential. Unless you are a specialty site, anyone can place anything up for auction. It is the customer's responsibility to arrange for the transfer of auctioned items. So it is entirely possible for someone in Zimbabwe to use your site to buy a lock of Elvis's hair from someone in Greenland.

E-BUSINESS MODEL/PAYMENT PROCESSING METHOD

E-business level 3 is most appropriate for an auction site. You will need some sophisticated software and online payment processing (if you are going to take care of the financial arrangements from your site) to be competitive in this market. For more information, see Part 1.

IMPORTANT BUSINESS ISSUES TO BE ADDRESSED

There is already a saturation of auction sites; some have proven to work and others have flopped. Getting the buyers to your site will be the biggest challenge, so once you build a somewhat dedicated audience, it's important to be responsive to their needs by incorporating a rating system that is regulated by the users of your auction site. You want to develop a system to ensure that you are paid your fee or commission if you don't handle the financial transaction from your site.

Niche auction sites still provide a great opportunity. Stamp auctions, coin collector auctions, and similar types of niche auctions provide for easier marketing.

ONLINE MARKETING TECHNIQUES

- By asking if your customers would like to be kept updated on any great deals in their field of interest, permission marketing could be one of your greatest assets. For example, an Elvis fan might be interested in knowing when an Elvis-related item comes up for auction.

- Banner exchange and banner advertising on sites that have the same target market you do can be very effective.

- Consider using viral marketing. This will allow your customers to invite friends to join the auction site. If users see something a friend might like, they will most likely pass on the information.

- Develop a sponsored listings campaign to bid on appropriate keywords with the popular search engines.

- Develop and implement a comprehensive link strategy.

For a more detailed description of these techniques, along with many other effective online marketing methods, I recommend the companion book *101 Ways to Promote Your Web Site*. You can also find tons of free resources at *http://www.susansweeney.com/resources.html.*

ADDITIONAL INCOME
Banner advertising can generate a substantial income as long as you have a lot of visitors to your site.

ONLINE EXAMPLES

eBay
http://www.ebay.com
eBay is synonymous with online auctions in the same way as Nike is synonymous with sneakers.

uBid
http://www.ubid.com
Another well-designed auction site. Not as omnipresent as eBay, but a well-laid-out site nonetheless.

6. Auto Advice

OVERVIEW OF BUSINESS MODEL
Through providing sound advice to visitors wondering how to solve a problem with their current automobile or whether or not to purchase a certain year or make of automobile, you have the opportunity to develop a nice little business.

If you offer your visitors quality auto advice, they will return to your site again and again to see how your advice can help them to maintain a better, longer-lasting automobile.

Advice Web sites allow you to "data-mine" in targeted markets. Consider your users as your source of income. The more visitors you have and the more information you gather from the people you counsel, the better. There are a lot of permission marketing opportunities available with this type of business. You can ask your visitors for permission to send them specific types of information and then you can charge a sponsorship or advertising fee to those suppliers who have information they want distributed to these opt-in lists.

Your main source of income will be from selling banner advertising on your site to businesses that share the same target market—automobile retailers, used car dealers, after-sale product suppliers, and auto parts suppliers. Since this type of business targets individuals interested in automobiles, you are providing an optimal banner advertising opportunity for all businesses in the auto industry.

Skills Needed

This form of business requires that you have expert knowledge in the area of automobiles. If you don't offer quality advice, your visitors will notice and will not return to your site. This could seriously hinder the profitability of your business.

Cost to Start This Business

The cost to start this type of business ranges from approximately $1,000 to $5,000. Initially you will have to pay for the design, development, and hosting of your Web site. Additional costs associated with starting this type of business include online and offline advertising costs.

Number of Employees Needed to Start

Typically, one part-time person is needed to run this type of business, depending on the volume of requests received from visitors.

International Potential

This business has high international potential.

E-Business Model/Payment Processing Method

E-business level 1 is most appropriate for this type of business. For more information, see Part 1.

IMPORTANT BUSINESS ISSUES TO BE ADDRESSED

It is important that you offer sound advice on your site. If you offer advice that is incorrect or inappropriate, it could seriously hinder your business potential. You should place a disclaimer on your site in case this problem arises. This will exclude you from any legal action that may result from accidents or damages resulting from your automotive advice.

ONLINE MARKETING TECHNIQUES

- Viral marketing with a catchy "Tell a Friend" element would be appropriate for this type of site.

- Make sure there are plenty of areas on your Web site that encourage users to provide their e-mail address—for example, "Click here if you would like to be notified when we update our advice column." You could also have product-specific mail lists to which visitors could opt in. Having an RSS feed to let subscribers know when you add new content is another neat feature to generate targeted traffic.

- Participate in newsgroups, mailing lists, and discussion forums related to automobiles with a cleverly designed signature file.

- Have your Web site listed and linked from as many auto-related directories, meta-indexes, and Web sites as possible.

- Develop a sponsored listings campaign to bid on appropriate keyword phrases with the popular search engines.

- Develop online press releases and have them distributed to as many automotive-related publications and e-zines as possible.

- Web ring participation can have a significant impact on traffic, as there are many auto-related Web rings accessible from Webring.org and Looplink.com.

For a more detailed description of these techniques, along with many other effective online marketing methods, I recommend the companion book *101 Ways to Promote Your Web Site*. You can also find tons of free resources at *http://www.susansweeney.com/resources.html*.

ADDITIONAL INCOME

There are plenty of avenues to create additional income in the advice Web site business. You can set up mailing lists targeted toward specific car owners and sell or provide sponsorship opportunities to industry partners that want to reach that target market. For example, you could have a Volkswagen mailing list, or for an even more targeted approach you could have a Volkswagen Beetle mailing list. The possibilities are endless. You can ask people if they would like to receive different auto maintenance advice via e-mail daily. This form of permission marketing enables you to send them an e-mail at their request. Proper use of these targeted lists could result in a tremendous money-making opportunity for your business due to the nature of readership.

ONLINE EXAMPLES

AutoAdvice.com
http://www.autoadvice.com
An in-depth site offering auto advice and tips on how to buy a new car.

FreeAutoAdvice.com
http://freeautoadvice.com
This site is operated by a collection of mechanics and technicians who repair cars.

7. Banner Ad Designer

OVERVIEW OF BUSINESS MODEL

One of the primary forms of advertising on the Internet today is through banner advertisements placed on high-traffic Web sites. Banner ads quite often are designed by a graphic designer. With the Internet growing at an exponential rate, more small businesses are going online. Most of these small businesses can't afford to have their own in-house graphic designer, so they have to outsource the creation of their ads to outside firms.

As a banner ad developer, you will take requests for banner ads via e-mail. After consulting with customers via e-mail or phone, you will construct a banner ad that meets their requirements and price. The revenue will come from the payment for these services.

SKILLS NEEDED

The most important set of skills for creating banner ads lies in superior graphic design abilities. Familiarity with the standard graphical programs is a must. More recently, however, animated banner ads have become quite popular. To create these types of ads, you will need to be familiar with the Java programming language or Macromedia Flash.

COST TO START THIS BUSINESS

Costs can be minimal to begin this business if you have a computer and the proper software needed to complete the work. Most graphic designers have the necessary hardware and software and are more than capable of designing and developing their own Web site.

NUMBER OF EMPLOYEES NEEDED TO START

One part-time person can start this business.

INTERNATIONAL POTENTIAL

The international potential for this business is without limits. If your graphics are catchy, your ads will be noticed and you no doubt will be contacted for your services. If a client requests banners in another language, have them provide the text and there should be no problem.

E-BUSINESS MODEL/PAYMENT PROCESSING METHOD

E-business level 1 or 2 is appropriate for this type of business. For more information, see Part 1. You will be taking requests through e-mail, but since the customers will desire input into the creative process, you will be in contact with them over the phone and they can pay you directly.

IMPORTANT BUSINESS ISSUES TO BE ADDRESSED

Online competition could be formidable. For this reason, great design and excellent customer service are very important. The graphical presentation of your own Web site is of particular importance. Show off your stuff and have an area for client samples and testimonials viewable to the public.

ONLINE MARKETING TECHNIQUES

- Develop a comprehensive link strategy. Establishing links from related sites such as online marketing e-zines, ad agencies, and newsletters is an excellent way to bring targeted business to your Web site.

- Circulate a series of dynamite banner ads for your own services.

- Develop a sponsored listings campaign to bid on appropriate keyword phrases with the popular search engines.

- Participate in marketing mail lists, Usenet newsgroups, and forums.

For a more detailed description of these techniques, along with many other effective online marketing methods, I recommend the companion book *101 Ways to Promote Your Web Site*. You can also find tons of free resources at *http://www.susansweeney.com/resources.html*.

ADDITIONAL INCOME
By increasing your services into related fields such as graphic corporate ID development, e-book covers, e-brochure development, and Web site development, you could expand your income.

ONLINE EXAMPLES

Addesigner.com
http://www.addesigner.com
This Web site lets you design your own banner ads in a short time and then download them if you are a member. The banner ads are of the simplest kind, but it is a good low-end solution for some businesses.

Mouser Art
http://www.mouserart.com
A typical small entrepreneurial Web site. However, the excellent site design and layout gives the site a really professional feel.

8. Beauty Products

OVERVIEW OF BUSINESS MODEL
Buying beauty products online is very popular with busy female professionals. They have certain brands they buy regularly, know what they want, and have very little time for shopping. Sometimes they are looking for special products that are not carried by regular vendors. Online beauty stores solve this problem by accommodating the needs of the business professional. Online beauty stores

can sell everything from lipstick and makeup to bath oils and aromatherapy products. With the increasing product demand for this industry, selling beauty products online provides an excellent online business opportunity.

SKILLS NEEDED

Knowledge of health and beauty products is a must.

COST TO START THIS BUSINESS

The cost to set up and run this type of business ranges from $1,000 to $100,000, depending on how much inventory you plan to carry. Initially, you will have to pay for the design, development, and hosting of your Web site along with your storefront solution and merchant account setup. All additional costs are associated with promoting your business online and offline as well as purchasing and holding inventory.

NUMBER OF EMPLOYEES NEEDED TO START

This business can easily be started by one individual. This business can also be started and run as a part-time venture.

INTERNATIONAL POTENTIAL

This online business has strong international potential as its products are of interest to consumers across the globe.

E-BUSINESS MODEL/PAYMENT PROCESSING METHOD

E-business level 3 or 4 is most appropriate for this type of business. Level 3 is appropriate when the business is online only. Level 4 is appropriate if you have a fairly large operation with many products or where you have an offline location as well, with a Web-compatible inventory system. For more information, see Part 1.

IMPORTANT BUSINESS ISSUES TO BE ADDRESSED

You will have to be very price competitive on those products that are generally available online or locally. Keep in mind that when purchasing from your online store, the customer will have to pay for shipping and handling in addition to product cost. To the extent that you specialize in niche products or hard-to-find items, this will be less of an issue.

ONLINE MARKETING TECHNIQUES

- Develop a strategic online banner advertising campaign on health- and beauty-related Web sites.

- Participate in newsgroups, discussion forums, and mailing lists related to health and beauty with a cleverly designed signature file.

- Offering health and beauty tips from your site would be a great way to encourage repeat traffic. Perhaps consider setting up a beauty tip of the day that you would send via an autoresponder.

- Practice permission marketing by asking visitors if they would like to be notified via e-mail when you add new products to your Web site.

- Participate in e-zines related to beauty, health, and hair care as well as those e-zines that have the same target market you do—busy professional women and teens. Your participation could be banner advertising, story or article submission, sponsorship, or providing a prize for their contests.

For a more detailed description of these techniques, along with many other effective online marketing methods, I recommend the companion book *101 Ways to Promote Your Web Site*. You can also find tons of free resources at *http://www.susansweeney.com/resources.html*.

Additional Income

In addition to selling beauty products, you can also sell accessories such as makeup cases, towels, lather-builders, handbags, and so on. By offering these products, you would not only add value to your online beauty store, you would also have the opportunity to generate additional income for your business. Gift certificates and gift baskets may provide an additional source of revenue. You can also sell banner advertising and sponsorship opportunities to companies that target the same group that you do.

Online Examples

Just for Redheads Beauty Products
http://www.justforredheads.com
This is a great online beauty store that uses a Yahoo! Storefront template service to sell its products online. It also has a very unique target market—redheads!

Life Plus Vitamins
http://www.lifeplusvitamins.com

This is a great online site that sells vitamins, beauty products, and other health- and hygiene-related products.

9. Blog Software/Blog Directory

OVERVIEW OF BUSINESS MODEL

A blog is a Web site or part of a Web site that can be used to post news, thoughts, and updates as well as interact with others. Many people use blogs and would be quite happy to use a blog service where they can quickly and easily develop and maintain their blog on a blog portal. The number of people using your blog service, the number of people they promote their blog to, as well as the number of references to publicly promoted blogs (in the case of maintaining a blog directory) will be the key to many visitors, and then your pages are in turn worth advertising dollars. Blogs can be as specific or as general as the owner pleases—some might relate to an individual's travels so friends and family can keep up to date with where they are and know that they are safe; others relate to corporate products and uses; others are used to provide useful information to customers and potential customers. There are as many uses for blogs as there are products and services.

Blogs are quite versatile; they offer posting options such as inviting friends to post, having your blog open to the public to post, or keeping the posting to yourself. Blogs are making it possible to hold ongoing conversations in public with thousands of people.

A blog software site or a blog directory has many revenue-generation op- portunities. You have banner advertising, sponsorship, and subscription oppor- tunities. You can promote additional products and services that you provide related to technology products and services.

SKILLS NEEDED

If you have the programming skills to build the blog software, portal, and di- rectory, you will be able to do this yourself. If you don't, you will have to outsource or contract these elements out.

COST TO START THIS BUSINESS

You will need a computer and the appropriate blog software. Start-up costs will also include the design, development, and hosting of your Web site, which will include the blog software, blog portal and the blog directory. The start-up costs for this type of business will generally run between $4,000 and $30,000, depending on how much of the programming you have to outsource.

NUMBER OF EMPLOYEES NEEDED TO START

Starting off you need only one employee—not even full-time if that's not what you can fit into your schedule.

INTERNATIONAL POTENTIAL

This business's international potential increases if it's translated into the major languages of the globe. English is widely accepted, however.

E-BUSINESS MODEL/PAYMENT PROCESSING METHOD

Ideally, a blog directory should charge advertisers throughout the year. E-business level 1 or 2 would be appropriate for this type of online business. See Part 1 for more details.

IMPORTANT BUSINESS ISSUES TO BE ADDRESSED

In order to utilize your blog software service to its full potential, you will want to invest in advanced blog tools as they are available. These tools today offer such things as e-mail notifications when updates are made, sending the blog content via e-mail to subscribers, and the option of collaborative authors; tomorrow, who knows, as this is a fast changing environment.

You should have a Web traffic analysis package on the server that hosts your site so that you can show advertisers accurate information about your site traffic.

ONLINE MARKETING TECHNIQUES

- Participating in newsgroups and discussion forums related to your target audience would be a great way to increase exposure of your blogs and the traffic to your Web site.

- Launching a strategic banner advertising campaign on topic-specific Web sites would generate targeted exposure for your blog.

- Develop links from as many Web sites, directories, and meta-indexes related to the topic of your blog as you can.

- Make sure your site is optimized for organic search engine positioning and also consider participating in pay-per-click campaigns with the more popular search engines.

- Develop a sponsored listings campaign to bid on appropriate keyword phrases with the popular search engines.

- Participating in publicly accessible opt-in mail lists related to the topic of your blog would be a great way to communicate with your target market.

For a more detailed description of these techniques, along with many other effective online marketing methods, I recommend the companion book *101 Ways to Promote Your Web Site*. You can also find tons of free resources at *http://www.susansweeney.com/resources.html*.

ADDITIONAL INCOME

Additional income comes into play by charging a fee if the blog is educational or is an area of expertise. Also, you may be able to host a blog directory, be it all the same topic or various types of blogs. You can join the affiliate programs of providers of products or services that your target market may be interested in.

ONLINE EXAMPLES

Free Webs
http://www.freewebs.com
A large online blog software provider. There is a chance to join the affiliate program and advertise as well on this site.

Globe of Blogs
http://www.globeofblogs.com
An online blog directory. This site is very easy to navigate.

10. Bookstore

OVERVIEW OF BUSINESS MODEL

Online bookstores are one of the most widely accepted forms of online businesses. You can start an online bookstore that sells many titles, but for a more targeted approach you may consider starting a bookstore that specializes in a particular type of book. This will differentiate you from the larger online booksellers like Amazon.com and BarnesandNoble.com, and will also allow you to use highly targeted traffic-building techniques.

Setting up a bookstore online gives you some leeway with distributors as compared to other online business opportunities. Typically, book distributors grant longer terms of credit than other distributors or wholesalers. This is great, since books can sit in your inventory for extended periods of time. You don't want to have to pay for stock that does not turn a profit for your online business.

To help enhance your online bookstore, you should try to develop a database of value-added reading for each selection you have listed on your site. This could be anything from author reviews and biographies to a chapter excerpt or table of contents. Whatever you decide to use to help enhance the listings on your online bookstore Web site, you will be adding more value to the products that you offer, which ultimately could decide whether a consumer will purchase the product or not.

SKILLS NEEDED

If you decide to launch a specialized online bookstore, you should have knowledge of the particular subject and you should understand what your target market's needs are. You will need to learn the retail book business—returns, remainders, and so on.

COST TO START THIS BUSINESS

Costs to set up this type of business can run anywhere from a low of about $3,000 for Web site design, development, and hosting (where the business is basically a member of Amazon or another bookstore's affiliate program and provides recommendations and links to specific books), to a setup cost in the millions for the design, development, and setup of the next Amazon.com. An online bookstore where you set up your own storefront and carry a small inventory will likely cost you between $3,000 and $10,000.

NUMBER OF EMPLOYEES NEEDED TO START

You can start this business with one person. In the beginning, this type of business could be run on a part-time basis.

INTERNATIONAL POTENTIAL

This business has high international potential.

E-BUSINESS MODEL/PAYMENT PROCESSING METHOD

E-business level 3 or 4 is most appropriate for this type of business if you are operating a storefront or catalogue. For more information, see Part 1.

IMPORTANT BUSINESS ISSUES TO BE ADDRESSED

A common issue that most online bookstores face is having an efficient delivery service. If you tell your clients that your products are available for shipment within a 24-hour period, you should follow through with it. Nothing displeases customers more than having a purchase arrive two to three weeks after they have made a purchase. To offer the best possible shipping methods for your customers, investigate your local postal carrier for the most effective way to ship your products.

Keeping inventory information current on your Web site is critical.

ONLINE MARKETING TECHNIQUES

- Developing a comprehensive affiliate/associate program would not only send referral business to your bookstore, it would also increase the overall awareness of your site.

- Launching a strategic banner advertising campaign on Web sites frequented by your target market will send high volumes of traffic to your Web site. Your banner ads could contain coupons for specific titles.

- You should enable visitors to tell friends about certain book selections directly from your site via e-mail. This viral marketing technique is a great way to increase traffic to your Web site.

- A comprehensive link strategy should be developed and implemented. Links should be developed from cybermalls, meta-indexes, and sites that relate to your bookstore's niche.

- You should develop a mail list where you will provide news on new releases, reviews, and author interviews.

- You could consider developing a loyalty program for frequent shoppers.

For a more detailed description of these techniques, along with many other effective online marketing methods, I recommend the companion book *101 Ways to Promote Your Web Site*. You can also find tons of free resources at *http://www.susansweeney.com/resources.html*.

ADDITIONAL INCOME

In addition to selling books, you might also consider selling other, related products such as bookmarks, book bags, or coffee mugs. Gift wrapping and custom cards could be additional services that you could provide to customers who are sending books directly to friends as gifts. You could offer gift certificates as well. These added features would enhance your Web site's overall appeal.

ONLINE EXAMPLES

Amazon.com
http://www.amazon.com
Amazon.com is arguably the world's most famous online bookstore.

Adventurous Traveler Bookstore
http://atb.away.com/index.html
A great specialty bookstore that targets a particular market segment.

11. Business Opportunity Center

OVERVIEW OF BUSINESS

Developing a business opportunity center is a great resource for your target market and a good way to bring in some additional income. On this site, people can post resumes and businesses can post available opportunities. You can earn money by selling advertising on your site and by allowing businesses to subscribe to your site, whereby they receive information pertinent to their needs, or you can allow businesses to feature their opportunity (e.g., franchise). In addition, you could provide resources for people looking for employment as well as entrepreneurial resources.

SKILLS NEEDED

If you are focusing on business opportunities within a specific sector, such as the dental industry, then knowledge of the industry is necessary. If you are going to provide a general business opportunity site, a general knowledge of computers, the Internet, and Internet marketing is what you need.

COST TO START THIS BUSINESS

To set up this informational resource, your costs will primarily consist of Web site design, development, promotion, research, and regular site maintenance. You will have computer hardware and software costs. You will likely have a database development cost, as all your opportunities likely will be stored in a searchable database. Expect costs to fall between $4,000 and $10,000.

NUMBER OF EMPLOYEES NEEDED TO START

One person can administer this business. Depending on the activity of the site, it's possible to do it part-time. You may wish to have an additional person to assist with site maintenance and visitor inquiries.

INTERNATIONAL POTENTIAL

This business offers very little international potential. In fact, as a small operation you may wish to focus on your local area rather than compete directly with the countrywide opportunity sites.

E-BUSINESS MODEL/PAYMENT PROCESSING METHOD

E-business level 1 is most appropriate for this type of business. If you want to automate the input process so that anyone can submit an opportunity and have it listed for a fee, you may want to use a level 3 model. For more information, see Part 1.

IMPORTANT BUSINESS ISSUES TO BE ADDRESSED

Make sure you have a plan laid out before you approach this topic—know how revenue will be generated and who the potential clients are in your area. Be aware that maintaining up-to-date information requires organization. You might want to look at a fully automated style for this business.

ONLINE MARKETING TECHNIQUES

- Participate in newsgroups, mailing lists, and discussion forums related to entrepreneurship or business with a cleverly designed signature file.

- Develop links from as many business-related Web sites, meta-indexes, and directories as possible.

- Develop a comprehensive link strategy. Establish links to your site from the classified sections of regional online publications.

- Develop a sponsored listings campaign to bid on appropriate keyword phrases with the popular search engines.

- Participate in business- and entrepreneur-related e-zines. You can do this by writing articles to be published in the e-zine or by purchasing advertising in the online publications.

For a more detailed description of these techniques, along with many other effective online marketing methods, I recommend the companion book *101*

Ways to Promote Your Web Site. You can also find tons of free resources at *http://www.susansweeney.com/resources.html.*

ADDITIONAL INCOME

Additional income would surround the sales of any products and services you offer that complement the primary function of your business. Perhaps you could offer resume writing or business plan development services. You may even choose to sell products relating to your topic, such as books on resume writing or business development.

ONLINE EXAMPLES

Bizopp.com—Business Opportunity Center
http://www.bizopp.com
A nice-looking business opportunity site with plenty of resources.

Business Opportunities Classifieds Online (BOC Online)
http://www.boconline.com
A list of business opportunity classifieds.

12. Business Broker

OVERVIEW OF BUSINESS MODEL

The number of people who want to go into business for themselves is increasing every day. There are thousands of potential entrepreneurs and investors searching for new business opportunities daily. This provides you with the perfect opportunity to capitalize on this entrepreneurship frenzy. There are two ways that you can approach this type of business. One is very simplistic; the other is more complex.

The simplistic approach to starting this business is by providing a listing of potential business opportunities on your Web site. To generate revenue, you can charge businesses a monthly or annual fee for having their business listed on your site. You can then offer businesses the opportunity to purchase banner ads on your site or to enhance their listings with a company logo, e-mail links, or direct links to their Web site. This is a very simple and easy approach to launching this type of business.

The more complex approach to starting your own online business brokerage firm is by actively seeking business opportunities for business buyers and investors to review. This requires a more in-depth knowledge of business fundamentals and excellent sales skills, as you are ultimately negotiating to sell someone else's business. Revenue is typically generated on a percentage-of-sales basis when you operate at this level. You typically list the businesses that you are selling directly on your Web site at no charge. You do this to expose the business opportunities to potential buyers.

SKILLS NEEDED

The skills necessary to launch this type of business vary depending on which approach you take. If you go with the more simplistic approach, experience with marketing online would be a definite asset, as you are going to want to actively promote your Web site and generate substantial traffic. If you decide to take the more complex approach, knowledge of business valuations would be an asset. There are also several designations available for business brokers. If you were to obtain one of these designations, you would add tremendous credibility to your business brokerage firm.

COST TO START THIS BUSINESS

Since you are providing a service that has no tangible inventory, your initial costs will be minimal. You will need a computer and appropriate software, of course. Initial costs will also include the design, development, and hosting of your Web site. The cost to start this type of business ranges from $3,000 to $10,000. If you take the simplistic approach, you are going to face more extensive costs associated with the development of your site in that a database will need to be designed and developed to list the businesses for sale. You will also need a strategy to develop considerable Web site traffic, as people are not going to pay to have their site listed on a site that receives no traffic. If you take the more complex approach, you will face different costs: You will have to develop professional marketing collateral and invest more in research and business promotion to find businesses that are looking to sell.

NUMBER OF EMPLOYEES NEEDED TO START

The number of employees needed to run this type of business will depend on which approach you take. The simpler approach can be started by one person part-time. The more complex business should have a full-time person ready and available to communicate with clients and meet with them at their convenience.

INTERNATIONAL POTENTIAL

This business has strong international potential, as business investments are of interest to people all over the world. Using the Internet as a medium to promote this type of business makes the potential for international investment even greater.

E-BUSINESS MODEL/PAYMENT PROCESSING METHOD

E-business level 1 is most appropriate for this type of business. For more information, see Part 1.

IMPORTANT BUSINESS ISSUES TO BE ADDRESSED

If you decide to use a more simplistic approach to this type of business, you should do whatever you can to develop traffic to your Web site. People are not going to want to purchase advertising or a listing on your site if you are not receiving any Web site traffic.

If you are taking a more complex approach to this business, you should monitor the quality of businesses that you are trying to sell. It can take months, even years, to close a business sale, so you want to ensure that you are not wasting any time on a business that will not provide you with a return on your investment. This is especially important because you are typically receiving payment based on sales commissions.

ONLINE MARKETING TECHNIQUES

- Participating in newsgroups and discussion forums related to your target audience would be a great way to increase the traffic to your Web site.

- Launching a strategic banner advertising campaign on business- and investment-related Web sites would generate targeted exposure for your business.

- Develop links from as many Web sites, directories, and meta-indexes related to business and investments as possible.

- Participating in mail lists and discussion groups related to business and investments would be a great way to communicate with your target market.

- Purchasing advertising in or contributing articles to e-zines related to your target market would help generate exposure and would enhance the professionalism of your brokerage firm.

For a more detailed description of these techniques, along with many other effective online marketing methods, I recommend the companion book *101 Ways to Promote Your Web Site*. You can also find tons of free resources at *http://www.susansweeney.com/resources.html*.

ADDITIONAL INCOME

In addition to providing brokerage services, you may also want to offer consulting services for struggling businesses. This would be a great way to earn additional income and would also add credibility to your brokerage services. You can provide business valuation services to businesses interested in selling, and you can help procure financing for those interested in purchasing a business.

ONLINE EXAMPLES

Business Brokers Network
http://www.bbn-net.com
America's largest business brokerage Web site, BBN-Net is the Net's largest database of quality businesses for sale.

International Business Brokers Association
http://www.ibba.org
IBBA is the largest international not-for-profit association operating exclusively for the benefit of people and firms engaged in the various aspects of business brokerage, and mergers and acquisitions.

13. Business Plan Writing Service

OVERVIEW OF BUSINESS MODEL

There are an abundance of budding entrepreneurs out there with great ideas but who lack the writing and organizational skills to produce a professional business plan. The Internet is the ideal medium to provide this service, so why not create a business plan writing service online?

Start-up businesses pay thousands of dollars to have business plans developed when they are trying to get a loan or receive funding for new projects. A poorly written business plan can seriously hinder the chances of receiving money from anyone, which is why most businesses choose to have their business plans written professionally. Since this market refreshes itself, there is a tremendous opportunity to make a lot of money with this business.

SKILLS NEEDED

Expert writing skills and knowledge of regular business practices are a minimum requirement for operating this type of business. The ability to develop financial projections can be developed through your business, may be outsourced, or would be provided by the client. Knowledge of how to work with bank officers and lenders is also an asset.

COST TO START THIS BUSINESS

The costs associated with starting this type of business range from $3,000 to $4,500. This covers the cost to design, build, and host your Web site as well as the necessary investment in computer hardware and software. Additional costs may result from promoting your services online and offline, as well as overhead costs such as office supplies and telecommunications bills.

NUMBER OF EMPLOYEES NEEDED TO START

One full-time capable writer is needed to run this form of business. It can initially be started as a part-time endeavor.

INTERNATIONAL POTENTIAL

This business has some international potential. Not only will people in your country be interested in this service, internationals looking to invest in your country may also need a professional business plan prepared.

E-BUSINESS MODEL/PAYMENT PROCESSING METHOD

E-business level 1 is most appropriate for this type of business. For more information, see Part 1.

IMPORTANT BUSINESS ISSUES TO BE ADDRESSED

A common problem with start-up operations is that banks and other lenders are unwilling to invest in the business idea. When this happens, entrepreneurs often abandon the business idea along with any commitments they have made while trying to start the business. This could seriously affect your business, so to avoid this problem you should ask for a 30 to 50 percent deposit up front. You can collect the remainder of the fee when the business plan has been completed.

ONLINE MARKETING TECHNIQUES

- Develop a comprehensive link strategy. Establish links from as many business- and entrepreneur-related Web sites, meta-indexes, and directories as possible.

- Participate in newsgroups and discussion forums related to online business, entrepreneurship, or business financing.

- Develop a sponsored listings campaign to bid on appropriate keyword phrases with the popular search engines.

- Launch a small-business advice column on your site to draw repeat traffic from entrepreneurs. Ask site visitors if they'd like to be notified when it is updated or if they'd like to receive a copy via e-mail. You could provide your advice column or articles to appropriate e-zines or opt-in mail lists as long as they provide you and your Web site with exposure.

For a more detailed description of these techniques, along with many other effective online marketing methods, I recommend the companion book *101 Ways to Promote Your Web Site*. You can also find tons of free resources at *http://www.susansweeney.com/resources.html*.

ADDITIONAL INCOME

In addition to writing business plans, you could also develop a referral service to other business service providers such as bookkeepers and tax preparers. You can receive a referral fee for every company that you refer to these businesses, and they could do the same for you. This is a great way for your business to receive some additional income.

ONLINE EXAMPLES

New Century Marketing Concepts
http://www.insmkt.com/plan.htm
A great business that offers business plan writing services.

GrowThink.com
http://www.growthink.com

A dynamite business that offers business plan writing and venture development services.

14. Cartoon/Joke Writer

OVERVIEW OF BUSINESS

There are many options available to you online if you have a knack for humor or cartoon sketching. A common trend found across humor sites is the inclusion of an opt-in mail list—a joke of the day, quote of the week, or the like. Many sites make their money by allowing other companies to sponsor their mail list or newsletter based on a CPM (cost per thousand) basis. These sites also often sell banner advertising opportunities as well. Some of these sites will allow reproduction of the cartoons or jokes they develop for a fee.

As a freelance artist, you have the option of doing custom work for other companies that they could then include in their media. Depending on your objectives, you may wish to expand your services to include Web icon design, gifts, cards, advertising, and apparel.

SKILLS NEEDED

Well-developed artistic or written skills, combined with a knack for humor.

COST TO START THIS BUSINESS

Web development and promotion costs will play a role in your start-up costs. Investment in equipment to develop the creative side of the business will also have to be incurred if you do not already own items such as a scanner or graphic editing software. Expect costs to run between $3,000 and $6,000.

NUMBER OF EMPLOYEES NEEDED TO START

This is a one-person business. This business can start as a part-time endeavor.

INTERNATIONAL POTENTIAL

International potential exists, but only if the foreign culture is similar to your own. What you may find funny, others may not. Also, if you're focusing on current happenings, these happenings may not be of great interest to foreign countries.

E-BUSINESS MODEL/PAYMENT PROCESSING METHOD

E-business level 1 is most appropriate for this type of business. For more information, see Part 1.

IMPORTANT BUSINESS ISSUES TO BE ADDRESSED

Copyright issues need to be addressed. If you are charging for the use of your cartoons, ensure that your contracts are very clear in the usage rights you are granting. Make it very clear whether the client has the exclusive rights, unlimited usage, or single usage rights.

ONLINE MARKETING TECHNIQUES

- Partner with popular e-zines to include your businesses jokes with their online e-zine distribution, identifying you as the source and providing a link to your Web site.

- Participate in newsgroups and discussion forums related to online advertising or the industries that your ad network targets.

- Online press release distribution and regular contributions to periodicals and publications will be a great asset when promoting your business.

- Develop a sponsored listings campaign to bid on appropriate phrases with the popular search engines.

- Develop links from as many comedy- or joke-related Web sites, meta-indexes, and directories as possible.

For a more detailed description of these techniques, along with many other effective online marketing methods, I recommend the companion book *101 Ways to Promote Your Web Site*. You can also find tons of free resources at *http://www.susansweeney.com/resources.html.*

ADDITIONAL INCOME

You can earn additional income by developing your own line of merchandise that depicts your comedic material and then selling it online or offline at local events, fairs, flea markets, and so on.

Online Examples

Funnyjokes.com
http://www.funnyjokes.com
A site containing clean humor, dirty jokes, tasteless cartoons, comic strips, greeting cards, free downloads, and a large daily mailing list.

Joke-of-the-Day.com
http://www.joke-of-the-day.com
All kinds of humor can be found here, including a few large mail lists. Their Joke-of-the-Day mail list has over a million subscribers.

15. Classified Ads

Overview of Business
Building an online classified ads business is proving to be a very successful concept. While people generally expect to be able to post text-based ads for free, you can generate income by allowing people to post enhanced advertisements (e.g., ads with pictures) or classified ads with hypertext links to a Web site. Additional revenue would come from direct advertising sales (e.g., banner ads). An option you may wish to consider is setting up an e-mail system for your users, where they can register for a free e-mail account. You could then send them advertisements based on their opt-in preferences.

Coupons, auctions, real estate information, and so on, are all related topics that would be appropriate for your site.

Skills Needed
All you need is the drive to succeed, basic computer skills, and a knowledge of Internet marketing.

Cost to Start This Business
Most of your costs will be attributed to Web design, development, and the initial promotion for your site. You will likely incur database development costs as well, because your site should include a searchable database of the various classified ads. Initial costs will likely run between $4,000 and $12,000.

Number of Employees Needed to Start
One employee is needed to run this business.

INTERNATIONAL POTENTIAL

There is lots of international potential for this type of business.

E-BUSINESS MODEL/PAYMENT PROCESSING METHOD

E-business level 3 is most appropriate for this type of business. For more information, see Part 1.

IMPORTANT BUSINESS ISSUES TO BE ADDRESSED

Organization is your biggest concern. A lot of confusion can come about from having a site with users posting classified ads. Clearly state the guidelines for posting and maintaining ads. You also have to be on the watch for inappropriate postings.

It will require a greater investment, but you might want to have a fully automated site developed where, upon paying a fee, the client has access to a form to enter the text and any graphics to be included in his or her ad.

ONLINE MARKETING TECHNIQUES

- Develop as many links as possible from related Web sites, meta-indexes, and directories.

- You should consider having your site listed with various cybermalls that are frequented by your target market.

- Participate in newsgroups, mailing lists, and discussion forums where you could easily promote your business with a cleverly designed signature file.

For a more detailed description of these techniques, along with many other effective online marketing methods, I recommend the companion book *101 Ways to Promote Your Web Site*. You can also find tons of free resources at *http://www.susansweeney.com/resources.html*.

ADDITIONAL INCOME

You can generate additional revenue by selling sponsorship opportunities for your mail list. Your mail list should encourage participation from your Web site by asking if the visitor would like to be notified when you update your classifieds or when a particular type of item is posted.

You can generate banner advertising revenue from your site. If you have high traffic volumes, your classified advertisers will be happy and your banner advertisers will generate higher revenue for you.

ONLINE EXAMPLES

Buy & Sell Online Classifieds
http://www.buysell.com
A Canadian buy-and-sell classified ads site.

The Ad Net!
http://www.theadnet.com
Internet classified advertising.

16. Collector Store—Rare Books and Records Finder

OVERVIEW OF BUSINESS

There are many people online who collect rare books, memorabilia, and antique items. A large number of these people head to the Web in search of what they want. If you're an enthusiast in this area, what better way to earn some extra money than using your knowledge of the subject to help others out in their search? The Internet is one of the first places people go to look for these types of items these days. You could also set up all or part of your site as an auction site where people can sell their items on your Web site. You would take a commission of the final sale or require users to pay an up-front fee (safer) to list their item.

SKILLS NEEDED

You would need to have an extensive knowledge of rare books, memorabilia, music, or other collectors' items, and would need to know their value and where to find them.

COST TO START THIS BUSINESS

The costs to start this business will include a computer, scanner, appropriate business software, Web design, development, and hosting, as well as storefront software. Total cost for the aforementioned could be $3,000 to $10,000. Other costs may include purchasing product for resale, and these costs are all dependent on what you carry and how much you carry as inventory. You might also want to consider purchasing a digital camera to capture graphics of the items you have available for sale.

Number of Employees Needed

This is a business you will likely run as a one-person operation; it can even be run on a part-time basis.

International Potential

There is lots of international potential in this business.

E-Business Model/Payment Processing Method

The level of e-business is dependent on what products and services you offer and how they are offered. If you provide a finder service, then level 1 is appropriate. If you offer only a few products for sale, then level 2 or 3 is appropriate. If a storefront is appropriate given the number of products you are selling, then level 3 is the appropriate model. If you are running an auction as well, you will want specialized software that you will likely want to be integrated with your back-end systems. For this you will want level 4. For more information, see Part 1.

Important Business Issues to Be Addressed

If your site follows the auction format and you plan to charge a commission on sales, be sure you have a secure system in place to ensure that you get paid. Know how you will track sales and how you will receive payment. If you are going to provide a search service, be sure you have the right connections and are able to quickly access items your clients are looking for.

Online Marketing Techniques

- Develop a comprehensive link strategy. Music sites, book sites, rarity sites, collectibles sites, and so on, are all appropriate locations to get yourself linked. Don't ignore relevant meta-indexes either.

- Participate in newsgroups, discussion forums, and mailing lists related to collectors, rare books and coins, memorabilia, and music with a cleverly designed signature file.

- Practice permission marketing by asking visitors if they would like to be notified via e-mail when you offer new products of the type they are interested in.

- Develop a mail list with news on new products and articles of interest to collectors. Prominently display your Subscribe button throughout your site.

- Provide a "Tell a Friend" program that would allow visitors to send an e-mail regarding any of your products to their friends.

- Links from cybermalls that focus on collectibles would be very appropriate for this type of business and could lead to significant traffic.

- Web ring participation should also be considered. There are all kinds of Web rings that focus on these types of products.

For a more detailed description of these techniques, along with many other effective online marketing methods, I recommend the companion book *101 Ways to Promote Your Web Site*. You can also find tons of free resources at *http://www.susansweeney.com/resources.html*.

ADDITIONAL INCOME

Think of all the items that go along with the territory. You can sell artwork reproductions or antique audio equipment, and maybe even perform restoration services if you have the necessary skills. Consider launching your own online publication too!

ONLINE EXAMPLES

Record Finders
http://www.recordfinders.com
A publication, but they also sell paraphernalia for out-of-print vinyl records and the music industry.

Bibliofind
http://www.bibliofind.com
They have a huge selection of old and rare books.

17. Commercial Cleaning

OVERVIEW OF BUSINESS

This type of business would operate offline, but would use the Web as a communication and promotional medium with its target market. Your Web site would promote your services, and you might decide to include a free-quote option or the ability to set up corporate accounts online. A few of the services you could include are:

- Carpet cleaning

- Furniture cleaning

- Wall washing

- Floor cleaning

- Draperies cleaning

- Water, smoke, and fire damage restoration

- Air-quality testing.

SKILLS NEEDED
Knowledge of cleaning supplies and what works best in certain situations would be a valuable asset. You may need to acquire certification to do some tasks, such as air-quality testing or specific types of cleaning.

COST TO START THIS BUSINESS
The development of your Web site and promotional materials will factor into your start-up costs. Any cleaning supplies needed and certification courses you are required to take will also factor in. Expect start-up costs to be between $1,000 and $3,000.

NUMBER OF EMPLOYEES NEEDED TO START
This depends on how much business you plan to take on. You can get started with yourself, and as business picks up you can slowly expand your work force. This type of operation can be started as a part-time business.

INTERNATIONAL POTENTIAL
There is very little international potential. Most of your business will be derived for your immediate area or surrounding communities.

E-BUSINESS MODEL/PAYMENT PROCESSING METHOD
E-business level 1 is most appropriate for this type of business. For more information, see Part 1.

IMPORTANT BUSINESS ISSUES TO BE ADDRESSED

Do your research. This is a very popular business idea, so you will want to understand who your competition is. You do not want to get involved in a business area that is overly saturated.

ONLINE MARKETING TECHNIQUES

- Participate in newsgroups and discussion forums related to commercial cleaning.

- Develop links from as many Web sites, meta-indexes, and directories related to commercial cleaning as possible. You should also have your site listed in as many online business directories as possible. You will want to focus on those that target your geographic area.

- Develop a sponsored listings campaign to bid on appropriate keyword phrases with the popular search engines.

- To increase repeat traffic, you might want to develop a newsletter offering helpful cleaning tips. This will encourage people to visit your site and find out more about your products and services.

For a more detailed description of these techniques, along with many other effective online marketing methods, I recommend the companion book *101 Ways to Promote Your Web Site.* You can also find tons of free resources at *http://www.susansweeney.com/resources.html.*

ADDITIONAL INCOME

If you are considering expanding your business into other product or service areas, you could generate additional income by selling cleaning products and supplies. If you want to expand the business itself, then you might consider setting up franchise opportunities.

ONLINE EXAMPLES

Regina's Maids
http://www.reginasmaids.com
A cleaning company located in Hoboken, NJ. They offer residential and corporate cleaning services to the tri-state area.

Capital Cleaning Services, Inc.
http://www.capitalcleaning.com
This is a Chicago-based business cleaning service for office, retail, and manufacturing buildings.

18. Community Events Web Site

OVERVIEW OF BUSINESS MODEL

This business takes advantage of several of the primary strengths of the Internet—dynamic presentation of information, easy updatability, and quick and easy accessibility. Community events usually are posted in the newspaper or occasionally are advertised on television. Finding and attending one of these events can be quite a hassle, especially for people working in an office all day. The purpose of a community event Web site is to provide easy, up-to-date access to a complete list of community events. By using the Internet to dynamically present this information, you will gain a significant advantage over newspapers and television. With the right online marketing strategy, you will have a lot of traffic. You will make your money primarily through advertising.

SKILLS NEEDED

Your staff must have basic computer skills. An ability to program in HTML and design graphics would be useful if you don't want to go through the time and expense to have a user-friendly database developed. You will want to develop online marketing expertise, as the more traffic you attract to your site, the greater your revenue will be.

COST TO START THIS BUSINESS

This is a relatively easy and inexpensive business to start online. You will need to invest in a computer, appropriate software, Web site design, development, and hosting. You should also invest in marketing both online and offline to create exposure and traffic for your site. Start-up costs will range from $3,000 to $10,000.

NUMBER OF EMPLOYEES NEEDED TO START

The number of employees needed depends on the skills of your employees. You will need at least one of each of the following: a Web developer, a graphic designer, and someone to keep your information up to date. A highly skilled and dedicated individual could perform all three jobs.

INTERNATIONAL POTENTIAL

The international potential of your business is extremely low. Only tourists visiting your city and looking for something to do during their stay would be interested in your site.

E-BUSINESS MODEL/PAYMENT PROCESSING METHOD

E-business level 1 is most appropriate for this type of business. If you choose to sell tickets for events online as well, then you will need to expand your service to a minimum of level 3 or level 4. For more information, see Part 1.

IMPORTANT BUSINESS ISSUES TO BE ADDRESSED

Since you are providing an information service, it is imperative that your information be up to the minute and constantly updated. This should be relatively easy, however, since your basic service is effectively free advertising for those interested in exposure for their event. If you choose to allow for online ordering of tickets, then you will need to arrange a place for your customers to pick the tickets up or a delivery mechanism.

ONLINE MARKETING TECHNIQUES

- Asking if your customers would like to be kept updated via e-mail on events in a specific field of interest is a great way to implement permission marketing.

- Develop coupons and discounts for various events to be used as an incentive. Ask site visitors if they would like to join your mail list to regularly receive these coupons and specials.

- You might also consider using a viral marketing technique like "Tell a Friend." This will allow your customers to promote your site to their friends.

- Develop a comprehensive link strategy. Request links from as many local Web sites as possible by offering them in return access to the updated information for their site visitors from your site.

- Develop a banner advertising campaign targeting local sites that get a lot of traffic. Having your banner ad prominently displayed on local newspaper sites generally is effective. Quite often you can trade the banner placement for a weekly posting of your Calendar of Events in their newspaper.

For a more detailed description of these techniques, along with many other effective online marketing methods, I recommend the companion book *101 Ways to Promote Your Web Site*. You can also find tons of free resources at *http://www.susansweeney.com/resources.html*.

ADDITIONAL INCOME

A way to expand your service is to allow for the online ordering of tickets to the events through your Web site. Depending on how you choose to do this, it could work one of two ways. You could make the ticket providers pay for the privilege of offering their tickets through your service. However, unless you are well known and have a significant volume of Web site traffic, this is unlikely to work. Usually you will charge a small fee to the purchaser for your efforts. You could provide Calendar of Events listings for free but charge a fee if they want a hypertext link to their site or enhanced graphics.

ONLINE EXAMPLES

The Maine Events Scheduler
http://maineevents.com
A list of events in the state of Maine.

Toronto.com
http://www.toronto.com
A beautiful site that covers most things you would want to do in the Toronto area. Plus it provides information on the events themselves.

19. Concierge Service

OVERVIEW OF BUSINESS MODEL

As the number of jet-set traveling business-people rises, a serious demand develops for concierge services that originate online and then turn into a high-touch service once the client is within your geographic area. Today's online concierge service has many advantages over what the word previously meant. The client finds and interacts with you through your Web site.

Here's how it works: Clients can e-mail you their schedule, tell you what they would like for a grocery list and where they might like to make dinner reservations, tell you what they need copied and couriered, tell you what transportation needs they have, and so on. You provide all the services that an assistant, housekeeper, and personal planner would, and you charge for your services based on the added value of having all these services done by one business or capable individual. It saves tons of time for a business traveler, and it's becoming popular.

SKILLS NEEDED

To operate this business, you need a personable manner and an organized method of doing things. Your clients will look to you for advice on how to best get along in the new city they have come to work in. Having knowledge of the area and knowing how to make a business traveler comfortable will ensure that you succeed in this business. You will need basic Web publishing skills to update your Web site and proper writing skills so your communication with clients is concise and professional.

COST TO START THIS BUSINESS

The cost to start this business will include a computer, appropriate software, and a printer. You will also incur costs related to the design, development, and marketing of your Web site. Suggested costs for these expenses is $3,000 to $7,000. There are no inventory or overhead costs that come out of pocket before your client pays for your services, so this business is perfect for someone looking to start from scratch.

NUMBER OF EMPLOYEES NEEDED TO START

To begin, you will need only one capable and organized part-time person. If you become busy, however, you will have to hire more help in order to continue to deliver high-touch personalized service.

INTERNATIONAL POTENTIAL

There is international potential for this business. Foreign visitors may be particularly in need of your services.

E-BUSINESS MODEL/PAYMENT PROCESSING METHOD

E-business level 1 is ideal for concierge services. There is no need for online payment processing because the client pays you directly. For more information, see Part 1.

IMPORTANT BUSINESS ISSUES TO BE ADDRESSED

In this business you want to be a careful money monitor. You may want to get a retainer upon signing the contract for out-of-pocket expenses. The client will be asking you to complete services that require paying up front, such as photocopying, dry cleaning, and buying groceries. You should have a budget for all the expenses and make sure you are not losing any profit due to poor bookkeeping. Remember that the service you are providing should be tailored to the individual. It's your job to make their days run as smoothly as possible. If you master this, many more jobs could come your way. It's a great business for referrals. You want to have your responsibilities and your client's budget and expectations for specific expenses clearly laid out in a contract.

ONLINE MARKETING TECHNIQUES

- Develop a comprehensive link strategy. Generate links with descriptive text describing your services on the main business services sites in your area—for example, the local chamber of commerce Web site. Get listed and linked from the regional online directories and publications that have content geared for the business traveler.

- Develop a sponsored listings campaign to bid on appropriate keyword phrases with the popular search engines.

- Gather client testimonials and publish these on your Web site.

For a more detailed description of these techniques, along with many other effective online marketing methods, I recommend the companion book *101 Ways to Promote Your Web Site*. You can also find tons of free resources at *http://www.susansweeney.com/resources.html*.

ADDITIONAL INCOME

Additional income could certainly come from tipping, which is widely practiced in this business. Other ways to increase your income are broadening your services to include more sophisticated skills such as taking notes at meetings and becoming more of an administrative assistant than a concierge. Once you have a working relationship with each client, providing all the services humanly possible for them will be the source of additional income. It all depends on how flexible you are.

Figure 2.2.   An excellent example of an online concierge service.

ONLINE EXAMPLE

Worldwide Assistance
http://www.worldwideassistance.com/concierge.htm
Virtual assistant and concierge services provided internationally.
Theconciergeforyou.com (Figure 2.2).

20. Cookbooks and Recipes

OVERVIEW OF BUSINESS MODEL

The popularity of online cooking and recipe Web sites is growing constantly.
Similar to purchasing a traditional offline cookbook at a bookstore, many people
are now turning to the Web to find their latest recipes and purchase their cookbooks online.

There are a few ways that you can generate revenue with this type of business. Since your site will receive highly targeted traffic, you will provide an

excellent advertising opportunity for cooking, food, or kitchen-related businesses. You can sell cookbooks and other cooking-related publications directly from your site. You can also charge a membership fee for this type of business whereby only members would be able to access certain sections of the site by way of a user ID and password.

This type of business also gives you a tremendous opportunity to practice permission marketing. You can ask people if they would like to be notified when you make updates to your Web site or if they would like to receive daily recipes via e-mail. This will encourage people to return to your site often and will also provide you with another advertising opportunity to offer cooking, food, or kitchen-related businesses. If you send out a daily or weekly newsletter, you could sell advertising space in your newsletter to cooking-related businesses. You may choose to develop a niche for yourself in this area. You could develop a heart smart cooking site, a low-cal cooking site, or a macrobiotic diet site.

SKILLS NEEDED

Since you will be offering your visitors cooking advice and recipes, knowledge of different foods and cooking techniques would be an asset. This will enable you to answer any questions your visitors may ask. The more you know about cooking, the more professional your business will appear.

COST TO START THIS BUSINESS

Initially you will have to pay for the design and hosting of your Web site, computer hardware, computer software, a scanner (to scan your cookbook covers), and a printer. If you currently have some of these items, your initial start-up costs will be considerably lower. If you plan on setting up a comprehensive mailing list system, you will also have to purchase mailing list software to help you organize and maintain your mail lists. Other costs that you will incur are related to the promotion of your Web site. Estimated cost is $5,000 to $10,000 to start.

NUMBER OF EMPLOYEES NEEDED TO START

One dedicated individual can run this type of business. You can start this venture while keeping your regular full-time job until your business's revenue surpasses your current income.

INTERNATIONAL POTENTIAL

This business has strong international potential. New recipes and cooking techniques are of interest to people all over the world.

E-BUSINESS MODEL/PAYMENT PROCESSING METHOD

Since you will be selling traditional offline cookbooks directly from your site, e-business level 2 or 3 would be most appropriate for this type of business. For more information on this, see Part 1.

IMPORTANT BUSINESS ISSUES TO BE ADDRESSED

You should ensure that the recipes that you publish on your site and in your cookbooks are original and have not been copied directly from another source. This is an issue that many cooking sites have faced in the past. To avoid copyright issues, always get permission in writing and cite where you have received the recipe from. This will avoid any future conflicts that you may face with competing businesses or copyrighted cooking publications.

ONLINE MARKETING TECHNIQUES

- Participating in newsgroups and discussion forums related to cooking would be a great way to generate traffic to your Web site. Always make a valuable contribution, and always include your signature file with a great tagline.

- Launch a strategic banner advertising campaign on Web sites frequented by your target market. These sites could include cooking sites, food-related sites, and kitchen accessory sites.

- Develop a viral marketing strategy where people can "Send This Recipe to a Friend" via your site. This will spread the word about your site.

- You could hold a weekly or monthly contest on your Web site for a free cookbook. You could ask people if they would like to be notified of the winner via e-mail. This e-mail will encourage them to return to your site to reenter your contest, thus re-exposing them to your site.

- Develop a discussion board on your site where visitors can interact with one another about cooking, great recipes, and past food experiences. This is a great way to encourage people to return to your site, as they will love to participate in your virtual cooking community. You can even participate in the discussion, which enables you to interact with your potential customers.

- You could choose to have a Visiting Chefs section on your site where you could profile a celebrity chef and provide some of his or her secret recipes. You might choose to post in advance the celebrity chef calendar and ask people if they'd like to be notified when you update the calendar. If you wanted to incorporate some higher-end technology, you could have a live webcast or downloadable video accessible from your site.

For a more detailed description of these techniques, along with many other effective online marketing methods, I recommend the companion book *101 Ways to Promote Your Web Site*. You can also find tons of free resources at *http://www.susansweeney.com/resources.html*.

ADDITIONAL INCOME

You could generate additional income for your cookbook and recipe site by selling a database of your favorite recipes on CD-ROM. This would be similar to your cookbooks. However, the low costs of developing this product would dramatically increase the overall revenue for your business.

ONLINE EXAMPLES

The Kitchen Link
http://www.kitchenlink.com
This is a large recipe site that uses several online marketing techniques to keep traffic coming to its site, including a newsletter, a mailing list, discussion boards, and a cooking advice column.

RecipeCenter.com
http://www.recipecenter.com
A dynamite recipe Web site with thousands of great recipes for visitors to read. A great feature about this site is that they have a "Tell a Friend" option, which enables them to practice viral marketing. Visitors can e-mail up to five friends at once to tell them about RecipeCenter.com, and if they do, their name is entered in a drawing for a free cookbook. This is a great strategy!

21. Copy Writing

OVERVIEW OF BUSINESS MODEL

Today advertisers are realizing that cleverly written copy can seriously affect the responsiveness to their ads and marketing collateral. Online and offline content has to be designed in a cleverly written manner to induce the reader to purchase the business's products or services, or otherwise do what the advertiser wants them to do. If you have excellent writing skills and have advertising copy-writing experience, this could be the ideal business venture for you.

SKILLS NEEDED

Excellent writing skills and past experience with writing creative advertising copy are essential to operating this type of business.

COST TO START THIS BUSINESS

Since you are providing a service that has no inventory, your initial costs will be minimal. You will have to pay for the design, development, and hosting of your Web site. You will have to invest in an appropriate computer, software, a scanner, and a printer. Other costs that you will incur are associated with promoting your copy-writing service online and offline. The cost to start this type of business will generally range from $4,000 to $10,000.

NUMBER OF EMPLOYEES NEEDED TO START

One full-time employee is needed to run this type of business. If your business requests exceed what you're capable of handling, you might consider hiring an additional employee.

INTERNATIONAL POTENTIAL

This business has strong international potential.

E-BUSINESS MODEL/PAYMENT PROCESSING METHOD

E-business level 1 is most appropriate for this type of business. For more information, see Part 1.

IMPORTANT BUSINESS ISSUES TO BE ADDRESSED

It is important to remember that if you are writing copy for a company from another culture, you should understand the culture for which you are writing the copy. In many instances advertising firms have designed and implemented a marketing campaign before understanding what the culture was all about. This has resulted in offending millions of individuals with advertisements that offend the home country's culture. If you decide to take on any international projects, make sure you do your research first before you write your advertising copy. One bad experience could seriously hinder the future of your copy-writing business.

ONLINE MARKETING TECHNIQUES

- Participate in newsgroups and discussion forums related to marketing and advertising with a cleverly designed signature file.

- Participating in advertising and marketing-related mailing lists would enable you to display your expertise while directing traffic to your Web site.

- Develop links from as many advertising, marketing, and business-service-related Web sites, meta-indexes, and directories as possible.

- Participate in marketing related e-zines through contribution of appropriate articles that feature your expertise and knowledge of your craft.

For a more detailed description of these techniques, along with many other effective online marketing methods, I recommend the companion book *101 Ways to Promote Your Web Site*. You can also find tons of free resources at *http://www.susansweeney.com/resources.html*.

ADDITIONAL INCOME

To earn additional income, you might want to consider offering graphic design services to your clients. Since this would complement your copy-writing service, you would be able to develop extensive promotional pieces for your clients.

ONLINE EXAMPLES

2Hot Designs
http://www.2hotdesigns.com
2Hot Designs is an image creation firm that specializes in Web design, graphic design, and creative copy-writing services.

Nick Usborne
http://www.nickusborne.com
Nick Usborne is a copy-writing business specializing in a strategic approach to copy writing online. They write and edit content to ensure that the message is concise, effective, and effortless.

22. Coupon Site

OVERVIEW OF BUSINESS MODEL

Everyone loves to save money. That is why we are witnessing the emergence of coupon networks online, where consumers can easily visit the site, view coupons, print them, and use them in a traditional offline store. Coupon networks can be targeted at both national and regional audiences, depending on your online objectives and marketing budget.

How does it work? It's simple. You charge businesses to advertise their coupons on your site. You then promote your site to the area that you are targeting (whether it be national or regional) and encourage your visitors to use the coupons available on your Web site. It's as easy as that!

SKILLS NEEDED

Strong online marketing skills would be an asset to run this type of business.

COST TO START THIS BUSINESS

The cost to set up and run this type of business ranges from $4,000 to $50,000. Start-up costs include computer hardware and software, a scanner, and a printer. Initially you will also have to pay for the design, development, and hosting of your Web site. You may want to develop a fully automated system where customers can have password-controlled access to forms online to input their coupons and pay for coupon placement. The development costs for the program would vary depending on the complexity. All additional costs are associated with promoting your business online and offline.

NUMBER OF EMPLOYEES NEEDED TO START

This business can be started with one person. However, to attract lots of visitors to your site and encourage them to come back often, you will want lots of coupons on your site. This is not easily accomplished by only one person.

INTERNATIONAL POTENTIAL

Since different countries have different pricing strategies and currencies, this type of business does not have strong international potential. It is better suited for a national or regional market.

E-BUSINESS MODEL/PAYMENT PROCESSING METHOD

E-business level 1 is most appropriate for this type of business initially. If you go for the fully automated system, you will want to progress to level 2. For more information on this, see Part 1.

IMPORTANT BUSINESS ISSUES TO BE ADDRESSED

Many of your coupon advertisers will provide repeat business for your coupon network if they get a good response; therefore, it is important to develop strong relationships with these advertisers and make sure a lot of their coupons are responded to. It is important to provide guidelines and tips on what makes an effective coupon. Don't do anything that may jeopardize your relationship with these advertisers as it may hinder the chances of their doing repeat business with your organization. One bad experience can turn multiple advertisers away from doing business with your coupon network. To ensure that you avoid this problem, you should consider implementing a strategic customer relationship management system.

Many of the people accessing the site will be home users and may have dial-up access. Large graphic files will take longer to download. The longer the download time, the more likely it is that the visitor will click away before the Web page is viewed. With coupons being graphic intensive, it is important that you have restrictions on acceptable file sizes to ensure quick and easy access to all pages of your site.

ONLINE MARKETING TECHNIQUES

- Develop a comprehensive link strategy. Generate links from as many related topic-specific Web sites, local Web sites with high traffic, appropriate directories, and meta-indexes as possible.

- Launch a strategic banner advertising campaign on Web sites frequented by your target market. These sites could include geographically targeted Web sites or industry-specific sites.

- Develop your own personal mailing list to communicate with your site visitors. You could ask people if they would like to be notified when you update the coupons offered on your site. This is a great permission marketing technique to increase the repeat traffic to your Web site.

- Develop a banner advertising campaign where your banners are the actual coupons from your site. These banners would be strategically placed on appropriate sites.

- Develop a sponsored listings campaign to bid on appropriate keyword phrases with the popular search engines.

- Develop a viral marketing strategy where people can "Send This Coupon to a Friend" via your site. This will help to spread the word about your site.

For a more detailed description of these techniques, along with many other effective online marketing methods, I recommend the companion book *101 Ways to Promote Your Web Site.* You can also find tons of free resources at *http://www.susansweeney.com/resources.html.*

ADDITIONAL INCOME

You might consider developing a coupon book that would be printed and sold offline. These are popular with fund raisers and would be a natural add-on for this type of business.

ONLINE EXAMPLES

CouponNetwork.ca
http://www.couponnetwork.ca
This is a dynamite coupon site for consumers in Nova Scotia, Canada.

CoolSavings.com
http://www.coolsavings.com
CoolSavings.com is a very popular U.S. coupon site offering a wide range of coupons to its consumers.

23. Craft Store

OVERVIEW OF BUSINESS MODEL

Online craft sites became popular as soon as the Internet became a household reality. One of the greatest benefits of the craft industry is the variety of items and the fact that they can be made at home. Much like the art market, customers will buy a craft based on their own preferences. They will tend to look at many sites before finding one that they like.

The content on the site should make each craft seem unique in every way, and there should be contests and interactive features throughout the Web site that keep the users coming back and entertained.

At start-up your craft store will most likely include only the products you produce yourself. However, if you know other people who produce crafts, you can ask if they would be interested in having their products sold online. Since your main source of income will be from selling crafts through your Web site, it is in your interest to work out a deal with your colleagues where you get paid a commission if and when their products are sold.

SKILLS NEEDED

The homemade craft industry operates in a unique and insular fashion. A broad familiarity with people in the homemade craft industry as well as a fairly comprehensive knowledge of the products will be required to gain the respect of the people involved and should be considered basic skills for this project. You will need Web publishing and digital imaging skills. You will have to manage the online store, process payments, and interact with customers regarding their orders and shipping details.

COST TO START THIS BUSINESS

The cost to set up and run this type of business ranges from $3,000 to $7,000. Your initial setup costs will include a personal computer, a scanner or digital camera, and the appropriate software to process the images and publish them on the Web site. You will also need to have your own Web site designed, developed, and hosted. Additional costs associated with opening your own business are the promoting of your business online and offline. If you have your own computer, then you can reduce your expenses accordingly.

NUMBER OF EMPLOYEES NEEDED TO START

This type of business can easily be started as a one-person part-time venture from the comfort of your home.

INTERNATIONAL POTENTIAL

Crafts are already an international industry. In fact, you should be prepared to have people all over the world showing interest and purchasing your crafts, depending on their size and the cost of shipping.

E-BUSINESS MODEL/PAYMENT PROCESSING METHOD

E-business level 3 is most appropriate for this type of business. For more information, see Part 1.

IMPORTANT BUSINESS ISSUES TO BE ADDRESSED

The value of crafts is a disputed topic. The prices should be reasonable and competitive with other craft sites on the Web. Make sure to align yourself with crafters who produce quality goods that do not get damaged easily during shipment.

ONLINE MARKETING TECHNIQUES

- Start an affiliate program where others can recommend and provide a link to your site. You will have to pay a referral fee for every order that comes to you via your associates' links.

- Joining or operating a Web ring related to crafts will likely generate substantial traffic to your site. The average person will tend to look through a few craft sites looking for something they like.

- Use a viral marketing approach by allowing your customers to send e-mails or screen shots to their friends of items of interest. These Tell a Friend programs are growing in popularity.

- Develop a sponsored listings campaign to bid on appropriate keyword phrases with the popular search engines.

- Use permission marketing. Ask if your customers would like to be notified when the new crafts for the season are up for sale—Christmas, Thanksgiving, and Valentine's Day, for example.

- Approach the operators of e-mail reminder services and get them to suggest your site as a good place to look for an affordable gift for their clients' loved ones.

For a more detailed description of these techniques, along with many other effective online marketing methods, I recommend the companion book *101 Ways to Promote Your Web Site.* You can also find tons of free resources at *http://www.susansweeney.com/resources.html.*

ADDITIONAL INCOME
You can sell banner advertising from your site or provide sponsorship opportunities in your mail list.

24. Custom-Made Calendars

OVERVIEW OF BUSINESS MODEL
Today, with access to the Internet, people have come to expect a certain level of personal choice. Many people enjoy having their own personal calendar set for personal use or as a gift for friends and relatives.

Custom calendars are a wonderful choice for a simple gift idea or a great way to spruce up the office. These are wonderful gifts for parents or grandparents, as each month or each day can have an interesting picture of the children or grandchildren. They are also great corporate gifts, where each location or each product can be presented on each page. The custom applications are endless.

Now, with the extensive set of specialty publication software and the power of personal computers, it can be moderately easy to set up a small publication firm.

SKILLS NEEDED

The most important set of skills needed for creating custom calendars is superior graphic design capabilities. Familiarity with the various graphics programs available to you, particularly products like Adobe Photoshop, is a must.

COST TO START THIS BUSINESS

The cost to set up and run this type of business ranges from $2,000 to $7,000. Your initial setup costs include a personal computer, a photo-quality printer, and the appropriate software. You will also need to pay for the design, development, and hosting of your Web site, and possibly your storefront solution and merchant account setup. All additional costs are associated with promoting your business online and offline, and purchasing and holding a limited amount of inventory.

NUMBER OF EMPLOYEES NEEDED

This business can easily be started with one part-time individual.

INTERNATIONAL POTENTIAL

Your market size will be large, and most English-speaking international markets will provide an opportunity. Be aware that there will be markets that are closed to you due to language barriers.

E-BUSINESS MODEL/PAYMENT PROCESSING METHOD

E-business level 2 is most appropriate for this type of business. For more information, see Part 1.

IMPORTANT BUSINESS ISSUES TO BE ADDRESSED

You may be faced with significant online competition. This business has a low cost of entry. For this reason, you many want to target your calendars toward one particular niche of online customers. You might decide to specialize in pet calendars or corporate calendars. Also consider what volume of calendars you will be producing. If you turn out only a few a month, then you may wish to use a high-quality desktop or industrial printer. However, as your volume increases, you may need to utilize the services of a professional printing service, which may prove costly with little room for errors.

ONLINE MARKETING TECHNIQUES

- Develop a comprehensive link strategy. Generating links from other, related sites is an excellent way to bring targeted businesses to your Web site. You will want to be linked from sites that cater to your target market. You might establish links from appropriate cybermalls, gift-suggestion sites, and other appropriate directories.

- Generate a few samples to display on your Web site. Perhaps you could include a few great testimonials on that page of your site as well.

- You might also consider using a viral marketing technique like Tell a Friend. This will allow your customers to bring their friends to your Web site. If they enjoy your product, they're guaranteed to pass the information to a friend.

- Develop a sponsored listings campaign to bid on appropriate keyword phrases with the popular search engines.

- You might want to participate in Web rings related to *gifts* or *unusual gifts* or *one-of-a-kind gifts*.

For a more detailed description of these techniques, along with many other effective online marketing methods, I recommend the companion book *101 Ways to Promote Your Web Site*. You can also find tons of free resources at *http://www.susansweeney.com/resources.html*.

ADDITIONAL INCOME

You could easily expand your product line once your calendars are selling. With e-cards popping up everywhere on the Internet, this too could be a logical next step for your site. You could consider custom engraving, custom e-books, custom screen printing, custom mousepads, or other products that require the skill sets and the technology in your organization.

ONLINE EXAMPLES

Custom Made Calendars
http://www.custommadecalendars.com
This site is a good example of a custom calendar site. They have used the addition of private photos to establish a niche for themselves.

AmerICan Calendars
http://calendarco.com
Specialty calendars may be more appropriate than custom calendars. This is an example of a high-volume printing operation.

25. Custom-Printed Products

OVERVIEW OF BUSINESS MODEL

Promoting your Web site or business these days is a fully integrated process of traditional and progressive marketing techniques. A popular way to do this is to have the logo, URL, or business name printed on various items that we see and touch each day—things that are kept around a computer so that your Internet address is front and center when your potential client is only a click away from your Web site. Custom-printed products like coffee mugs, mouse pads, sticky notes, pens, and pencils are ideal promotional items to be used as giveaways at a trade show. Many businesses are promoting their Web addresses even more visibly on building signage, vehicle signage, or window awnings.

The Web is a perfect place to showcase and provide this service. Graphic files with corporate logos can be zipped and sent to you via e-mail. You can electronically send these files to all the production businesses that you hire to fulfill each order if you choose to outsource this activity. Clients probably should pay online for their order, but it's not absolutely necessary.

SKILLS NEEDED

You will need experience and contacts within the custom-printing business and a firm grasp of graphic design techniques. If you decide to do the design yourself, you could save more money than if you outsourced this work.

COST TO START THIS BUSINESS

Your initial setup costs include a personal computer and the appropriate software. You will also need to pay for the design, development, and hosting of your Web site, and possibly your storefront solution and merchant account setup. All additional costs are associated with promoting your business online and offline. The cost to set up and run this type of business ranges from $3,000 to $15,000.

NUMBER OF EMPLOYEES NEEDED TO START

This business can easily be started with one part-time individual.

INTERNATIONAL POTENTIAL

There is international potential for this type of business. You can reach businesses everywhere online, and many will be interested in this type of promotional product if it is marketed properly.

E-BUSINESS MODEL/PAYMENT PROCESSING METHOD

E-business levels 2 and 3 are most appropriate for this type of business. For more information, see Part 1.

IMPORTANT BUSINESS ISSUES TO BE ADDRESSED

This business has a low cost of entry. For this reason, you may want to target your printed products toward one particular niche of online customers. You might decide to specialize in customized items for the workplace that promote the company's URL. You might decide to provide unique products for the software industry. Choose a niche that promotes heavily, has a substantial budget for marketing, or participates in trade shows where giveaways are popular.

Make sure to keep yourself up to date on the best deals for the products you print on, and try to arrange a preferred customer or volume discount with the printing house you use so you can increase profits. As custom products have no market value to anyone else, you might want to get a deposit with the orders or have them prepaid.

ONLINE MARKETING TECHNIQUES

- Develop a comprehensive link strategy. Generate links from appropriate cybermalls, trade show supplier directories, and business product directories.

- Generate some great samples to display on your Web site. Perhaps you could include a few great testimonials on that page of your site as well.

- You might develop a mail list so that visitors can request notification whenever you add new products to your product line.

- Develop a sponsored listings campaign to bid on appropriate keyword phrases with the popular search engines.

- Develop an associate/affiliate program whereby other sites can recommend your service, provide a link to your site, and receive a commission or referral fee every time a customer links through and makes a purchase.

- Develop a banner advertising campaign targeted at trade show sites and business product sites.

For a more detailed description of these techniques, along with many other effective online marketing methods, I recommend the companion book *101 Ways to Promote Your Web Site*. You can also find tons of free resources at *http://www.susansweeney.com/resources.html.*

ADDITIONAL INCOME

You could easily expand your product line once your customized items are selling. Remain open to customer suggestions and new ideas for customizing.

ONLINE EXAMPLES

Mousepads.com
http://www.mousepads.com
Mousepads.com develops custom mousepads for businesses.

Giftmugs.com
http://www.giftmugs.com
Giftmugs.com prints business cards, corporate logos, and other pertinent information on mugs.

26. Cybermall Owner/Operator

OVERVIEW OF BUSINESS MODEL

Cybermalls are Internet shopping centers and are popular online businesses. A cybermall is basically a Web site that contains different categories of online stores that people can visit to purchase goods and services that they are interested in. There are typically four types of cybermalls: (1) geographically specific cybermalls (e.g., New England Craft Mall), (2) product- or service-specific cybermalls (e.g., Outdoor Adventure Mall), (3) industry-specific cybermalls (e.g., Financial Services Mall), or (4) demographic-specific cybermalls (Seniors Mall). The type of cybermall that you will start depends on your online objectives, your target market, and the types of products and services that you sell.

Cybermalls usually offer businesses two options: (1) The business can have its site listed in the cybermall with a link out to its Web site, or (2) the business can have a storefront developed within the cybermall.

There are several ways that you can generate revenue with this type of business. Typically, businesses pay the cybermall an initial setup fee for having their site listed in the cybermall, and then they pay a monthly listing fee or a percentage of all sales made from the referral. You can also sell advertising in the different categories of your cybermall. This advertising is usually very appealing to online businesses as the exposure is highly targeted.

SKILLS NEEDED

Knowledge of online advertising techniques is an asset to run this type of business. If you decide to launch a cybermall, you are going to have to ensure that you are generating as much traffic as possible to your site to make it appealing to possible vendors. To do this, you are going to have to dedicate a lot of time implementing various Internet marketing techniques to create a constant flow of traffic to your site. Knowledge about electronic storefronts, shopping carts, and electronic commerce would also be an asset.

COST TO START THIS BUSINESS

Initially you will have to pay for the design and hosting of your Web site, computer hardware, computer software, a scanner, and a printer. If you currently have some of these items, your initial start-up costs will be considerably lower. You should expect the cost for Web hosting to be considerably larger than that for a typical online business due to the high volumes of traffic that your site is going to receive and the space needed to set up vendors on your storefront. Either you will have to purchase storefront software, equipped with electronic shopping cart features, or you will be responsible for developing this in-house. If you plan on setting up a mailing list, you will also have to purchase mailing list software to help you organize and maintain your mail lists. It would probably be in your best interest to purchase comprehensive Web traffic analysis software to track where your Web site visitors are coming from. This information can be great for future marketing opportunities. Other costs that you will incur are related to the promotion of your Web site. Estimated cost is $10,000 to $30,000 to start.

NUMBER OF EMPLOYEES NEEDED TO START

The number of employees needed to run this type of business is one full-time individual and potentially one part-time employee. Initially you are going to be responsible for the mass promotion of your cybermall through various online mediums. This is going to be a very time-consuming task as a high volume of traffic is imperative for the success of a cybermall.

INTERNATIONAL POTENTIAL

This business has strong international potential. Since you are representing businesses that are selling their goods or services online, your cybermall would appeal to everyone.

E-BUSINESS MODEL/PAYMENT PROCESSING METHOD

E-business level 3 would be appropriate for this type of business. For more information, see Part 1.

IMPORTANT BUSINESS ISSUES TO BE ADDRESSED

You should ensure that your home page has an attractive interface with easy navigation throughout your site. Just like in a traditional retail outlet, visitors will not stay on your site if the environment is not appealing. Also, if some of your vendors choose to simply be listed on your site with a link out to their site, you should develop the interface so that the visitor doesn't actually leave your site. What you can do is have your vendor's site appear within a frame on your site. This enables the visitor to continue to navigate throughout your site without having to click back in his or her browser.

To keep your cybermall fresh, you should try to update your site on a regular basis. Consider having a What's New page on your site. You could ask visitors if they would like to be notified via e-mail when new items or affiliates are added to your cybermall. This would be a great way to generate repeat traffic from your site.

If you are going to provide vendors with merchant account and payment-processing services, you should ensure that none of your vendors engage in fraudulent activities. Since they are going to be using your merchant information, you should ask for credit references before allowing your vendors to do this.

Vendors are going to want to be listed in your cybermall for one reason—increased exposure. To ensure that this happens, you are going to have to do whatever you can to promote your business online and offline.

ONLINE MARKETING TECHNIQUES

- Launch a strategic banner advertising campaign on Web sites frequented by your target market. These sites could relate to the specific products, industry, or geographic location that your cybermall represents.

- Develop a viral marketing strategy whereby people can "Tell a Friend about This Product" via your site. This will spread the word about your site.

- You could hold a weekly or monthly contest on your Web site for a free product offered by one of your vendors. The vendor donating the product could be your Featured Vendor. You could ask people if they would like to be notified of the winner via e-mail. This e-mail will encourage them to return to your site to reenter your contest, thus re-exposing them to your site.

- Develop a sponsored listings campaign to bid on appropriate keyword phrases with the popular search engines.

- Develop as many links as possible from Web sites, directories, and meta-indexes related to your target market. These sites should relate to the specific products, industry, or geographic location that your cybermall represents.

For a more detailed description of these techniques, along with many other effective online marketing methods, I recommend the companion book *101 Ways to Promote Your Web Site*. You can also find tons of free resources at *http://www.susansweeney.com/resources.html*.

ADDITIONAL INCOME

As a cybermall operator, you can also offer additional services to vendors such as secure online ordering and payment processing, product search capabilities, and electronic shopping cart features. You can also provide vendors with a standard storefront development model, which enables them to easily set up their virtual presence in your cybermall. All of these features are available to potential vendors at a price, which means that there are many different ways for your cybermall to generate additional income.

ONLINE EXAMPLES

The Travel Mall
http://www.oztravel.com.au
Everything you need to plan your trip down under.

247Malls.com
http://247malls.com
The place to buy anything online.

Hsn.com
http://www.hsn.com

A beautiful craft site, well laid out with fully integrated e-commerce. It also has an enormous selection of products divided neatly into categories.

Inspirational Images
http://www.inspirationalphotoimages.com
A well-done site dedicated to inspirational art photography.

27. Desktop Imagery

OVERVIEW OF BUSINESS
Are you a graphic designer? Do you have a large gallery of desktop images that you randomly display on your computer? If so, why not turn your talent into a profitable business? Many graphic designers are now making money for using their natural talents. Desktop imagery is something that everyone likes to use to help brighten up his or her computer. So why not cash in on this opportunity?

You can set up a desktop imagery Web site where people can pay a monthly or annual membership to be able to enter a secure section of your site and download your hottest desktop images. You don't even have to design all of the images yourself. You can partner with other graphic designers and sell their images on your site. You can give them a percentage of the revenue generated from your site memberships in accordance with the number of their images that have been downloaded. It's as easy as that!

SKILLS NEEDED
Excellent graphic design skills are essential to run this type of business.

COST TO START THIS BUSINESS
Your talent is free, but if you plan to attract people to your site, you are going to have to design a dynamite Web site. Since you will be hosting rather large images on your site, you will take up more storage space on the server you're hosting your site on; thus, you can expect the costs of hosting your site to be higher than those for a typical Web site. To start this business you will need a computer, appropriate software, a printer, and a scanner. You will also incur costs associated with the design, development, and hosting of your Web site. The costs to start this type of business will range from $3,000 to $10,000.

NUMBER OF EMPLOYEES NEEDED TO START
One full- or part-time employee is needed to run this type of business.

INTERNATIONAL POTENTIAL
Very high! As explained earlier, everyone loves desktop imagery!

E-BUSINESS MODEL/PAYMENT PROCESSING METHOD
E-business level 2 is most appropriate for this type of business. For more information, see Part 1.

IMPORTANT BUSINESS ISSUES TO BE ADDRESSED
You want to ensure that you continuously add quality artwork to your site. If you begin to lower your standards with what you place on your site, you will decrease the chances that someone will renew their membership with your business. If you find that you cannot publish quality artwork on a continuous basis, ask a fellow graphic designer if he or she would be interested in joining your business on a commission basis. You will want to address copyright and usage issues where you have artwork provided by others. You may want to provide several downloads for free on a trial basis to get people using your service.

ONLINE MARKETING TECHNIQUES

- Develop a comprehensive link strategy. Generate links from as many desktop-imagery-related Web sites, directories, and meta-indexes as possible.

- Launch a strategic banner advertising campaign on Web sites frequented by your target market.

- Develop your own personal mailing list to communicate with your site visitors. You could ask people if they would like to be notified when you update the imagery offered on your site.

- Develop a sponsored listings campaign to bid on appropriate keyword phrases with the popular search engines.

- You could hold a weekly or monthly contest on your site for a free membership to your desktop imagery Web site. You could ask people if they would like to be notified of the winner via e-mail. This will encourage them to return to your site to reenter your contest.

For a more detailed description of these techniques, along with many other effective online marketing methods, I recommend the companion book *101*

Ways to Promote Your Web Site. You can also find tons of free resources at *http://www.susansweeney.com/resources.html.*

ADDITIONAL INCOME

In addition to offering downloadable desktop imagery from your Web site, you could also sell CD-ROM compilations filled with past desktop favorites. This would be a great way to generate revenue for your business.

ONLINE EXAMPLES

DigitalBlasphemy.com
http://www.digitalblasphemy.com
This is a great site that has a terrific selection of popular desktop imagery available to its members.

Themes.Org
http://www.themes.org
Although they don't charge a membership fee, this exciting Web site offers the most comprehensive collection of UNIX window manager themes anywhere. Instead of charging a membership fee, this site makes money through advertising.

28. Dining Guide

OVERVIEW OF BUSINESS MODEL

This one is super easy to start and run for someone who loves the art of critiquing cuisine and sharing it with an audience. This business, although online, is regionally based because one should go to the restaurant and eat the meals to write the review. The content should remain current, and revenue can be generated primarily from advertising by local restaurants and eateries that want to be featured within the guide.

Your dining guide could be a simple searchable database of dining establishments in your local area or a comprehensive site with full menus updated on a regular basis, links to the restaurants' Web sites, and even reservation-taking capability. Alternatively, your site could be an independent restaurant review site.

SKILLS NEEDED

To run the Web site single-handedly, you should have basic Web publishing and digital imaging skills. If you choose to run a restaurant review site, you should have a knack for writing about food, presentation, and service. It would be advantageous to have prior experience in the restaurant or culinary-preparation industry.

Cost to Start This Business

The approximate cost to start this business is $2,000 to $5,000. To start this business you will need to design, develop, and host your Web site. Ongoing costs will include the time you commit to writing and publishing the guide.

Number of Employees Needed to Start

Only one! But eventually you may want to expand the guide regionally, and being online, this should be easy to do. You could establish a sales force to generate listings for inclusion, or for the food review site you could invite food critics at large to contribute their articles and increase the advertising potential of the site.

International Potential

There is not very much international potential to this online business because it is based on actual restaurants that you can go to rather than recipes, but there is potential for international action.

E-Business Model/Payment Processing Method

The e-business model suitable for the restaurant review site is level 1. The more comprehensive restaurant guide could be developed to be fully automated, where the restaurant owners could update their menus and specials through password-protected access. If you progress to this stage, you could use the level 3 e-business model as described in Part 1.

Important Business Issues to Be Addressed

The dining guide should have images to capture the visitor's interest and provide richly detailed reviews of the chosen dishes, with proper credit given to all the restaurants included together with links to their Web sites and so on. The content should encourage browsers to interact with the guide. There should be a facility for visitors to submit their own reviews and to win a free meal, for example.

The information on your site should always be current so that the menus you mention are available when a reader decides to go to a restaurant mentioned on your guide. The past reviews should be indexed in an archive and be accessible at all times.

ONLINE MARKETING TECHNIQUES

- You might also consider using a viral marketing technique like "Tell a Friend about This Restaurant." If one of your visitors is planning a dinner out with friends, this can be very effective. A novel feature like this might be worthy of developing a press release for distribution to your local newspaper for added exposure.

- You will want to develop a comprehensive link strategy. You will want to establish links from local Web sites that have large traffic volumes as well as links from sites that relate to restaurants.

- You may want to participate in geography-specific cybermalls.

- You may want to consider developing interactive press releases and distributing them to local publications, and also national and international food-related publications and e-zines.

- Get linked from online advertising directories.

- Develop a sponsored listings campaign to bid on appropriate keyword phrases with the popular search engines.

- You might want to hold regular contests where the prize is a dinner for two donated by one of the restaurants on your site. You can add an element of permission marketing here, asking site visitors if they want to be notified when you have a new contest.

For a more detailed description of these techniques, along with many other effective online marketing methods, I recommend the companion book *101 Ways to Promote Your Web Site*. You can also find tons of free resources at *http://www.susansweeney.com/resources.html.*

ADDITIONAL INCOME

Extra revenue potential is available if you add an e-commerce component to the site. For example, your guide could begin storing popular recipes in a virtual database and you could act as a reseller. Clients could purchase recipes and download them directly from the site. There is plenty of potential for advertising and paid feature articles in the dining guide.

Figure 2.3. Dineaid.com is a very popular dining guide for the Atlantic Canada region.

You could participate in the affiliate or associate programs of sites that sell gourmet or food-related items. You could recommend specific recipe books from Amazon.com or other online stores that have affiliate programs. You can sell banner advertising or sponsorship space to restaurants for added exposure.

ONLINE EXAMPLES

Dineaid.com
www.dineaid.com
You can view over 4,300 restaurant listings in Atlantic Canada, as well as menus, coupons, specials, and more (Figure 2.3).

RestaurantRow.com
http://www.restaurantrow.com
One of the world's largest online dining guides. View over 170,000 restaurants; make reservations, as well as look at menus.

29. Direct Marketing/Direct Mail

OVERVIEW OF BUSINESS MODEL

The Internet is the mecca for direct-marketing services. A virtual database is the most flexible and useful way to store and access the contacts needed to operate this business, and the Web is a perfect place to showcase your direct-marketing materials and skills. Most of the clientele will likely be other businesses, and the revenue will come from the payment for marketing services and access to targeted mail and e-mail lists.

SKILLS NEEDED

You should be organized, with experience in direct-marketing methods, and be sensitive to the different socioeconomic demographics encountered in global marketing pursuits. You should have computer skills and be familiar with design. You can provide the services yourself or perhaps contract out some of the components of each campaign, depending on your expertise and resources.

COST TO START THIS BUSINESS

The cost to get this business up and running will include the computer hardware and software costs, and the costs related to the design, development, and hosting of the Web site, and it is suggested that the lists of contacts be stored in a virtual database. The approximate cost to begin operation is $4,000 to $10,000.

NUMBER OF EMPLOYEES NEEDED TO START

The direct-marketing business can be started with one person, but for many projects undertaken, part-time help may be needed to complete the job. Portions of various contracts can also be outsourced.

INTERNATIONAL POTENTIAL

The international potential of this business depends entirely on which clients you are involved with and what their target markets are.

E-BUSINESS MODEL/PAYMENT PROCESSING METHOD

The e-business model suitable for this business during the first stage of development is level 1 or 2. For more information, refer to Part 1.

IMPORTANT BUSINESS ISSUES TO BE ADDRESSED

Issues to be addressed here are the cautions that come with any direct-marketing initiative, which are simply the responsible use of direct contact information and a strict policy that protects the privacy of the individuals within your database. You will want to have a double opt-in policy in place for the collection of contact information. You will need to clean your database often to eliminate stale or outdated addresses. Direct marketing is called such because it is designed to be targeted and high-touch in nature.

ONLINE MARKETING TECHNIQUES

- Organic search engine optimization as well as participating in a pay-per-click campaign with the major search engines

- Links from media partners and clients who are known to use your services as well as from appropriate directories related to direct-mail services and appropriate cybermalls

- Testimonials from successful campaigns circulated in timely newsletters to your clientele

- Articles in online direct-marketing industry publications or e-zines about your unique approaches and strategies.

For a more detailed description of these techniques, along with many other effective online marketing methods, I recommend the companion book *101 Ways to Promote Your Web Site*. You can also find tons of free resources at *http://www.susansweeney.com/resources.html*.

ADDITIONAL INCOME

Extra income comes into play once you have proven the effectiveness of your marketing techniques and the responsiveness of the contact lists you possess in your database. Consulting on various progressive direct-marketing strategies holds potential for additional income. Additional services could include list brokering, mailing list rentals, mailing list label production, and order fulfillment.

ONLINE EXAMPLES

Postmaster Direct
www.postmasterdirect.com
Postmaster Direct is the granddaddy of online e-mail rental list companies.

Alphamedia Direct Marketing
http://www.Alphamedia.co.uk
This site offers one-stop direct-mail shop list brokering and management, database design and management, label production and printing, fulfillment house, and full computer bureau services.

30. Do-It-Yourself Site

OVERVIEW OF BUSINESS MODEL

This business is a fun online pursuit because you can utilize your own interests and knowledge for the benefit of others. Enthusiasts all over the world use the Web to locate information and tips on how to tackle household projects by themselves. Another advantage to this business is the wide variety of topics you may consult on—everything from how to install three-prong electric sockets to gardening tips. Revenue can come from advertisers who are looking to target the do-it-yourselfers, such as Home Depot, Lowe's, and Canadian Tire.

SKILLS NEEDED

Obviously, being handy is a must for the operator of this business. Competent writing skills, Web publishing know-how, and basic digital imaging will be necessary to run the Web site.

COST TO START THIS BUSINESS

The start-up cost of this business is minimal. A ballpark range is $2,000 to $5,000. You will need a Web site, hosting, and a solid business plan.

NUMBER OF EMPLOYEES NEEDED TO START

To begin, only one employee is needed. If the demand for more tips and areas of interest increases, then you may want to hire a part-time do-it-yourself assistant to help in updating the Web site and continuing to market the site online and to potential advertisers.

INTERNATIONAL POTENTIAL

The international potential is immediate and is probably governed by household type and climate. If the tips are translated into other major languages, your international potential increases. There are online translators who charge by the word to assist you, should you decide to try it.

E-BUSINESS MODEL/PAYMENT PROCESSING METHOD

To begin, the revenue will probably come from advertisers that want to target your niche market. The budget-sensitive consumer is savvy on the Internet and knows how to find a deal. Contacting the suppliers with the lowest prices overall is a good idea. Stay away from the higher end. E-business level 1 is the most appropriate level for the do-it-yourself Web site. For more information, see Part 1.

IMPORTANT BUSINESS ISSUES TO BE ADDRESSED

An important thing to note in this business is that your site will have to balance the look and feel between professional and amateur because the browsers will want to feel as though you are doing the projects yourself. Therefore, you have to remain sensitive to budget, the tools you use, and so on. You must make sure not to alienate your target market, which will be looking to save money. This market may include a large number of women.

ONLINE MARKETING TECHNIQUES

- Organic search engine placement.

- Reciprocal linking with related do-it-yourself Web sites and other related-content Web sites.

- Get linked from online do-it-yourself directories.

- Provide articles for publishing in e-zines that focus on homemaking and hobbies.

- Develop an opt-in mail list to provide a regular newsletter filled with do-it-yourself tips.

For a more detailed description of these techniques, along with many other effective online marketing methods, I recommend the companion book *101 Ways to Promote Your Web Site*. You can also find tons of free resources at *http://www.susansweeney.com/resources.html*.

ADDITIONAL INCOME

Additional income could possibly come from participation in affiliate programs of suppliers that sell products to the do-it-yourself market. You can sell sponsorship and banner advertising opportunities on your mail list.

ONLINE EXAMPLES

DoItYourself.com
http://www.doityourself.com
Obviously one of the major do-it-yourself sites on the Web. However, it is only home repair, with no other do-it-yourself options offered.

Remodeling Online
http://www.remodelonline.com

A similar but much more diverse site than DoItYourself.com. They cover gardening as well as decorating and other things a homeowner may care about.

31. E-Books

OVERVIEW OF BUSINESS MODEL

E-books are gaining popularity. A popular example of a fiction e-book potential is Stephen King's success in publishing his latest horror novel in e-reader format on the Amazon Web site. The multitude of users attempting to download the book crashed the server! Obviously there is a demand. E-books can be written on a multitude of subjects, from Internet marketing to how to get through the teenage years to building a sailboat—the subjects are endless.

SKILLS NEEDED

You will need to be knowledgeable on your topic and be able to write well.

COST TO START THIS BUSINESS

The cost to begin this business depends on which approach you take. If you want to develop your own e-books and have them purchased and downloaded from your site, the cost will be negligible. If you decide to become a reseller or an online marketing outlet for e-books, the cost is significantly lower to begin. You will incur start-up costs related to design, development, and hosting of your Web site as well as expenses related to any storefront and payment-processing capability. Expect a ballpark price of $3,000 to $5,000 to begin.

NUMBER OF EMPLOYEES NEEDED TO START

This business can be started by one person who is organized and possesses an avid interest in reading and the supporting technology needed for e-books to be distributed. Eventually you may want to get technical support if you decide to have the e-books downloaded and purchased directly from your site.

INTERNATIONAL POTENTIAL

The international potential is immediate and depends heavily on online marketing strategy. Depending on the language of the e-books you feature, the market is international from the onset.

E-BUSINESS MODEL/PAYMENT PROCESSING METHOD

The e-business model suitable for this business during the first stage of development is level 1, but if you should decide to accept payment and allow download of the e-books from your site, level 3 is more appropriate. For more information, refer to Part 1.

IMPORTANT BUSINESS ISSUES TO BE ADDRESSED

To operate an e-business that sells and markets e-books, you have two basic options: to become a reseller affiliate for larger sites that already have the books loaded on their server, or to set up your site so that the e-books are purchased and downloaded from your own Web site.

ONLINE MARKETING TECHNIQUES

To market e-books online, you should consider the target audience and your niche. We suggest the following:

- Spend time researching where the niche of e-book buyers are surfing and work to become linked or advertised on the top sites you find in this research.

- Consider organic search engine optimization and participating in search engine pay per click campaigns.

- Establishing a viral marketing campaign like "Tell a Friend about This Book" might be very effective.

- Developing a targeted banner advertising campaign where readers of specific titles are visiting could generate significant traffic.

- Develop a mail list where visitors could opt in to receive notification as new titles are available. This could also be made available through an RSS feed.

- Get linked from online e-book directories.

- Links should be established from book-related cybermalls and e-book-related Web rings.

For a more detailed description of these techniques, along with many other effective online marketing methods, I recommend the companion book *101 Ways to Promote Your Web Site*. You can also find tons of free resources at *http://www.susansweeney.com/resources.html*.

ADDITIONAL INCOME

Additional income could come from advertising if the traffic reaches a sustained and healthy level. You may provide a service for new authors who want to publish in e-book format only, and this would give the content of your site an original edge, because people cannot obtain it anywhere else. You could provide an e-book development service for others.

ONLINE EXAMPLES

eBooks
http://www.ebooks.com
A site that holds assorted novels for download.

Adobe
http://www.adobe.com/epager/ebooks/main.htm.
Adobe's site deals with e-books being released in PDF format. There are links to many sites.

32. Educational Products

OVERVIEW OF BUSINESS MODEL

The sale and promotion of educational products online is a popular and growing business. Already there are online schools and courses that are accessible at any time from anywhere in the world. Downloadable educational software holds major possibilities in the future of learning. Niche-marketing opportunities can be exploited by choosing a particular set of subjects or age groups to cater to. Becoming the benchmark for a particular field of study would be wise considering that there are and will continue to be many Web sites offering educational materials via download.

SKILLS NEEDED

It is a good idea to have a background in the education market and some awareness of product availability in this market. You should have basic Web publishing skills and proper writing capabilities.

COST TO START THIS BUSINESS

The cost to start the ball rolling with your educational products online business consists of developing the Web site. Depending on how extensive the site is, and assuming that you will want to sell the products online, the estimated cost to start up is $3,000 to $7,000.

NUMBER OF EMPLOYEES NEEDED TO START

During the onset of this online business, one experienced individual should be capable of running things.

INTERNATIONAL POTENTIAL

If the products are suitable for all languages, the global potential is huge. The subject areas of the educational products you provide will determine how international the market is.

E-BUSINESS MODEL/PAYMENT PROCESSING METHOD

We recommend e-business level 3 for this online business. Refer to Part 1 for more information.

IMPORTANT BUSINESS ISSUES TO BE ADDRESSED

The first thing to do when setting up this business is establish a product base and define relationships with suppliers of these products. One must make sure that the wares that are provided are respected educational tools and materials within the subjects you concentrate on. The prices have to be competitive, and the content on your site should be geared to attract the buyer of the products, not necessarily the end user.

ONLINE MARKETING TECHNIQUES

Your site should be simple and user-friendly, not to mention easily found on the Internet's search engines and on education-related Web sites. We recommend the following techniques for marketing your business online:

- Organic search engine optimization as well as developing a sponsored listings campaign to bid on appropriate keyword phrases with the popular search engines.

- Developing a comprehensive links strategy. Links should be established with affiliated learning sites and suppliers of educational products.

- Real reviews and testimonials from users of the products available for sale on your site should be published on the site as well as in appropriate e-zines and newsletters.

- Viral marketing strategies like Tell a Friend should be employed.

- Permission marketing techniques should be employed. Ask visitors if they would like to be notified via e-mail when you add new educational products to your product offering. The updates could also be provided by RSS feed.

- You could have regular contests where the prize is one of your educational products or, alternatively, you could find other contest sites and offer one of your educational products as a prize with exposure for your site and a link to it.

For a more detailed description of these techniques, along with many other effective online marketing methods, I recommend the companion book *101 Ways to Promote Your Web Site.* You can also find tons of free resources at *http://www.susansweeney.com/resources.html.*

ADDITIONAL INCOME

Educational products and downloads are among the most widely distributed items on the Internet. As the market expands, quality will decrease. There is value in a rating system or guide that helps users make the right choice. Turning a portion of your site into a product review message board would be a wise idea. The traffic generated from this could lead to advertising opportunities.

ONLINE EXAMPLES

NASA
http://spacelink.nasa.gov/Instructional.Materials/NASA.Educational.Products/ .index.html
The NASA Web site is a good example of how to market educational products.

Teachernet
http://www.teachernet.com
This is an excellent Web site that deals with many educational products but also includes ideas for teachers and a discussion area for exchanging ideas and such.

American Educational Products
http://www.amep.com
This is a single corporation selling its products online. This is basically an Internet advertisement for its products.

33. Electronics Store

OVERVIEW OF BUSINESS MODEL

What better place to sell technological gadgets! The following are necessary to ensure success in this type of business: a reliable and robust supplier with a shipping system in place, and an up-to-date e-store with detailed descriptions, images, and reviews of products. This site would sell electronics directly to customers with payment processing happening online. (There's too much competition already to start at a lower level of operation.)

SKILLS NEEDED

The operator of this business should have experience dealing within the electronics industry and a proper gauge on value and product shelf life. He or she should have a firm grasp of Web publishing, writing promotional copy for products, and operating an online store.

COST TO START THIS BUSINESS

The budget to begin this endeavor is in the area of $3,000 to $10,000. Your initial setup costs include a personal computer and the appropriate software. You will also need to pay for the design, development, and hosting of your Web site, your storefront solution, and your merchant account setup. All additional costs are associated with promoting your business online and offline.

NUMBER OF EMPLOYEES NEEDED

Depending on how many products you are selling and where the inventory is stored, you might need two dedicated individuals to operate the business efficiently.

INTERNATIONAL POTENTIAL

The global reach of selling electronics online is almost guaranteed. Electronic devices are not restricted by regional or cultural boundaries such as language or lack of power sources. If the descriptions in the online store are available in several of the world's languages and the payment area has a tool to convert currency, there should be fantastic international opportunity.

E-BUSINESS MODEL/PAYMENT PROCESSING METHOD

The e-business model suggested for this type of operation is level 3, which includes an e-store and payment processing online. Refer to Part 1 for more information.

IMPORTANT BUSINESS ISSUES TO BE ADDRESSED

Selling electronics requires a high-tech, user-friendly site. The information on the site must be absolutely current, and you have to watch inventory as mass orders could come in at any time. The content and policy should encourage repeat business and provide support with upgrades and troubleshooting. The customer service department of your business should be highly responsive and be in touch with the shipping segment of the business.

ONLINE MARKETING TECHNIQUES

Your major target market will be high-tech gadget-prone online buyers, so you want to conduct a thorough market research project to determine where they are surfing. Once you have found these sites, establish relationships with them and exchange links. Here are some basic tips to get you started:

- Developing a comprehensive affiliate/associate program would not only send referral business to your electronics store, it would also increase the overall awareness of your site.

- Launching a strategic banner advertising campaign on Web sites frequented by your target market will send high volumes of traffic to your Web site. Your banner ads could contain coupons for specific products.

- You should enable visitors to tell friends about specific products directly from your site via e-mail. This viral marketing technique is a great way to increase traffic to your Web site.

- A comprehensive link strategy should be developed and implemented. Links should be developed from electronics cybermalls, meta-indexes, and electronics-related sites.

- You should develop a mail list where you will provide news on new products, product reviews, and specials to those site visitors who choose to opt in to the mail list.

- You could consider developing a loyalty program for frequent shoppers.

- Real reviews and testimonials from users of the products available for sale on your site should be published on the site as well as in appropriate e-zines and newsletters.

- Develop a sponsored listings campaign to bid on appropriate keyword phrases with the popular search engines.

- You could have regular contests where the prize is one of your electronics products or, alternatively, you can find other contest sites and offer one of your electronics products as a prize with exposure for your site and a link to it.

For a more detailed description of these techniques, along with many other effective online marketing methods, I recommend the companion book *101 Ways to Promote Your Web Site*. You can also find tons of free resources at *http://www.susansweeney.com/resources.html*.

ADDITIONAL INCOME

There is an opportunity to generate revenue through sales of banner advertising space and sponsorship of your mail list. Ads may be permitted in your mail list for a nominal fee.

ONLINE EXAMPLES

VoltexPC.com
http://www.voltexcomputers.com
This site offers an attractive presentation of hot items up for sale, is easy to navigate, and can easily be found in the search engines.

Cambridge Sound Works
http://www.cambridgesoundworks.com/store/category.cgi?category=0
This site is easily navigated, has a professional design, and offers a wide variety of products for sale *plus* articles on how to burn CDs and other technical tips for the benefit of users.

TigerDirect.com
http://www.tigerdirect.com
Specializing in PC and hardware sales, this company is known for its high-quality customer service and fast delivery.

34. E-Mail Reminder Service

OVERVIEW OF BUSINESS MODEL

As a provider of e-mail reminders, the basic service you would provide is creating a Web site with a software-driven automated e-mail reminder application.

The operator of this business will have to design comprehensive input forms not only to gather the important dates and occasions from all the clients and enough other information to be able to send them the reminder, but also to make appropriate gift suggestions.

For example, a client may want to be reminded of all of his or her nieces' or nephews' birthdays. In addition to gathering the birthdates, you would also want to gather the child's name, age, sex, and toy preferences. By doing this you can customize the reminder e-mail to read something like this:

> *Dear Susan,*
>
> *Your niece Mykhala's birthday is coming up in 10 days. Mykhala will be 9 years old, and she likes Barbie dolls, Gamecube games, and Nancy Drew books. Click here to find links to some of these gifts should you want to take care of her birthday gift today.*
>
> *Regards,*
>
> *Sarah*

These links would be from your site to retailers online where you belong to their affiliate program and will receive a referral fee for any sales that come from your site.

Dates such as birthdays, anniversaries, graduations, Valentine's Day, Secretary's Day, special days (Mother's Day and Father's Day), and corporate special occasions are what you will usually be reminding clients of. However, where your service includes recommendations, you may find clients including dates like Christmas, Easter, Hanukkah, and various cultural and religious holidays.

The trick to this operation is providing the service for free and having a high number of clients, because your income will be generated, for the most part, from banner advertising and affiliate program revenue. You will want to have this service fully automated, either by developing a program or by purchasing software that can perform this function. High traffic caused by repeat users will attract various online advertisers, resellers, alliances, and affiliates.

SKILLS NEEDED

The e-mail reminder service is perfect for someone who is punctual, organized, and a clear communicator via e-mail.

COST TO START THIS BUSINESS

The cost to start this business will include the cost of designing, developing, and hosting your Web site. You will need a computer, appropriate software, a printer, and an Internet connection. The e-mail reminder service software should be flexible and should match or exceed what the competition is using. We estimate the start-up costs for this business to run between $5,000 and $20,000. The advantage to this type of business is that there is no inventory.

NUMBER OF EMPLOYEES NEEDED TO START
This business can easily be started with one part-time individual.

INTERNATIONAL POTENTIAL
The global potential of this business is governed solely by language barriers.

E-BUSINESS MODEL/PAYMENT PROCESSING METHOD
E-business level 1 is most appropriate for this type of business. You will collect payment offline, and your income will come from affiliate commissions and banner advertising revenues. For more information, see Part 1.

IMPORTANT BUSINESS ISSUES TO BE ADDRESSED
The advertising opportunities must be seized or the business will not make a profit, since the actual reminder service is free. Utilizing the timely e-mail contact you have with clients is the key to success. Gather personalized information from your users so that when an announcement comes along, you are able to suggest what gifts to purchase for their family, loved ones, bosses, co-workers, and friends. Join affiliate programs for popular e-stores and market their wares in your e-mails. You'll make profits off the click-through and sales commissions.

ONLINE MARKETING TECHNIQUES

- Develop a comprehensive link strategy. Generating links from other, related sites is an excellent way to bring targeted businesses to your Web site. You will want to be linked from sites that cater to your target market (busy professionals with tight schedules). You might establish links from gift suggestion sites, e-stores, calendar and event management software sites, and other, related directories.

- Include testimonials from clients who have used your service in the past.

- You might include a viral marketing technique like Tell a Friend on your Web site. This will allow your customers to tell their friends about your service directly from your Web site.

- Get linked from online gift site directories.

- Develop a sponsored listings campaign to bid on appropriate keyword phrases with the popular search engines.

- Launch a banner advertising campaign or, better yet, join an ad network that can pinpoint the niche markets for your service and place your banners in the best locations.

For a more detailed description of these techniques, along with many other effective online marketing methods, I recommend the companion book *101 Ways to Promote Your Web Site.* You can also find tons of free resources at *http://www.susansweeney.com/resources.html.*

ADDITIONAL INCOME
Additional income could come from other services rendered through e-mail such as wish lists, wedding gift list e-mail updates, and reminders of this nature.

ONLINE EXAMPLES

Candor
http://www.candor.com/reminder/default.asp
This service is free.

P C Reminder
http://www.pcreminder.com
Choose from reminding yourself, reminding another person, or having someone remind you.

35. Employment Agency

OVERVIEW OF BUSINESS MODEL
Unemployed people and employed people looking for a change in employment all over the world search for work each day and are using the Internet to do it. Businesses are searching for new employees on the Web as well, but the process is hit or miss. Online employment agencies can simplify this process. An online employment agency bridges the gap between the prospective work force and the employers who need access to it.

The primary service of this business is providing an outlet for people to send in their resumes or portfolios and simultaneously matching them with prospective employers that are seeking people with similar credentials. There are many online employment sites on the Web now, but the selection has to be more refined and organized by employment type and location. Your site should include resources for job seekers. The employment agency's role is to understand the needs of its primary client—the employer.

Revenue can be generated in a number of ways from this type of site. You could charge individuals to submit their resumes. You could charge employers to post their employment opportunities. You could choose to allow posting of resumes and opportunities for free and generate revenue through banner advertising or selling ancillary services to employers or applicants. You could also run this business as an executive recruitment or placement service, where you publicize positions available and actually interview and recommend individuals to the employer.

SKILLS NEEDED

To run this business you need basic Web publishing skills. It would help significantly if you have a history working with an employment agency and have experience with resume writing, interviewing, and the development of employment opportunity descriptions.

COST TO START THIS BUSINESS

To start this business you need appropriate computer hardware, software, and a printer. You will incur design, development, and hosting costs related to your Web site. You will want to have a searchable database as part of your Web site and perhaps an automated, password-controlled, input area for job and resume postings. This will add to the development costs of your Web site. The costs to start this type of business online will range between $5,000 and $50,000 depending on the level of automation and the sophistication of your database.

NUMBER OF EMPLOYEES NEEDED TO START

To start this business you will need one or more experienced people, depending on the volume, the services you offer, and the level of automation.

INTERNATIONAL POTENTIAL

There is limited international potential in this type of business.

E-BUSINESS MODEL/PAYMENT PROCESSING METHOD

The recommended e-business level depends on how you choose to run your business. If you charge for the posting of resumes or job descriptions, you will want level 2. If you do not charge for the postings but generate your revenue through advertising or other services, level 1 would be more appropriate. See Part 1 for more details.

IMPORTANT BUSINESS ISSUES TO BE ADDRESSED

Have a solid business plan that clearly defines the service you will provide for your clients. If you provide recruitment and recommendation services, you will want to develop contracts or agreements that clearly spell out your fees, the services you will provide, and a payment schedule. Make sure to include plenty of useful resources and information on your site for job seekers (resume tips, links to resume sites, etc.).

ONLINE MARKETING TECHNIQUES

Marketing this business on the Web should prove to be somewhat easy because employment sites are sought after quite aggressively by job seekers. You are marketing to two separate groups, job seekers and prospective employers. The following steps should be taken to properly address your online marketing strategy:

- Ensure that your site is search engine friendly by including appropriate page titles, keyword meta-tags, description meta-tags, and so on, and then register with the major search engines and directories.

- Develop a comprehensive link strategy. The more links there are to your site, the more traffic you will see. You should generate links from related sites such as employment-related meta-indexes, resume writing services, business services, and secondary education sites.

- Submit articles to e-zines that promote and give examples of the success rate of your services, and be sure to include testimonials from both employers and job seekers.

- Develop a targeted banner advertising campaign. Have your ads appear on sites that job seekers and employers frequent.

For a more detailed description of these techniques, along with many other effective online marketing methods, I recommend the companion book *101 Ways to Promote Your Web Site*. You can also find tons of free resources at *http://www.susansweeney.com/resources.html.*

ADDITIONAL INCOME

There are all kinds of opportunities for additional income with banner advertising, sponsorship, and the expansion of your services. If you decide to focus on one field of work, training and retraining could be added to your services. You could establish a weekly newsletter to all your job seekers with ad links to sites that want to market themselves to your target group. You could include resume writing and job description writing services to your offering. You could provide membership opportunities for employers, giving them an unlimited or a specific number of job postings.

ONLINE EXAMPLES

ADECCO—The employment people
http://www.adeccous.com
This is a small but very nice job agency that has both an employer and an employee section.

PHDS LTD
http://www.phds-jobs.co.uk
This site specializes in engineering recruitment in the United Kingdom.

Monsterboard.com
http://www.monsterboard.com
This is a dynamite employment site.

36. Event and Meeting Planning

OVERVIEW OF BUSINESS MODEL

Planning a meeting or an event can be a time-consuming task for most people, and a well-done event usually requires a professional's touch. Since most events are special occasions, the customers are usually more flexible regarding pricing but are still seeking the best deal possible.

Web-based event planners make their money using basically the same method as their real-world counterparts. You research your client's objectives, needs, and requirements. You then develop a plan and program for the meeting or event, have it approved by the clients, and then make all the necessary arrangements and carry out the plan, taking care of all the details.

Meeting and event planners are paid a fee for their services or earn a commission from the suppliers of the services and products for the event or meeting. Often an event planner will be asked to arrange and be responsible for all the minute details for an event. In this case, you must be ready for that degree of involvement and be willing to shoulder the responsibility.

SKILLS NEEDED

Good organizational and communication skills are an absolute must. Unless you are fortunate enough to be operating in your local area, you will be required to arrange all the details long distance.

COST TO START THIS BUSINESS

The cost to set up and run this type of business will range from $1,000 to $20,000. Initially you will have to pay to develop your Web site along with all costs associated with this (e.g., hosting service). Additional costs associated with opening this business include online and offline advertising costs, and any offline promotion that you may implement.

NUMBER OF EMPLOYEES NEEDED

This type of business can be started with one person. It can start off as a part-time venture.

INTERNATIONAL POTENTIAL

This online business has strong international potential, since you will provide services that are universally beneficial.

E-BUSINESS MODEL/PAYMENT PROCESSING METHOD

Since you will be taking requests and dealing directly with the customer, e-business level 1 or 2 is most appropriate for this type of business. For more information, see Part 1.

IMPORTANT BUSINESS ISSUES TO BE ADDRESSED

Unless your customer or the meeting is in your immediate area, you will need to acquire a list of suppliers in the area where the event or meeting is taking place. An excellent source for this kind of information is event publications. One other major point to be aware of is that often event planners are called upon to set up the entire event. This requires a great deal of commitment and organization, especially at long distances.

ONLINE MARKETING TECHNIQUES

- Develop a comprehensive link strategy. Request links from sites related to meeting and event planning, appropriate directories and meta-indexes, and targeted cybermalls.

- Developing a strategic online banner advertising campaign could greatly increase targeted traffic to your site. You can outsource this activity to an advertising agency or ad network, or you can develop your advertising campaign in-house. Regardless of your approach, by placing a banner ad on a Web site or search engine that is frequented by your target market, you can develop a significant amount of traffic to your Web site.

- Participate in targeted mail lists, Usenet newsgroups, and discussion forums where participants are looking for advice on meeting planning, speakers, and venues. Always make a valuable contribution and attach your signature file.

- Develop a sponsored listings campaign to bid on appropriate keyword phrases with the popular search engines.

- Participate in e-zines and online publications that are read by your target market. You can contribute appropriate articles that display your area of expertise.

For a more detailed description of these techniques, along with many other effective online marketing methods, I recommend the companion book *101 Ways to Promote Your Web Site*. You can also find tons of free resources at *http://www.susansweeney.com/resources.html*.

ADDITIONAL INCOME

In addition to providing your organizational expertise, you could also start your own affiliate program with your suppliers. That way, even if your customers choose not to use your services directly but use your Web site to locate a specific supplier, you will earn a referral fee from the business that you helped your supplier get.

ONLINE EXAMPLES

All Time Favorites
http://www.alltimefavorites.com
Listed on their main page (Figure 2.4) are the types of events they specialize in. They also have a searchable database that allows users to find event resources in their local area.

Eventplanner.com
http://eventplanner.com
This site is dedicated to helping event planners themselves by making the tools they need readily accessible. Also, the site includes a directory of event planners and attempts to build an online community for event planners.

Figure 2.4. All Time Favorites has a database for local users.

37. E-Zines (Online Magazines)

OVERVIEW OF BUSINESS MODEL

E-zines are online publications or online magazines. The content draws eyeballs and then your pages are worth advertising dollars. E-zines can be as specific or as general as the writers please, but the wise idea is to focus on a particular interest group that is active on the Web today and approach advertisers who are targeting that particular group for a source of profit.

There are Web-based e-zines where the visitor views the e-zine at the e-zine Web site and travels though the e-zine by clicking through the pages of the site. These types of e-zines have the look and feel of traditional magazines as far as page layout and graphics go.

There are also e-mail-based e-zines where a subscriber receives a copy of the e-zine on a regular basis via e-mail. These types of e-zines are generally short on graphics and heavy on content. They are generally very topic-focused and include three or four text-based articles on the subject matter.

Both types of e-zines have banner advertising, sponsorship, and subscription opportunities.

SKILLS NEEDED

An e-zine is a great idea for someone who loves to write passionately and concisely about any given topic of shared interest. The ability to use an HTML publishing program is a must. Web-based e-zines need images, so you should be able to process images optimized for the Web either through scanning or via digital photography.

Cost to Start This Business

You are creating content that comes from your own mind, so the biggest investment is your time. You will need a computer and the appropriate software along with a scanner and printer. You may want to invest in a digital camera for those pursuing Web-based e-zines. Start-up costs will also include the design, development, and hosting of your Web site. The start-up costs for this type of business will generally run between $3,000 and $20,000. Ongoing costs will be your time and occasionally paying guest or staff writers for their stories.

Number of Employees Needed to Start

Starting off, you need only one employee, not even full-time if that's not what you can fit into your schedule. For more content, you may want to take on some other writers who contribute, and for this you can usually pay them per story.

International Potential

This business's international potential increases if it's translated into the major languages of the globe. English is widely accepted, however.

E-Business Model/Payment Processing Method

Ideally, an e-zine should charge advertisers quarterly throughout the year. There is no real need for online payment processing. E-business level 1 is appropriate for this type of online business. See Part 1 for more details.

Important Business Issues to Be Addressed

E-zines are pretty straightforward. Be careful to write in a clear and precise manner and remember the audience the whole time you are composing articles; make sure you continue to appeal to the same niche of readers; and watch for other sites encroaching on your content. It happens all the time.

Have a detailed Web traffic analysis package on the server on which your site is hosted so that you can show advertisers accurate information about your site traffic.

Online Marketing Techniques

- Participating in newsgroups and discussion forums related to your target audience would be a great way to increase exposure of your e-zine and traffic to your Web site.

- Launching a strategic banner advertising campaign on topic-specific Web sites would generate targeted exposure for your e-zine.

- Develop links from as many Web sites, directories, and meta-indexes related to the topic of your e-zine as possible.

- Develop a sponsored listings campaign to bid on appropriate keyword phrases with the popular search engines.

- Participating in publicly accessible opt-in mail lists related to the topic of your e-zine would be a great way to communicate with your target market.

For a more detailed description of these techniques, along with many other effective online marketing methods, I recommend the companion book *101 Ways to Promote Your Web Site*. You can also find tons of free resources at *http://www.susansweeney.com/resources.html*.

ADDITIONAL INCOME

Additional income comes into play by selling your stories to other e-zines and being hired to write articles. Also, if you are talented in publishing HTML articles, other writers may hire you to produce their content in Web format.

You can join the affiliate programs of providers of products or services that your target market may be interested in. For example, if your e-zine is about Internet marketing, you could join Amazon's affiliate program and recommend great books like *101 Ways to Promote Your Web Site*.

ONLINE EXAMPLES

eWire Riding and Music E-Zine
http://www.ewirezine.com
eWire is an e-zine that is devoted to BMX riding and music.

Any Swing Goes
http://www.anyswinggoes.com
This is a full e-zine covering everything related to swing music.

38. Fund Raiser

OVERVIEW OF BUSINESS MODEL

Online fund raising has serious potential for success because of how affordable the Internet is as a marketing medium, communication tool, and place to present information. There are many choices available if you want to provide fund-raising services. The number of potential customers for this type of business is signifi-cant—charitable organizations, schools, hospitals, not-for-profit associations, and so on. Most organizations do not have the personnel to run fund-raising cam-paigns in-house and are quite happy to use an outside service. Fund-raising cam-paigns for each organization are usually run at a specific time of year, so the trick will be to have clients who run their campaigns at different times.

Skills Needed
This business is perfect for someone who has experience in philanthropy and telemarketing. You have to be organized and have a great telephone manner. Basic Web publishing skills and familiarity with managing a contact database are needed.

Cost to Start This Business
To start this business you will need a computer, appropriate software, and a printer. You will incur costs related to the design, development, and hosting of your Web site. You may need to purchase direct mail lists as well if your clients don't provide them. The approximate cost to start this business is between $3,000 and $10,000.

Number of Employees Needed to Start
One dedicated and knowledgeable person can start this business from home and part-time to begin.

International Potential
The potential of this business is mainly national. International telephone rates and foreign languages are drawbacks to international delivery of this type of service.

E-Business Model/Payment Processing Method
E-business level 1 is most appropriate for this type of business. For more infor-mation, see Part 1.

Important Business Issues to Be Addressed
It is important to consider how your revenues are generated. One option is to collect a fee or percentage of the money you raise for any given charity or group. The other is by selling a product to be used in a fund-raiser. Obviously you will gain a profit through the sale of such items. The best way to increase revenues is to provide both services.

Online Marketing Techniques

- Develop a comprehensive link strategy. If you do not provide products for fund raisers, link to sites that do and vice versa. Also develop links from appropriate directories, meta-indexes, and Web rings.

- Register your site throughout the major search engines and optimize your site for organic search engine placement with effective keyword phrases such as *fund-raising services*. You can also consider participating in a pay-per-click strategy with the popular search engines.

- Arrange reciprocal links with a wide variety of philanthropic sites.

- Participate in news and discussion groups for fund raisers to share their techniques and successes.

- Participate in mail lists that your target market participates in relative to fund raising.

For a more detailed description of these techniques, along with many other effective online marketing methods, I recommend the companion book *101 Ways to Promote Your Web Site*. You can also find tons of free resources at *http://www.susansweeney.com/resources.html*.

Additional Income

Avenues for additional income are banner and hyperlink advertising on your Web site if the traffic levels are high. Other ways to gain more revenue from your fund-raiser Web site would be to expand your services and offer to coach others for a fee on how to begin a fund-raising project. You can also provide products that can be used in fund raising.

Online Examples

JustGiving.com
http://www.justgiving.com
This is an online fund raiser dedicated to both donating and raising money.

Charity Mania
http://www.charitymania.com

Based in California, this organization provides inexpensive ways for schools, churches, sports teams, and the like to sell raffle tickets.

39. Genealogy Research

OVERVIEW OF BUSINESS MODEL

Running an online genealogy research business is a great part-time venture. If you have an interest or expertise in human history, family trees, or a particular region or community, this could be the venture for you. The way it works is simple. You research incoming genealogical requests for a fee. The Internet is the perfect place to conduct many stages of your research, market your services, and communicate with clients. Revenue comes from the fees for researching genealogy information and advertising for related businesses, such as software for building family trees.

SKILLS NEEDED

The operator of this business should have a very real interest in genealogy, researching skills, and Web publishing skills. It is important to communicate clearly via e-mail with clients. Extensive knowledge of a certain community or family will help to differentiate your services from the competition.

COST TO START THIS BUSINESS

To begin this business you will need a computer, appropriate software, and a printer. You will also incur the costs of designing, developing, and hosting your Web site. The cost to start this business will be between $3,000 and $5,000.

NUMBER OF EMPLOYEES NEEDED TO START

One part-time skilled individual can start this business from home.

INTERNATIONAL POTENTIAL

The international potential of this business is both highly possible and hard to predict. Depending on your field of expertise in the genealogy department, you could be receiving requests from anywhere in the world. You never know where someone's relatives or descendants have moved. The further away they are, the more likely they are to seek your help.

E-Business Model/Payment Processing Method

The genealogy research Web site requires e-business level 1. For more information, see Part 1.

Important Business Issues to Be Addressed

The genealogy research business is founded on documentation. Clients will want proof of your research results. You will want to charge by the hour for your time on each project, so be sure to work out a solid business plan where you indicate your rates for different services. Have these clearly posted on your Web site and make sure that they are competitive with other genealogical Web sites' rates.

Online Marketing Techniques

Your online marketing strategy for this business should include the following key elements:

- A comprehensive link strategy that will get you links from as many genealogy-related sites as possible, as well as appropriate directories, meta-indexes, and Web rings.

- Banner advertising on high-traffic resource sites that target your niche market. For example, if you specialize in Irish genealogy, then you should advertise on sites that appeal to this crowd.

- Participation in publicly accessible mail lists related to the discussion of genealogy. Provide valuable contribution to show your area of expertise.

- Participation in online chats, discussions, and forums about your field, including a descriptive signature file.

- Building a mail list of clients and perspective clients who would like to receive your regular newsletters with the latest discoveries you have made and related family-tree-type news.

For a more detailed description of these techniques, along with many other effective online marketing methods, I recommend the companion book *101 Ways to Promote Your Web Site.* You can also find tons of free resources at *http://www.susansweeney.com/resources.html.*

ADDITIONAL INCOME

A couple of additional ways to earn income from your genealogy research site include:

- Joining affiliate e-stores that sell products of interest to your target group.

- Offering consulting services over the phone or via live chat on how to properly research your family tree.

As requests come in, you will begin to see where potential for extra income exists depending on your skills, time, and resources.

ONLINE EXAMPLES

A+ Genealogy Research Service, LLC
http://www.genealogy-research.com
Allows you to research your family history and can answer numerous genealogical questions you may have.

Genealogy Pro
http://genealogypro.com
Genealogy Pro is the directory with the largest choice of independent genealogy related services and products including: professional genealogists, adoption and missing people researchers, translators, military and historical researchers, heraldry specialists, heir and estate researchers, photographers, and more!

40. Gift Baskets

OVERVIEW OF BUSINESS MODEL

Online gift basket stores are becoming as popular as their traditional offline counterparts. These stores make it easy for consumers to go online, purchase a gift basket, and have it shipped to a family or friend as a gift. The level of customization provided by some of these online retailers is amazing. You can do everything from picking out a customized gift basket to choosing what type of wrapping paper and gift card you want to dress the gift with.

There are several ways to earn income from this type of business. Of course, you're going to generate revenue from the sale of gift baskets and other gift-related items; however, like any business, you can generate significant revenue from value-added services—things such as gift wrapping, personalized gift cards, special shipping options, or unique customizable products (e.g., engraved gift boxes). You can also generate revenue from selling online advertising to noncompeting Web sites that target the same audience. Since you are targeting the same audience, you can provide potential advertisers with a dynamite opportunity for exposing their products or services.

SKILLS NEEDED

First and foremost, knowledge of the products that you are representing is a must. This enables you to answer any questions that your clients or potential clients might have about your products. Knowledge of online advertising techniques is also an asset to run this type of business. If you decide to launch a gift basket Web site, you are going to have to ensure that you are generating as much traffic as possible to your site to develop your client base. To do this, you are going to have to dedicate a lot of time implementing various Internet marketing techniques to create a constant flow of traffic to your site. Knowledge about electronic storefronts, shopping carts, and electronic commerce would also be an asset.

COST TO START THIS BUSINESS

Initially you will have to pay for the design, development, and hosting of your Web site, computer hardware, computer software, a scanner, a printer, and a digital camera so that you can take photos of your gift baskets. If you currently have some of these items, your initial start-up costs will be considerably lower. In order to set up your storefront, you will have to purchase storefront software equipped with electronic shopping cart features, use an application service provider, or be responsible for developing this in-house. If you plan to set up a mailing list, you will also have to purchase mailing list software to help you organize and maintain your mail lists. You should also purchase comprehensive Web traffic analysis software to track where your Web site visitors are coming from. This information can be great for future marketing opportunities. Other costs that you will incur are related to the promotion of your Web site and the purchase of inventory. Minimum estimated cost to start is $10,000 to $20,000.

NUMBER OF EMPLOYEES NEEDED TO START

You can start this type of business with one person. If you do your online marketing well and generate significant visitors and customers, you will quickly expand. Approximately one to three full-time employees will be needed in full operation for this type of business. At least one staff member will be responsible for the daily online promotion of your site, while the others will handle all administrative, accounting, shipping, and inventory tasks required to run the business smoothly.

INTERNATIONAL POTENTIAL

This business has strong international potential. People from all over the world will be able to visit your Web site and order your gift baskets to send to their loved ones. However, before you offer your products to foreign countries, you should ensure that your parcels would easily pass through customs. Some countries may have regulations as to what types of products can enter their country or may have significant duties and taxes that may be levied.

E-BUSINESS MODEL/PAYMENT PROCESSING METHOD

E-business level 3 or 4 would be most appropriate for this type of business. For more information, see Part 1.

IMPORTANT BUSINESS ISSUES TO BE ADDRESSED

Since you are promoting your products to an online audience, it is extremely important for you to generate as much traffic as possible to your site. There are multiple ways for you to do this; however, it is essential that you allocate a significant amount of time to the daily online promotion of the site.

You should also remember never to offer a product on your site that is not in stock. Stock-outs can seriously hinder the success and reputation of any online retailer. Nothing would be more disappointing than searching through your storefront, finding a dynamite gift basket to purchase, ordering it, and then finding out that you don't have it in stock. This could discourage visitors from ever returning to your site to make a future purchase. To avoid this problem, it is suggested that you monitor your inventory levels closely and have the capability to remove items easily from your online catalogue.

ONLINE MARKETING TECHNIQUES

- Developing a comprehensive affiliate/associate program would not only increase the awareness of your gift basket site, it would also send referral business to your site.

- Launching a strategic banner advertising campaign on Web sites frequented by your target market would be a great way to increase traffic to your site. Sites on which you could place banner ads include noncompeting gift sites, holiday-specific Web sites (e.g., Mother's Day sites, Valentine's Day sites, etc.), and other Web sites that would be of interest to your target market.

- You could hold a weekly or monthly contest on your site for a free gift basket. You could ask people if they would like to be notified of the winner via e-mail. This would encourage them to return to your site and re-enter your contest, thus re-exposing them to your products.

- Develop a sponsored listings campaign to bid on appropriate keyword phrases with the popular search engines.

- Develop as many links as possible from Web sites, directories, meta-indexes, and Web rings frequented by your target market.

- You could develop a Featured Gift Basket page on your site. You could change this product every week. People will continue to return to your site to see what the featured gift basket is. You could even ask people if they would like to be notified of your featured gift basket via e-mail. This would be a great way to encourage repeat traffic.

For a more detailed description of these techniques, along with many other effective online marketing methods, I recommend the companion book *101 Ways to Promote Your Web Site*. You can also find tons of free resources at *http://www.susansweeney.com/resources.html*.

ADDITIONAL INCOME

In addition to selling gift baskets from your site, you could also sell complementary items. Things such as preserves, candles, soaps, ornaments, and other novelty items that you could sell in a gift basket you can also sell individually. These products would not only complement your gift basket product, but would also expand your product line. You can offer several levels of gift wrapping at various price points.

ONLINE EXAMPLES

PEI Preserve Company
http://www.preservecompany.com
This is a terrific online business (Figure 2.5) that sells homemade preserves to people all over the world. They use several effective Internet marketing techniques to increase the traffic to their site, including a mailing list that enables them to communicate with their clients.

GiftBaskets.com
http://www.giftbaskets.com

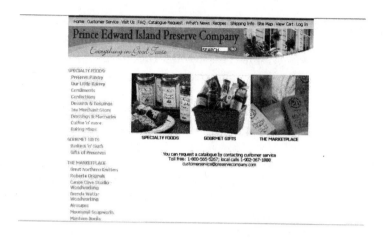

Figure 2.5. PEI Preserve Company sells homemade preserves to people all over the world.

This is a dynamite site that offers a wide range of gift basket products to its clients.

41. Gift Registry (Online Wish List)

Overview of Business Model

Many people today use gift registries to help their family and friends with gift purchases for weddings or other special occasions. In the traditional model, gift registries are often limited to one store. Now on the Internet, under the guise of wish lists, the idea of the gift registry has come into its own.

An online wish list is a service that can be connected to many online stores. When people are having a special occasion, such as a wedding, they simply register on the wish list site and list the items they would like to receive that can be purchased anywhere online. Their family and friends then go online to the wish list and can choose items of interest to the couple as well as ensure that they are not getting the same item as someone else.

An online wish list service participates in the affiliate programs of many online stores. Whenever someone using your service buys a product from an affiliated site, you receive a small percentage of the sale (usually anywhere from

5 to 25 percent). If your wish list is particularly well designed and is popular, then you can also collect a membership fee from your member businesses or sell them preferred space or banner advertising.

SKILLS NEEDED

Some familiarity with marketing online is necessary. In addition, this sort of business deals with a number of advanced concepts and components of the Internet, so you will need to have a firm grasp of the way affiliate programs work before pursuing this concept. Finally, you will need a computer programmer to write and maintain your wish list software.

COST TO START THIS BUSINESS

The cost to initially set up your gift registry/online wish list will range from $8,000 to $30,000. These costs include a high-end computer, appropriate software, and a printer, as well as the costs related to the design, development, and hosting of your Web site. Other initial costs you will incur include the development of your wish list software as well as the marketing and advertising of your Web site.

NUMBER OF EMPLOYEES NEEDED TO START

The maintenance of your Web site and creation of your wish list software will require a lot of work. You will also need to launch a massive promotional campaign. It is possible that one or two dedicated people could start up this business.

INTERNATIONAL POTENTIAL

Your service does not actually perform any shipping or other functions that sometimes restrict an online business. There are no barriers, with the exception of language, preventing you from capitalizing on the global market.

E-BUSINESS MODEL/PAYMENT PROCESSING METHOD

E-business level 1 is most appropriate for this type of business. For more information, see Part 1.

IMPORTANT BUSINESS ISSUES TO BE ADDRESSED

A large part of the setup of an online gift registry is related to successfully linking up with online retail stores and their affiliate programs. You will have to develop a dynamite Web site and specialized software related to the gift registry. You will also have to develop a comprehensive Internet marketing strategy to generate significant traffic to your site.

ONLINE MARKETING TECHNIQUES

- When people visit your Web site to register or to purchase a gift for a friend who is registered with your site, you have a perfect opportunity to encourage the use of viral marketing techniques like Tell a Friend. If they found your site and service useful, then they will pass that information on to their friends.

- You should develop and implement a targeted banner advertising strategy. You will want to place banner ads on appropriate wedding-related and other special-occasion Web sites.

- Develop and implement a comprehensive link strategy. You should be linked from as many gift-related Web sites, directories, meta-indexes, and Web rings as possible.

- Participate in publicly accessible mail lists related to wedding planning.

- Develop a sponsored listings campaign to bid on appropriate keyword phrases with the popular search engines.

- Participate in newsgroups, discussion forums, and chats related to wedding and other special-occasion planning.

For a more detailed description of these techniques, along with many other effective online marketing methods, I recommend the companion book *101 Ways to Promote Your Web Site*. You can also find tons of free resources at *http://www.susansweeney.com/resources.html*.

ADDITIONAL INCOME

You can add e-cards or a reminder service to your product offering. You can sell banner advertising to Web sites that are targeting the same demographic that you are.

ONLINE EXAMPLES

Wishlist.com
http://www.wishlist.com
One of the major online gift registries. It also has a few special features.

Giftregistry21.com
http://www.giftregistry21.com

A good site, but you have to register before you can use most of its services, though it does provide good confidentiality.

42. Graphic Designer

OVERVIEW OF BUSINESS

If you do graphic design work, there is a huge market for your services throughout the world. You can generate revenue from the design of everything from signs and brochures to Web sites and corporate ads. The possibilities are endless. To promote your services, you could simply design a dynamite Web site that contains a portfolio of your work for visitors to see. This should contain your best work, because this is what your clients will judge your talent and professionalism against. Your Web site will basically be your online resume for potential business opportunities, so make sure you do a good job on the site design and layout!

How does it work? You simply have to develop a request form on your site. Here visitors can easily fill out their contact information and a brief description of the type of design work they would like to have you provide to them. You can then follow up on their service request via e-mail or telephone. This is a very easy way to run this type of business.

SKILLS NEEDED

Excellent graphic design skills are essential to run this type of business. Knowledge of various graphic design software programs would also be a must.

COST TO START THIS BUSINESS

Initially you will have to pay for the development and hosting of your Web site, computer hardware, computer software, a scanner, a printer, and possibly a digital camera for your graphic design work. Since you can handle the graphic design work for your Web site, you can work closely with a Web site designer during the development stage of your site if you are not capable of writing code. If you currently have some of these items, your initial start-up costs will be considerably lower. If you plan to set up a mailing list, you will also have to purchase mailing list software to help you organize and maintain your mail lists. Other costs that you will incur are related to the promotion of your Web site. Estimated cost is $10,000 to 25,000 to start.

NUMBER OF EMPLOYEES NEEDED TO START

One dedicated individual is required to operate this type of business. In the beginning you may be able to work at this business part-time while keeping your regular job; however, as requests increase, you will be able to make this business a full-time venture. You might also have to hire an extra employee to handle all administrative tasks associated with running this business.

INTERNATIONAL POTENTIAL

This type of business has high international potential due to the high demand for graphic design services.

E-BUSINESS MODEL/PAYMENT PROCESSING METHOD

E-business level 1 is most appropriate for this type of business. For more information, see Part 1.

IMPORTANT BUSINESS ISSUES TO BE ADDRESSED

When dealing with graphic design work, you should insist on a deposit before you undertake each project. Graphic designers have been known to deliver the digital format of their work to their client for review and then never hear from the client again. To avoid this, it is suggested that you collect a 30 to 50 percent deposit up front, and then collect the remainder after you complete the project.

ONLINE MARKETING TECHNIQUES

- Develop a comprehensive link strategy. You want to get as many links as possible from appropriate Web sites, directories, and meta-indexes related to your target market. There are thousands of graphic design-related Web sites on the Internet that would provide a great linking opportunity for your site. You should also attempt to develop links from business service link sites and directories. These sites will provide highly targeted traffic to your site.

- Participate in newsgroups and discussion forums related to graphic design or business services. Remember to use a cleverly designed signature file with a catchy tagline and hypertext link that will send readers to your site.

- Providing valuable contributions to graphic design-related mail lists would be a great way to create exposure for your business. Again, a cleverly designed signature file with a catchy tagline would be a great way to send traffic to your site.

- Show before-and-after examples of any work where you are updating logos, corporate IDs, or the "look and feel" of Web sites.

- Develop a sponsored listings campaign to bid on appropriate keyword phrases with the popular search engines.

- Hosting your own graphic design advice column for up-and-coming graphic designers would be a great way to encourage repeat traffic to your site. You could offer advice related to using specific software programs or about different design techniques. You can ask people if they would like to be notified via e-mail whenever you update your advice column. This will encourage people to return to your site to view your latest advice.

For a more detailed description of these techniques, along with many other effective online marketing methods, I recommend the companion book *101 Ways to Promote Your Web Site*. You can also find tons of free resources at *http://www.susansweeney.com/resources.html*.

ADDITIONAL INCOME
To complement your graphic design talents, you could offer Web design and development services. Since these two services complement each other, you would be adding tremendous value to your graphic design business while earning additional income from Web development projects.

ONLINE EXAMPLES

Jeff Gutterud Publishing
http://www.jgpublish.com
This is a graphic design firm that offers some Web-based publishing as well as professional logo design.

JBF Designs
http://www.jbfdesigns.com
This one-person operation offers both graphic design and Web site design services.

43. Health Guide

OVERVIEW OF BUSINESS MODEL
Health and fitness are becoming important to everyone these days. People are eating better, exercising more, and trying to live a healthier lifestyle. The prob-

lem is that many people are not as educated as they would like to be on how to accomplish these tasks. This online business can provide people with this information. You can offer your site's visitors healthy recipes, new exercise techniques, and information about the health industry. You'll be surprised how many people will continuously visit your site to learn more about how to improve their quality of life.

This type of site can recommend and provide links to health-related products that can be purchased online. Income can be generated through affiliate program revenue from these sites.

This type of site can also generate revenue from selling targeted online advertising to businesses related to health and fitness. Since your Web site's visitors are obviously coming to your site to view information about health and fitness, you will be able to provide businesses with a highly targeted advertising opportunity. You will want to have a link directly on your home page that says something like "Advertise with Us." This link will lead the visitor to a page where he or she can view Web site traffic statistics and a listing of benefits of advertising on your site. Testimonials from past advertisers would also be an asset. This would easily encourage businesses to advertise on your site.

Skills Needed

Knowledge of health and fitness is essential if you're operating this type of business. Strong research techniques would also be an asset, as you are constantly going to be searching for new health-related information to provide to your visitors. Knowledge of effective online advertising techniques would also be an asset, as this type of business requires a high number of Web site visitors.

Cost to Start This Business

Initially you will have to pay for the design, development, and hosting of your Web site, computer hardware, computer software, a scanner, a printer, and possibly a digital camera so that you can take photos of various foods or exercise techniques. If you currently have some of these items, your initial start-up costs will be considerably lower. If you plan to set up a mailing list to communicate with your Web site visitors, you will have to purchase mailing list software to help you organize and maintain your mail lists. You will also have to purchase comprehensive Web traffic analysis software to track where your Web site visitors are coming from. You can use this information to help sell advertising on your Web site. Other costs that you will incur are related to the promotion of your Web site. Estimated cost is $5,000 to $10,000 to start.

NUMBER OF EMPLOYEES NEEDED TO START

Approximately one to three full-time employees will be needed to operate this type of business. At least one staff member will be responsible for the daily online promotion of your site, while the others will handle all administrative, accounting, and sales activities associated with running the daily business operations.

INTERNATIONAL POTENTIAL

This business has strong international potential as health consciousness has increased across the globe. Everyone will be interested in your health and fitness news and advice.

E-BUSINESS MODEL/PAYMENT PROCESSING METHOD

E-business level 1 would be most appropriate for this type of business. For more information, see Part 1.

IMPORTANT BUSINESS ISSUES TO BE ADDRESSED

Since you are promoting health and fitness advice online, it is extremely important for you to generate as much traffic as possible to your site. There are multiple ways for you to do this; however, it is essential that you allocate a significant amount of time to the daily online promotion of the site.

Since you will be viewed as a professional in your field, it is very important that you not offer any health or fitness advice that might inflict injury or sickness on one of your visitors. If you suggest that a particular diet or exercise is effective, make sure that (1) people can't hurt themselves following your advice, and (2) there are no side effects that will harm your visitors sometime down the road. If you don't do this, it could prove detrimental to the success of your online health and fitness guide business.

ONLINE MARKETING TECHNIQUES

- Launching a strategic banner advertising campaign on Web sites frequented by your target market would be a great way to increase traffic to your site. Sites that you could place banner ads on include noncompeting health sites, exercise sites, and food and cooking Web sites (for those interested in following a healthy diet).

- You could hold a weekly or monthly contest on your site for free health-related merchandise. Perhaps an exercise tape or a treadmill could be the prize, depending on your business model and the availability of sponsors to donate the prize. You could ask people if they would like to be notified of the winner via e-mail. This would encourage them to return to your site and re-enter your contest, thus re-exposing them to your Web site.

- Develop as many links as possible from Web sites, directories, and meta-indexes frequented by your target market. There are thousands of health- and fitness-related Web sites online. These are the sites that your target market will visit if they are looking for information about health and fitness.

- You could develop an Ask the Experts section on your site where visitors could ask you questions about health and fitness. This would be a great way for you to interact with your visitors. You could provide an RSS feed for those who want to be notified when you update this feature.

- You could contribute articles to health-related e-zines. Make sure you are credited with the article and ensure that there is a link provided back to your Web site.

- Develop a sponsored listings campaign to bid on appropriate keyword phrases with the popular search engines.

- Developing a mail list would be a great way to stay in touch with your visitors. You could have a Health Tips newsletter that could go out monthly, weekly, or even daily to all of your subscribers. This is a great way to encourage visitors to return to your site and will also help enhance the professionalism of your site.

For a more detailed description of these techniques, along with many other effective online marketing methods, I recommend the companion book *101 Ways to Promote Your Web Site*. You can also find tons of free resources at *http://www.susansweeney.com/resources.html*.

ADDITIONAL INCOME

In addition to selling online advertising on your Web site, you might also consider selling health-related products. You could sell vitamins, nutrition supplements, fitness books, videos, or clothing. This would be a great way to make additional income for your business; however, you will have to purchase the appropriate storefront software to operate at this level of e-business.

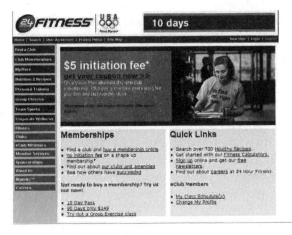

Figure 2.6.   Anyone can get free online fitness advice at 24 Hour Fitness.

ONLINE EXAMPLES

24 Hour Fitness
http://www.24hourfitness.com
This is a dynamite Web site (Figure 2.6) offering health and fitness advice to its visitors. They also have an Ask the Experts section where visitors can ask the professionals at 24 Hour Fitness questions. This is a great way for the site to enhance its professionalism.

Health World Online
http://www.healthy.net
This site has multiple interactive features to promote personal well-being and a healthy lifestyle.

44. Hobby Store

OVERVIEW OF BUSINESS MODEL
We all have hobbies. Even though we may not perceive our recreational activities as "hobbies," they are. Playing video games is a present-day hobby, and so

is collecting a video library of all the best flicks. Collecting is a traditional hobby. Huge hobby markets you might want to consider are model building, sports, coin and stamp collecting, antiques, and crafts.

The advantages of creating a hobby site begin with the guarantee that people will always look for these products in their spare time and they will often use the Net to do it.

Most hobby sites focus on a particular age group or gender. This is a good idea because you will want browsers to stick around on your site. You must provide a significant amount of information and interactivity that suits their hobby preference in order to make this happen.

Revenue will come from online sales of hobby products that you showcase on your site and also through affiliate relationships with manufacturers and distributors of the hobby paraphernalia that pertains to your target niche.

SKILLS NEEDED

Familiarity with online marketing techniques is a definite plus. Understanding the hobby industry will help you to design a site that stands up to other hobby sites on the Web that target your niche group. Focusing on a hobby you enjoy personally would be beneficial, since you may need to answer related questions. Basic Web publishing skills are needed to update your Web site.

COST TO START THIS BUSINESS

The cost to initially set up your hobby store will range from $5,000 to $10,000. These costs include a computer, administrative and e-commerce software to sell the hobby products in your online store, a printer, a scanner, and a digital camera. In the start-up phase, you may wish to join affiliate programs and recommend specific products from your site. This will reduce start-up costs because you will not need to purchase inventory or the software for the online store. You will also incur the cost of having your Web site designed, developed, and hosted. Other initial costs to consider include your inventory and the advertising of your Web site.

NUMBER OF EMPLOYEES NEEDED TO START

After the initial setup, this business requires so little time that it is ideal for those who decide to keep their full-time jobs. The number of employees required is dependent on the volume of business you will be handling. You can easily start this business with one employee if your order volume is low.

INTERNATIONAL POTENTIAL

Doing business on the Internet gives you international reach. People all over the world share hobbies, and they don't even know it. Hobby Web sites are a perfect way for hobby enthusiasts to meet each other and discuss their hobby. The only foreseeable barriers are language, tariffs, and shipping costs.

E-BUSINESS MODEL/PAYMENT PROCESSING METHOD

E-business level 1 or 2 is most appropriate for this type of business if you want to begin by taking the affiliate program approach. If you want to have your own online storefront, carry inventory, and sell products on your site, then level 3 is recommended. For more information, see Part 1.

IMPORTANT BUSINESS ISSUES TO BE ADDRESSED

The pertinent issues in the hobby business revolve around your target market. While planning out your business strategy, make sure to carefully research all the interests and traits of the individuals who most likely will be interested in the hobbies you promote on your site.

People love to talk about their hobbies because it's a source of joy for them, so make sure to have plenty of outlets on your site for the users to communicate with each other. Message boards, chat rooms, polls, mail lists, and allowing featured hobbyists to be introduced on the site are ways to do this. Make sure to have plenty of links to resources and create strategic alliances with noncompetitive partners so that you can provide a full set of services for your users.

ONLINE MARKETING TECHNIQUES

- Develop a comprehensive link strategy. Generate as many links as possible from targeted Web sites, cybermalls, directories, meta-indexes, and Web rings that relate to your hobby niche.

- Participate in publicly accessible opt-in mail lists that talk about your hobby. Provide a valuable contribution to the discussion, and attach your signature file with a catchy tagline to all correspondence.

- Participate in e-zines that relate to your hobby niche. You can submit articles, send press releases, sponsor a section of their Web site or outgoing promotion, or do banner advertising.

- Participate in appropriate newsgroups, discussion groups, and forums that talk about your hobby niche. Again, always include your signature file with a catchy tagline with all correspondence.

- Develop a sponsored listings campaign to bid on appropriate keyword phrases with the popular search engines.

- Run contests on your site with the prize being a product of interest to your target market. Ask people if they'd like to be notified as you have new contests and new prizes.

- Have a viral marketing element included in your site where visitors can "Tell a Friend" about your site.

For a more detailed description of these techniques, along with many other effective online marketing methods, I recommend the companion book *101 Ways to Promote Your Web Site*. You can also find tons of free resources at *http://www.susansweeney.com/resources.html*.

ADDITIONAL INCOME

Additional income can be generated through banner advertising revenue generated from advertisers that are interested in reaching the same target market that you do.

ONLINE EXAMPLES

eHobbies
http://www.ehobbies.com/Home.do
This site has a huge selection of anything you can think of as a hobby.

Hobbyshop.com
http://www.hobbyshop.com
This hobby Web site is built using Vstore.com's storefront templates. It sells the usual assortment of hobby items; however, it lacks any craft-related items.

45. Hotel Guide

OVERVIEW OF BUSINESS MODEL

The entire travel industry has been making a rapid transition to online service. A lot of people travel frequently, and they need to arrange their accommodations long before they get to where they're going. Hotel guides make it much easier for tourists and business travelers to do this, and they are in high demand all over the world.

The way this business works is by building a database of hotels in the area you choose. You may choose to build your database from a specific town or city, a specific state, or a specific country. Your site should be set up so that hotels can add their listing at your Web site and you can build the database from your end. The information on each hotel should include details such as what type of accommodations they have, address, parking, wheelchair access, amenities, number of rooms, nearby restaurants and attractions, and if they have a pool or hot tubs—all the details.

Basic listings are free for hotels, and the revenue can be made by charging a monthly, biannual, or annual fee for a hypertext link from the database listing to the hotel's Web site. Revenue is generated through the enhanced listings and banner advertising.

Your site should have a robust content area such as an e-zine that includes articles about all the fun things to do in the immediate area and pertinent information for business travelers (such as where to get dry cleaning and fax, e-mail, and printing services). Your site should feature a different hotel each week, and you should run contests for free accommodations and related things to attract repeat visits and keep your "stickiness" factor high.

SKILLS NEEDED

A broad familiarity with the travel industry in your area is needed. However, you will expand this knowledge as your hotel database progresses. The hotel database and the Web site will require a high level of maintenance, which will include constant updating and editing. Therefore, you will need experience in operating a database and in Web publishing skills.

COST TO START THIS BUSINESS

The cost to initially set up your hotel guide will range from $25,000 to over $50,000. These costs include a high-end computer and database software such as ColdFusion, Oracle, or SQL. You will need to have a Web site designed, developed, and hosted. Some other costs you will incur are the monthly advertising costs for your Web site.

NUMBER OF EMPLOYEES NEEDED TO START

If you outsource the database development, this business can be started and run by one individual.

INTERNATIONAL POTENTIAL

Information businesses face none of the usual hindrances common to the online retail models. Without shipping costs and import restrictions to contend with, there is nothing preventing your business from succeeding on an international level. Your only restriction to complete international penetration is language barriers. For this reason, you may wish to include on your Web site several language options.

E-Business Model/Payment Processing Method

E-business level 2 is most appropriate for this type of business. For more information, see Part 1.

Important Business Issues to Be Addressed

There are thousands of hotels worldwide, so the database you construct can be huge. To ensure customer satisfaction, your database will have to be as efficient as possible. Unfortunately, efficiency is what drives the cost of databases up. Keeping in touch with all the hotel operators is important. Create a form on your site where hotels can go to update information if anything should change in their details.

Make sure you have a solid invoicing strategy linked into the database so that hotels can pay with a credit card for their hypertext link or enhanced listing.

Online Marketing Techniques

- Develop a comprehensive link strategy. Generate as many links as possible to your site from appropriate travel-related Web sites, directories, meta-indexes, Web rings, and travel-related cybermalls.

- Develop a contest that will be run on a regular basis. The prize can be provided by companies in your database. Ask visitors if they'd like to be reminded when you run a new contest. This will get your name in front of your target customers on a regular basis.

- Develop a sponsored listings campaign to bid on appropriate keyword phrases with the popular search engines.

- You could be a contributing editor of a syndicated "Featured Hotel" article for travel related e-zines.

- A mail list or newsletter can also be used to advertise your deals and keep consumers interested in your services.

For a more detailed description of these techniques, along with many other effective online marketing methods, I recommend the companion book *101 Ways to Promote Your Web Site*. You can also find tons of free resources at *http://www.susansweeney.com/resources.html*.

ADDITIONAL INCOME

You can generate additional revenue through the sale of banner advertising throughout your site.

ONLINE EXAMPLES

USAHotelGuide.com
http://www.usahotelguide.com
A beautiful and well laid out Web site that not only lets you reserve hotel rooms but also lets you set up a car rental and book a flight.

Hotelguide.com
http://www.hotelguide.com
This site has a huge directory of hotels for every conceivable location, including Timbuktu! It also has incorporated wireless technology into its Web site. You can now arrange a hotel in Timbuktu from a cell phone.

46. Hunting and Fishing Supplies

OVERVIEW OF BUSINESS MODEL

Hunting and fishing are two of the oldest outdoor sports. The number of potential customers online with an interest in these sports is huge. The specialty equipment that is available for these two sports is amazing. There is so much special equipment that it would be almost impossible for any store to carry the full range—especially in a small populated region. The Internet is the serious huntsman's or fisherman's dream come true. Any product or piece of equipment is available with the click of a few buttons online.

You will want to have an online storefront to provide pictures of the products you sell as well as textual information about the product. Make sure that the storefront option you choose is very user-friendly.

Make sure you carry a broad enough range of products so that your target customers will consider your site a one-stop shop for all their needs. You may also choose to have a section of your storefront where you can advertise products that you can get if the enthusiast is willing to wait a little longer, granting access to even the rarest items for the part-time enthusiast.

You will make your money primarily by selling hunting and fishing equipment through your Web site. The huge variety of equipment for these two sports will necessitate a huge online catalogue unless you limit yourself initially. It may be a good idea to focus on a niche to start.

Skills Needed

You will need to have some familiarity with hunting and fishing products and the laws regarding their sale and use. Knowing something about marketing on the Internet would also be a very useful skill.

Cost to Start This Business

Costs will range from $10,000 to $250,000. This includes the purchase of a computer, appropriate software, a printer, a scanner, and a digital camera. You will need to purchase your initial inventory. You will also need to have your Web site designed, developed, and hosted. The start-up cost for this business will be higher than most other businesses due to the higher cost of your inventory items.

Number of Employees Needed to Start

This business can be started fairly easily with only one employee. Once the Web site is set up, most of your effort will be concentrated on updating your Web site, advertising your Web site, and shipping your product.

International Potential

The international potential of this business is relatively high. There are hunters and fishermen in most countries, and some of the products and specialty equipment may not be readily available in their local stores. Some items used for hunting are of a quasi-legal nature, especially firearms. In many countries these are controlled items with special import laws. It is important that you find out the import laws for the countries that you think you will be doing business with.

E-Business Model/Payment Processing Method

E-business level 3 is most appropriate for this type of business. If you have an offline store as well, you may want to look at level 4. For more information, see Part 1.

Important Business Issues to Be Addressed

Several legal issues arise from selling hunting and fishing products internationally. Firearms are the most obvious restricted item; however, importing certain knives may be illegal as well.

ONLINE MARKETING TECHNIQUES

- Developing a comprehensive affiliate/associate program would not only increase the awareness of your hunting and fishing supplies site, it would also send referral business to your site.

- Launching a strategic banner advertising campaign on Web sites frequented by your target market would be a great way to increase traffic to your site. Sites that you could place banner ads on include noncompeting hunting and fishing sites, and other Web sites that would be of interest to your target market.

- You could hold a weekly or monthly contest on your site for a free gift. You could ask people if they would like to be notified of the winner via e-mail. This would encourage them to return to your site and re-enter your contest, thus re-exposing them to your products.

- Develop as many links as possible from Web sites, directories, meta-indexes, and Web rings frequented by your target market.

- You could develop a Featured Product page on your site. You could change this product every week. People will continue to return to your site to see what the featured hunting- or fishing-related product is. You could even ask people if they would like to be notified of new featured products via e-mail. This would be a great way to encourage repeat traffic.

- Develop a sponsored listings campaign to bid on appropriate keyword phrases with the popular search engines.

- Online coupons and discounts can be used as an incentive to have visitors return to your site. You can ask if your visitors would like to be part of your preferred customers program, where they are notified weekly of specials and provided with coupons for online purchases.

For a more detailed description of these techniques, along with many other effective online marketing methods, I recommend the companion book *101 Ways to Promote Your Web Site*. You can also find tons of free resources at *http://www.susansweeney.com/resources.html*.

Figure 2.7.   If you like the great outdoors, visit Cabela's Web site.

ADDITIONAL INCOME

To generate additional income, you could expand your Web site to include equipment for other outdoor adventure sports. Several adventure sports can be categorized with hunting and fishing—including camping, hiking, gliding, and boating. You should be able to add any of these sports without compromising the feel of your Web site too much.

ONLINE EXAMPLES

Cabela's
http://www.cabelas.com
The site includes hunting, fishing, camping, and boating. It also has several useful features for the outdoors person. (See Figure 2.7)

Order Outdoors
http://www.orderoutdoors.com
This is mostly a fishing Web site. However, it does cover firearm laws and has some hunting equipment.

47. Image Consultant

OVERVIEW OF BUSINESS MODEL

This business is ideal for someone with knowledge of the importance of first impressions and how to present yourself in various settings, primarily the corporate or professional world and in the media. The way this business works is that you provide one-on-one image consulting to clients and possibly group seminars about image-related issues such as wardrobe, appropriate colors, cosmetic application, posture, and self-confidence. Clients can pay by the hour for your services, or you may choose to have a contract at a set amount for specific services—it's up to you. The Web site is the perfect place to showcase your services and your clients' success stories, and to market your business.

SKILLS NEEDED

To successfully operate this business, you will need experience in beauty, cosmetics, and fashion consulting. The Web site maintenance will require basic Web publishing skills, and you will need clear communication skills via e-mail, phone, and in person. To inspire confidence and style in your clients, you need to walk the walk as well.

COST TO START THIS BUSINESS

The cost to start this business will include the design, development, and hosting of your Web site, as well as a computer, appropriate software, a printer, a scanner, and a digital camera. You can start this venture from home and on a part-time basis. The approximate start-up cost ranges between $3,000 and $4,000.

NUMBER OF EMPLOYEES NEEDED

One experienced and competent individual can start this business single-handedly.

INTERNATIONAL POTENTIAL

The international potential for this business depends on the way you choose to communicate with your clients. If you would like to have customers send in images of themselves and communicate via e-mail to conduct consulting, then the global potential will be restricted only by language. Most image consultants operate face to face with clients, however, and this is preferred throughout the industry.

E-Business Model/Payment Processing Method

The e-business model suggested for the image consulting business is level 1. Clients will pay you directly for your services, so there is no need for online payment processing or a database. For more information, see Part 1.

Important Business Issues to Be Addressed

The image consulting business is highly personalized and everchanging due to today's rapid and progressive styles. Your advice should be tailored to the particular careers of your clients. Make sure your prices are competitive and your Web site clearly defines your capabilities and clientele.

Online Marketing Techniques

- Develop a comprehensive link strategy. You want to generate as many links as possible from appropriate Web sites, directories, Web rings, and meta-indexes related to your target market. There are many sites related to business services that would be appropriate link sites. Ensure that you get listed in sites that target your local area as well as your area of expertise.

- Participate in local newsgroups, mail lists, chat rooms, and discussion forums related to style, beauty, and image issues such as weight loss and makeup application in efforts to create awareness of your services and to attract new clients.

- Organize a reciprocal linking arrangement with regional beauty salons, fashion boutiques, stores, and publications in order to make your business apparent to the professional women who frequent them.

- Get testimonials from clients whom you've helped already and post them on your Web site—maybe even include before and after pictures.

- Develop and send articles about the benefits of using an image consultant to e-zines that focus on related topics.

- Develop a viral marketing strategy where people can "Tell a colleague about this service" via your site. This will spread the word about your site.

- Ensure that you submit your site to the search engines and directories.

- Promotion through related mail lists and newsletters is important. You could even develop your own newsletter or mail list to stay close with your target market.

- Participation in cybermalls related to business services in your geographic area would be very appropriate.

For a more detailed description of these techniques, along with many other effective online marketing methods, I recommend the companion book *101 Ways to Promote Your Web Site*. You can also find tons of free resources at *http://www.susansweeney.com/resources.html*.

ADDITIONAL INCOME

Extra income can come from reselling and advertising beauty products and fashions for preferred distributors. You can generate additional revenue from banner advertising and sponsorship by companies that are interested in reaching your target market.

ONLINE EXAMPLES

Your Best Image
http://www.yourbestimagepid.com
This site offers image consulting services to women in the professional world.

Victoria Brink-Guillot—International Image Consultant
http://www.guillotinternational.com
Victoria does on-site image consulting for brides and professionals. Her site features before and after images that are extremely effective in attracting new clients.

48. Information Broker

OVERVIEW OF BUSINESS MODEL

The information brokerage business is extremely popular these days, and need for the service will only increase as the value of information becomes more critical. The Internet is information, so if you have a talent for researching and accessing public and some private records, databases, and other forms of data warehousing, this is the business for you.

What types of information are clients looking for? Information requests can take many forms. Lawyers may be looking for specific information to strengthen their case. Corporations need market research to support their marketing plans. Businesses may be looking for competitive analysis or information.

How does it work? Clients request information on a certain subject, and you do the research, provide the client with your findings, and get paid for your effort. This operation has fantastic international potential but also has serious legal issues surrounding it, so make sure to have a firm grasp of your liability before embarking on this venture. There is good news: Information brokering can help a lot of people, so your job can be very rewarding and it's easy to get referrals.

Skills Needed

To successfully operate this business, you will need expertise in researching and accessing public, and in some cases private, information over the Internet and through traditional sources such as libraries, microfiche archives, and so on. To update your Web site, you will need basic Web publishing skills. Your communication skills should be concise and descriptive.

Cost to Start This Business

The cost to start this business will include the design, development, and hosting of your Web site as well as a computer, appropriate software, and a printer. The approximate start-up cost ranges between $3,000 and $7,500.

Number of Employees Needed

One experienced and competent individual with superior online researching skills and resources can start this business single-handedly.

International Potential

The international potential for this business is unlimited. There is no telling where a client may reside. If you have access to the information they seek, it's most likely that you can e-mail it to them, and this makes the borders of your business purely virtual and governed solely by language.

E-Business Model/Payment Processing Method

The e-business level suggested for the information brokerage business is level 1 or 2. For more information, see Part 1.

IMPORTANT BUSINESS ISSUES TO BE ADDRESSED

The information brokerage business sometimes infringes on the privacy of others, and whenever this happens there are legal ramifications. Before entering the business, you should research your liability and risk factor.

Sometimes in this business you will be under tight deadlines. Ensure that you have additional resources you can call upon to provide a professional service.

The pricing should be clearly outlined on your site for various services that are defined by the nature of information the client is searching for. The costs should be competitive and reflective of the amount of time it takes to conduct each search.

ONLINE MARKETING TECHNIQUES

- Develop a comprehensive link strategy. It is important to be linked from as many business service Web sites as possible, as well as related directories, business service cybermalls, Web rings, and meta-indexes.

- Develop extensive registration in all of the major search engines with focus on the information brokerage business and on sites where those searching for private or inaccessible information would most likely go. You can also develop a pay-per-click strategy with the popular search engines.

- Organizing a reciprocal linking arrangement with private investigators, public records organizations, libraries, and security sites will make your business apparent to your target demographic.

- Participating in market research and other business services-related mail lists and newsgroups may be an effective way to reach your target market online.

For a more detailed description of these techniques, along with many other effective online marketing methods, I recommend the companion book *101 Ways to Promote Your Web Site.* You can also find tons of free resources at *http://www.susansweeney.com/resources.html.*

ADDITIONAL INCOME

Extra income can come from conducting extensive searches and aiding private investigators and security specialists by doing online research that they cannot conduct. You may also advertise and recommend the services of private investigators, genealogists, and security specialists.

ONLINE EXAMPLES

Sterling Information Broker
http://www.sterlingcommerce.com
Sterling Information Broker provides delivery of business-critical documents with end-to-end audits and controls.

Information Broker Ireland
http://indigo.ie/~findinfo
This company finds and extracts any information in the public domain in Ireland and forwards it to you for a fee.

49. Interior Design

OVERVIEW OF BUSINESS MODEL

This business has a lot of online potential. The design of living and office space is becoming more important to us each time we realize how much our environment influences our mood and productivity at work. If you are an interior designer or work in a related field, this business could create an opportunity for self-employment and extra income.

Here's how it works: Clients find your site and learn of your services. You consult with the clients via e-mail and in person to determine their particular design needs. You provide the required design services and deliver the final product or services. These services may be billed on an hourly basis or be provided on a contract fee basis. Your advice should be budget-conscious so that the client can implement your realistic suggestions.

SKILLS NEEDED

You will need interior design skills, credentials, and experience. Basic Web publishing skills would be a bonus. Sometimes you will be communicating with your clients via e-mail to describe suggestions and perhaps using Adobe Photoshop or other image-editing software to convey your ideas for decorating and remodeling. You may want to use CAD (Computer Aided Design) software. You should be able to clearly define and explain interior design principles and be receptive to your clients' desires.

Cost to Start This Business

The cost to start this business will include the design, development, and hosting of your Web site as well as a computer, appropriate software, a printer, a scanner, and a digital camera. You can start this venture from home and on a part-time basis. The approximate start-up cost ranges between $5,000 and $10,000.

Number of Employees Needed to Start

One experienced and competent individual can start this business single-handedly.

International Potential

The international potential for this business depends on the way you communicate with your clients. If you would like to have customers send in images of their homes and communicate via e-mail to conduct consulting, then the global potential will be restricted to language barriers only. Most interior designers, however, make several house calls and operate face to face with clients, and this is preferred throughout the industry.

E-Business Model/Payment Processing Method

The e-business level suggested for online interior design is level 1. In the beginning clients will pay you directly for your services, so there is no need for online payment processing or a database. For more information, see Part 1.

Important Business Issues to Be Addressed

Interior design is an ever-changing and competitive business. To offer your clients quality service, your Web site should have a rich resource area where users can surf the Web for ideas, tips, and tools to help them decide what they would like to have done to their home or office.

Online Marketing Techniques

- Developing a comprehensive affiliate/associate program with fellow industry partners such as wall and floor covering manufacturers and distributors would increase the awareness of your interior design services and send referral business back and forth.

- Develop extensive registration in all of the major search engines that focus on the region in which you reside and on sites where people in the mood to redecorate would most likely go.

- Participate in local mail lists, chat rooms, and discussion forums related to interior design, remodeling, and decorating in efforts to create awareness of your services and to attract new clients.

- Organize a reciprocal linking arrangement and advertise with regional distributors of decorating and construction supply stores in order to make your business apparent to the folks who frequent them.

- Develop a sponsored listings campaign to bid on appropriate keyword phrases with the popular search engines.

- You might want to include a testimonial section on your Web site or a before-and-after section displaying some of your more successful projects.

For a more detailed description of these techniques, along with many other effective online marketing methods, I recommend the companion book *101 Ways to Promote Your Web Site*. You can also find tons of free resources at *http://www.susansweeney.com/resources.html.*

ADDITIONAL INCOME

Extra income in the interior design business can come from many avenues because of the wide variety of manufacturers and distributors you can recommend, resell for, and advertise for without threatening your own business. When you are in the position to consult, it's easy to recommend certain products and services. Everything from plumbing and electrical work to dry wall installation can be suggested by you, and it's highly possible to have an advertising and referral commission arrangement with local service and sales industry partners.

ONLINE EXAMPLES

Decorating Studio
http://www.decoratingstudio.com
An entire online interior design service site. You can hire consultants, get color schemes, and much more.

Huber Décor Inc.
http://www.huberdecor.com
Private interior design firm specializing in commercial, office, and mall interior design.

50. Mail List Service

OVERVIEW OF BUSINESS MODEL

The key to running a successful mail list service is attaining and growing a number of targeted mail lists that you can make available to clients to increase the value and responsiveness of each direct e-mail campaign.

You gather income from the renting of the list based on how targeted and how big it is. You have choices in this business as to how involved you are in your clients' marketing campaigns. You can rent the list and let them provide you with the communication they want sent out, or you can work with the client to develop the marketing message, deliver the personalized messages to the list, and provide tracking reports on the results. You can work with long-term clients to do A/B and other testing to increase the effectiveness of the campaigns. It depends on how much time you would like to commit to the business.

You can also develop a mail list online related to a particular topic. With this mail list you should not rent the list but certainly could accept advertising or sponsorship dollars. With opt-in mail lists, people join because they are interested in the topic of the mail list and are interested in receiving information related to that topic. Many of these opt-in mail lists are quite comprehensive—many have over 500,000 names on their list.

SKILLS NEEDED

Knowledge of online advertising techniques and e-mail capture is an asset to run this type of business. You will need experience in sorting, cleansing, and building lists using a database of some kind. You will need basic Web publishing skills to update your Web site and competent organizational skills.

COST TO START THIS BUSINESS

You will have to pay for the design, development, and hosting of your Web site. If you do not own a computer, this obviously will have to be purchased. The database software to manage your lists, whether it is stored on a server or on your desktop, will be a necessary start-up expense. Estimated cost is $3,500 to $5,500 to start.

Number of Employees Needed to Start

The number of employees needed to run this type of business is one dedicated individual, and you can start this venture from home while keeping your regular full-time job.

International Potential

This business has strong international potential, since targeted mailing is an important part of the marketing strategy for many businesses in all countries.

E-Business Model/Payment Processing Method

E-business level 1 or 2 would be appropriate for this type of business in the beginning. Once you develop an extensive group of lists that can be viewed (yet not copied) and ordered online and distributed via download, you may want to upgrade to level 3. For more information, see Part 1.

Important Business Issues to Be Addressed

The database and administration software you purchase to administer the mail lists should be researched and suitable to your level of operation. You should be available by phone for prospective and current clients to contact you. Concentrate on associating yourself with online marketing resource Web sites and remain current within your market when it comes to the effectiveness of your lists and pricing. The mail list services business is competitive.

Online Marketing Techniques

- Develop a comprehensive link strategy. Get links to your site from appropriate Web sites, Web rings, directories, and related cybermalls.

- Participate in newsgroups and discussion forums related to online advertising or the industries that your mail lists target.

- Develop a sponsored listings campaign to bid on appropriate keyword phrases with the popular search engines.

- Consider providing a reduction in fee when you include your clickable logo at the bottom of each of your clients' outbound messages.

- Launch a strategic banner advertising campaign on Web sites frequented by your target market.

For a more detailed description of these techniques, along with many other effective online marketing methods, I recommend the companion book *101 Ways to Promote Your Web Site*. You can also find tons of free resources at *http://www.susansweeney.com/resources.html*.

ADDITIONAL INCOME

You could generate additional income for your mail list by providing data-mining reports and effectiveness tests on your lists and others. This additional service would add value to your online business.

ONLINE EXAMPLES

D&B Sales and Marketing Solutions (see Figure 2.8)
http://www.zapdata.com/HomePage.do
This site makes lists available for a fee. They are downloadable from the site once you define criteria and pay a fee.

Women in Agriculture
http://www.wia.usda.gov/listserv.htm
This is an example of a targeted mail list available on the Net.

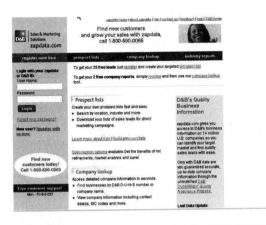

Figure 2.8. A great example of an online mail list service.

51. Map and Tourist Information

OVERVIEW OF BUSINESS MODEL

Tourism is definitely one of the industries that has the greatest opportunity online today. Travelers are avid Web surfers because they know the information they seek is plentiful and quickly accessible online. There are many tourism-related sites on the Net today, but there is still a need for sites that cater to niche markets. The possibilities are endless for map and travel content.

Maps can be provided digitally from your site and be available for download by the site visitor. There are many map sites popping up throughout the Internet with access available at no fee. These are provided to generate traffic and to complement travel-related sites.

At this stage the best route for any start-up online home business involving travel is targeting a very specific type of traveler, travel experience, or location and making your site the mecca of travel information for the niche you choose. For example, you could create a site for honeymooners who want to find a location for their honeymoon. The content should have maps, links to romantic travel operations that cater to honeymooners, and stories written by actual honeymooners who enjoyed these destinations and experiences in the past.

Your site must be very user-friendly. It must have all the information people in your niche market would look for when planning their trip. You'll need information on car rentals, accommodations, resorts, cruises, bicycle rentals, hot air balloon rides, beaches, tourist attractions, and other things of interest to your target market.

Revenue can be generated through the sale of advertising on your site, map digitizing services, referral fees from tourism-related sites promoted on your site, and selling travel-related products from your site.

SKILLS NEEDED

Knowledge of tourism content writing is an asset to run this type of business. Basic Web publishing and digital-imaging skills are needed to update the Web site. You will have to have clear communication skills via e-mail to service your clients.

COST TO START THIS BUSINESS

You will need a computer, software, a printer, and Internet access. You will have to pay for the design, development, and hosting of your Web site. Estimated cost is $3,000 to $7,500 to start.

NUMBER OF EMPLOYEES NEEDED

The number of employees needed to run this type of business is one talented, travel-savvy person, and you can start this venture while keeping your regular full-time job.

INTERNATIONAL POTENTIAL

The global potential of the online maps and tourist information business is obvious and guaranteed. The only limitation is language, but translation services exist that are affordable and well worth the cost to ensure the success of your venture.

E-BUSINESS MODEL/PAYMENT PROCESSING METHOD

The primary source of revenue will come from advertising, providing content, and perhaps booking commissions depending on how involved you intend to get in the travel planning side of the business. To begin with, it is suggested that e-business level 1 or 2 would be appropriate for this type of business. If you plan to have an online storefront to sell travel-related products, you will want the e-business level 3 model. For more information, see Part 1.

IMPORTANT BUSINESS ISSUES TO BE ADDRESSED

The travel business is fiercely competitive, so make sure that when you construct your business plan you research carefully and pick a niche demographic of travelers that is not covered heavily by another site already dominating in the search engines.

Keep your site updated and archive the old stories in a library. Remember, a travel story is never outdated; there are so many readers on the Net that the content is new to some browsers even though the content has been there for quite some time.

ONLINE MARKETING TECHNIQUES

- Develop a comprehensive link strategy. Generate as many links as possible to your site from appropriate Web sites, travel-related cybermalls, directories, and meta-indexes.

- Develop a sponsored listings campaign to bid on appropriate keyword phrases with the popular search engines. Make sure your site is designed to be search engine friendly for organic search placement.

- Participate in e-zines that your target market is reading. Make sure to provide your contact information and a link to your site.

- Develop and provide downloadable podcasts on various destinations from your Web site.

- Incorporate viral marketing techniques like "Tell a Friend" throughout your Web site.

- Participate in newsgroups, mail lists, and discussion forums about travel in the area in which your site specializes.

- Launch a strategic banner advertising campaign on Web sites frequented by your target market.

For a more detailed description of these techniques, along with many other effective online marketing methods, I recommend the companion book *101 Ways to Promote Your Web Site*. You can also find tons of free resources at *http://www.susansweeney.com/resources.html*.

ADDITIONAL INCOME

Extra income in the online map and tourism information Web site business can come from several avenues. If you are an avid travel writer, there are opportunities to get paid by travel operators to test out their accommodations, tours, or travel services and write a promotional story about them. There are many affiliate sales programs on the Net for travel content providers to join. You can sell travel-related products like travel insurance and long distance phone cards.

ONLINE EXAMPLES

Mapquest
http://www.mapquest.com
The largest and most popular map resource site in the world, and it's free!

Maps.com
http://www.maps.com
Provides maps and travel resources.

Virtual Tourist
http://www.virtualtourist.com
A huge travel site that encourages tourists to share experiences and communicate with other travelers. Included are searchable maps, archives of travel stories, and much more.

52. Market Research

OVERVIEW OF BUSINESS MODEL

In today's competitive marketing world, careful research is a must if you want to put advertising dollars into the right places. The Internet is now the fastest and most bountiful marketing research environment our world has ever seen. If you have experience in marketing data-collection methods and producing reports to prove specific theories, this is the business for you. The business would gain revenue from payment for research analysis reports and related industry reports for clients it attracts.

SKILLS NEEDED

Knowledge of online research methods is a must for this operation to run successfully. Creating professional reports of your research data and theories is also needed. You will need basic Web publishing skills to manage your Web site and client and partner mailing lists.

COST TO START THIS BUSINESS

You will have to pay for the development, design, and hosting of your Web site. If you do not own a computer, this obviously will have to be purchased along with the requisite software and printer. You will also need Internet access to do the research. The estimated cost is $3,500 to $5,500 to start.

NUMBER OF EMPLOYEES NEEDED TO START

The number of employees needed to run this type of business is one dedicated individual, and you can start this venture from home while keeping your regular job. Remember that you will need connections in the market analysis community so that you can access accurate information in reasonable time.

INTERNATIONAL POTENTIAL

This business has strong international potential. The global nature of the Internet creates a need for specific or niche online interest groups. The international potential for this business will depend on how much marketing you do and the languages in which you are capable of developing your reports.

E-BUSINESS MODEL/PAYMENT PROCESSING METHOD

E-business level 1 or 2 would be appropriate for this type of business in the beginning. Clients can pay you directly by check, money order, and so on. Once you develop an extensive group of clients or sell your reports via download from your site (big chance for money here!), you may want to upgrade to level 3. For more information, see Part 1.

IMPORTANT BUSINESS ISSUES TO BE ADDRESSED

Being accurate and providing data reports that make sense is the only way to get ahead in this business. Make sure that your prices are competitive and that the reports you develop are based on studied information. Selling your completed reports via download from your site is a great way to garnish income.

ONLINE MARKETING TECHNIQUES

- Develop a comprehensive link strategy. Make sure you are linked from as many market research and business service Web sites as possible, as well as appropriate directories, cybermalls, and meta-indexes.

- Participate in newsgroups and discussion forums related to online market analysis, advertising, or the industries that your clients are targeting.

- Develop a sponsored listings campaign to bid on appropriate keyword phrases with the popular search engines.

- Launch a strategic banner advertising campaign on Web sites frequented by your target markets.

For a more detailed description of these techniques, along with many other effective online marketing methods, I recommend the companion book *101 Ways to Promote Your Web Site*. You can also find tons of free resources at *http://www.susansweeney.com/resources.html*.

ADDITIONAL INCOME

More income can come from banner advertising and sponsorship of your mail list from companies that are targeting the same market as you are.

ONLINE EXAMPLES

OutLink
http://www.outlink.com
This company publishes the Firewall (Web security) report and also does standard market research.

Survey.com
http://www.survey.com
In their own words, this company is "the first e-research company." Many, many bells and whistles.

53. Monogramming

OVERVIEW OF BUSINESS MODEL

The monogramming business has great potential on the Internet. Customers can view all your services and products with clear images that they can enlarge. They can order from anywhere in the world and pay online. If you have experience in the custom embroidery and printing business, this venture has your name all over it.

Here's how it works: The entire catalogue displaying your monogramming services and products is put on your Web site so that browsers can view your wares and place orders. Your online storefront will make it easy for your customers to put many items in their shopping cart and identify the monogramming they want on each item. You will have to provide an opportunity for your corporate clients to send you their logo in digital format for their online purchases. The opportunity for repeat business is great in this industry.

SKILLS NEEDED

Experience in the monogramming industry and the ability to find quality products such as sweaters and T-shirts on which to embroider is required. You will need to have basic Web publishing and computer skills. Your products will be for sale in an online store, so familiarity with merchant software and secure payment processing methods is necessary.

COST TO START THIS BUSINESS

The cost to start this business will include the design, development, and hosting of your Web site as well as a computer, appropriate software, a printer, a digital camera, and a scanner. An online storefront, payment processing software, and a merchant account are required to make this operation work. You will also need to have the embroidery equipment and a small inventory to perform these services. You can start this venture from home and on a part-time basis. The approximate start-up cost ranges between $4,000 and $25,000.

NUMBER OF EMPLOYEES NEEDED

One experienced and competent individual can start this business single-handedly.

INTERNATIONAL POTENTIAL

The international potential of the online monogramming business is promising. Most products that you can embroider on are cloth, so they can be shipped anywhere.

E-BUSINESS MODEL/PAYMENT PROCESSING METHOD

The suggested e-business level recommended for this operation is 2 or 3. To maximize the potential sales of your monogramming business, customers should be able to order and pay online and include extensive details about their personalized monogramming needs. For more information, see Part 1.

IMPORTANT BUSINESS ISSUES TO BE ADDRESSED

Maintaining a strict budget while producing each order is what will ensure the profit of this business. The orders are unique and personal, so your online store should have many options and areas for the customer to include special notes and details such as the thread count of the cotton T-shirt and where the design is to be printed or embroidered.

ONLINE MARKETING TECHNIQUES

- Launching a strategic banner advertising campaign on Web sites frequented by your target market would be a great way to increase traffic to your site. Sites that you could place banner ads on include noncompeting gift sites, direct-marketing sites, trade show promotion sites, and other Web sites that would be of interest to your target market.

- Develop as many links as possible from Web sites, directories, meta-indexes, and Web rings frequented by your target market.

- You could develop a Featured Product page on your site. You could change this product every week. People will continue to return to your site to see what the featured product is. You could even ask people if they would like to be notified of your featured product via e-mail. This would be a great way to encourage repeat traffic to your site. You can also provide access to the updates via RSS.

- Developing a comprehensive affiliate/associate program will increase the awareness of your monogramming business and generate referral business.

- Register in all the major search engines after making sure your site has been optimized for search engine friendliness. You can also consider participating in pay-per-click programs with the popular search engines.

- Create a mailing list of all your clients and have a section on your Web site where potential customers may join the list to find out about up-coming promotions and so on.

- Organize a reciprocal linking arrangement with marketing agencies, publications, and corporations with obvious branding.

For a more detailed description of these techniques, along with many other effective online marketing methods, I recommend the companion book *101 Ways to Promote Your Web Site*. You can also find tons of free resources at *http://www.susansweeney.com/resources.html*.

ADDITIONAL INCOME

You can expand your business by providing services such as gift registry for weddings, christenings, showers, and other special events. You can offer several levels of gift wrapping, which will help to generate additional income for this business.

You can sell banner advertising to Web sites that are noncompeting but sell to the same target market.

ONLINE EXAMPLES

Ashton Whyte
http://www.ashtonwhyte.com
Nice Web site, but apparently this is only an advertisement for their real-world store. They do mention that they are willing to help customers over the phone.

Thread Heads
http://www.threadheads.com
I list this only for resource value. This site is a directory of most of the monogramming sites on the Web.

Image Builders
http://www.imagebuilders.com
You call the shop, discuss what you want, and they will make it and then ship it for you.

54. Movie Review Site

OVERVIEW OF BUSINESS

If you're a huge movie fan and enjoy discussing the latest movies, then this opportunity may be for you. You could develop a movie review site. You can provide your site's visitors with information on upcoming movie releases, reviews of currently released movies, and listings of recently released movies. You can also provide visitors with the latest information on the movie industry or entertainment industry.

There are several ways for this type of site to generate revenue. You can sell advertising space to entertainment-related businesses promoting movies, television, or other related products. You could also sell movie paraphernalia such as T-shirts, toys, stickers, posters, sound tracks, DVDs, and other merchandise related to the entertainment industry.

SKILLS NEEDED

Since you will be reviewing movies, excellent analytical skills are required. You need to be able to convey your message to your target market clearly and effectively, so excellent writing skills will also be necessary. Since the success of your movie review site depends largely on the number of visitors that your site receives, knowledge of online marketing techniques would be an asset.

COST TO START THIS BUSINESS

Initially you will have to pay for the development, design, and hosting of your Web site, computer hardware, computer software, a scanner, and a printer. It would probably be in your best interest to purchase comprehensive Web traffic analysis software to track where your Web site visitors are coming from. This information can be great for future marketing opportunities and will also enable you to report traffic statistics to potential advertisers. If you decide to sell movie merchandise on your site, you will have to purchase storefront software equipped with an electronic shopping cart feature or be responsible for developing this in-house. If you plan to set up a mailing list, you will also have to purchase mailing list software to help you organize and maintain your mail lists. Other costs that you will incur are related to the promotion of your Web site. Estimated cost is $5,000 to $10,000 to start.

NUMBER OF EMPLOYEES NEEDED TO START

This business can be started as a one-person operation on a part-time basis. To grow the business, you will require one or two full-time employees. Since this site requires that you develop an enormous number of site visitors, one employee's time should be focused on implementing Web site traffic-building techniques. The other employee(s) can be responsible for writing the movie reviews and handling all administrative, accounting, and sales associated with operating this type of business.

INTERNATIONAL POTENTIAL

There is very little international potential for this type of business. Movies available in your geographic area may not be playing in other parts of the world due to cultural conflicts, release dates, or lack of interest.

E-BUSINESS MODEL/PAYMENT PROCESSING METHOD

E-business level 1 is most appropriate for this type of business. For more information, see Part 1.

IMPORTANT BUSINESS ISSUES TO BE ADDRESSED

Advertisers are going to want to advertise on your movie review site for one reason—increased exposure. To ensure that this happens, you are going to have to do whatever you can to promote your business online and offline. It is also important to integrate all of your online and offline promotions. All colors, images, and themes should be consistent between your online and offline promotional efforts.

Be sure to display your contact information in a prominent location on your site. You want potential advertisers to be able to contact you easily. You could even have a section of your site dedicated to potential advertisers. An Advertising Information button could be linked to a page where potential advertisers could review traffic statistics, site reviews, and other information that would convince them to advertise on your site. This would be a dynamite way to encourage people to advertise on your site.

ONLINE MARKETING TECHNIQUES

- Launch a strategic banner advertising campaign on Web sites frequented by your target market. These sites could relate to movies, television, or other topics related to the entertainment industry.

- Develop a viral marketing strategy where people can "Tell a Friend about This Review" via your site. People will be able send a movie review to their friend if they are trying to decide which movie to see. This will spread the word about your site.

- You could hold a weekly or monthly contest on your Web site for free movie merchandise offered by one of your advertisers. This merchandise could include free passes to a movie premiere, T-shirts, a copy of the movie sound track, or other promotional merchandise. You could ask people if they would like to be notified of the winner via e-mail. This e-mail will encourage them to return to your site to re-enter your contest, thus re-exposing them to your site.

- Develop as many links as possible from appropriate Web sites, directories, and meta-indexes related to your target market. These sites should relate to movies, television, or the entertainment industry.

- Develop a sponsored listings campaign to bid on appropriate keyword phrases with the popular search engines.

- You should develop a What's New or a New Releases page for your site. This will encourage people to return to your site on a regular basis to see which movies were released. You could ask people if they would like to be notified via e-mail whenever you make updates to your site. This will encourage them to return to your site.

For a more detailed description of these techniques, along with many other effective online marketing methods, I recommend the companion book *101 Ways to Promote Your Web Site*. You can also find tons of free resources at *http://www.susansweeney.com/resources.html*.

ADDITIONAL INCOME

In addition to providing movie reviews from your site, you could also partner with a newspaper or entertainment publication to have your movie reviews published on a regular basis. This would not only generate exposure for your movie review site, it would also generate additional revenue for your business.

ONLINE EXAMPLES

Cinephiles—Movie Reviews and Analysis
http://www.cinephiles.net
Objective film reviews of new releases, user forums, and an online store.

CinemaReview.com
http://www.cinemareview.com
Tons of movie-related information. The site encourages the user to subscribe
for additional membership benefits.

55. Music Center

OVERVIEW OF BUSINESS MODEL

Music has enjoyed phenomenal success online. Due to the file type called
MP3, a myriad of Web sites such as CDNow, Napster, and Kazaa have proved
there is no question that music on the Internet is an award-winning combi-
nation. Selling of musical items online has the advantage of providing users
with a huge selection that spans a wide diversity throughout the music industry. This leaves plenty of space for businesses to avoid competing with
each other.

You will make money with your online business by selling musical items
online. What you sell can vary from store to store, but the inventory often
includes CDs, musical instruments, related paraphernalia, and sheet music.

You will have an easy-to-use online storefront and include many features
on your Web site to encourage repeat visitors, encourage your visitors to stay
awhile, and encourage visitors to tell their friends about your site.

SKILLS NEEDED

A music center is not just about selling music items and instruments online, but
also about providing a wealth of useful information to your customers. To provide the level of information your customers will expect, you will need to be
familiar with the types of music and instruments that your music center sells
and services.

COST TO START THIS BUSINESS

The cost to initially set up your music center will range from $5,000 to $20,000.
These costs include a computer, administrative and e-commerce software, a
printer, a scanner, and a digital camera. Your Web site will need to be designed,
developed, and hosted. Other initial costs (not included in the amount above)
to consider include your inventory and the advertising of your Web site.

NUMBER OF EMPLOYEES NEEDED TO START

Depending on the way you begin the venture, this can be a great part-time
start-up business for one individual. If you wish to provide a more comprehen-

sive service or begin to sell high volume, you would have to increase your staff size accordingly.

INTERNATIONAL POTENTIAL

Using the Internet, you have access to the global market. However, high shipping costs and the different musical tastes between continental markets may limit you to your home continent.

E-BUSINESS MODEL/PAYMENT PROCESSING METHOD

E-business model level 3 is most appropriate for this type of business. If you have an offline store as well, you might want to consider a level 4 model. For more information, see Part 1.

IMPORTANT BUSINESS ISSUES TO BE ADDRESSED

You will have to be competitive with your pricing as your customers will be looking for the best price online. Be aware of sites like Amazon.com and CDNow.com that offer generous discounts.

Sites like MP3.com, where music can be downloaded to a local computer and then burned to a CD, will have an impact on CD sales online.

ONLINE MARKETING TECHNIQUES

- Developing a comprehensive affiliate/associate program would not only increase the awareness of your music center site, it would also send referral business to your site.

- You could run a daily or weekly contest on your site for a free music product. You could ask people if they would like to be notified of the winner via e-mail. This would encourage them to return to your site and re-enter your contest, thus re-exposing them to your products.

- Develop as many links as possible from appropriate music-related Web sites, directories, meta-indexes, and Web rings frequented by your target market.

- You could develop a Featured Product page on your site. You could change this product every week. People will continue to return to your site to see what the featured music product is. You could even ask people if they would like to be notified of your featured product via e-mail. This would be a great way to encourage repeat traffic.

- Developing and distributing a great music newsletter or being the moderator for a music-related discussion group will build up a sense of community with your users. This will help create an affinity for your Web site in the hearts of your hardcore music fans. In other words, it is a great way to generate repeat customers.

- Launching a strategic banner advertising campaign on Web sites frequented by your target market would be a great way to increase traffic to your site. Sites that you could place banner ads on include noncompeting music sites and other Web sites that would be of interest to your target market.

- You can develop a discount center or offer coupons giving customers a deal, thus enticing them to return. Both discounts and coupons also allow your customers to join your permission-marketing campaign.

- Host live chats with local talents and store live audio recordings on the Web site of jam sessions, concerts, and so on.

For a more detailed description of these techniques, along with many other effective online marketing methods, I recommend the companion book *101 Ways to Promote Your Web Site*. You can also find tons of free resources at *http://www.susansweeney.com/resources.html*.

ADDITIONAL INCOME

You can expand your product line. If you are selling just CDs or just musical instruments, you could expand your service to include the other one. The music industry is renowned for product endorsements, so you can capitalize on this by selling musical paraphernalia such as T-shirts, hats, or other items with band logos.

ONLINE EXAMPLES

iMusic.com (Figure 2.9)
http://www.imusic.com
Great site with featured artists, latest news, contests, downloads, and much more for the music enthusiast.

Haight Ashbury Music Center
http://www.haight-ashbury-music.com

Figure 2.9.   iMusic.com features everything for the music enthusiast.

A very nicely laid out music center. This site has a wide selection of instruments and music available.

56. Newsletter Developer

OVERVIEW OF BUSINESS MODEL

Newsletters are a compelling way to create brand awareness and awareness about a company's products and services. There are all different kinds of newsletters being circulated on the Internet. Some are sent out daily; others are sent weekly or monthly. The higher the frequency of circulation, the more work is required to manage the development and circulation of the newsletter. Most newsletters are free, so the revenue comes from advertising, sponsorship, and mail list management.

In many cases, traditional businesses want to integrate the e-mail newsletter into their marketing strategy and would prefer to hire someone to manage this task for a fee. It would be possible to develop and circulate newsletters for several businesses and make a profit.

SKILLS NEEDED

To operate this online business, you will need experience in developing copy for public viewing, which demands a catchy and terse writing style to get the message across clearly and in few words. Basic Web publishing skills are needed to update the Web site where you market your services as a newsletter developer.

COST TO START THIS BUSINESS

You will need a computer, appropriate software, a printer, and an Internet account. The main expense will be the design, development, and hosting of your Web site. The estimated cost is $3,000 to $7,500 to start.

NUMBER OF EMPLOYEES NEEDED TO START

The number of employees needed to run this type of business is one dedicated individual, and you can start this venture while keeping your regular full-time job.

INTERNATIONAL POTENTIAL

This business has strong international potential if the newsletters are translated into several languages and the content appeals to a demographic that spans across the globe. E-mail can go anywhere, so the possibilities of having a global business are high.

E-BUSINESS MODEL/PAYMENT PROCESSING METHOD

Some newsletters are free, and the revenue is earned by the development, distribution services, and advertising. In the case of the free newsletter e-business, level 1 or 2 would be appropriate. If the newsletters you manage contain information that people are willing to pay for, then e-business level 2 may be suitable in the long run. For more information, see Part 1.

IMPORTANT BUSINESS ISSUES TO BE ADDRESSED

The development and management of newsletters and the mailing lists that they are associated with is becoming a more valuable business as the traditional print version of the newsletter becomes obsolete. Make sure the pricing of your services is competitive with other newsletter developers, and carefully plan how much time you will spend on each circulation.

You must be aware of e-mail courtesy and privacy guidelines so you do not spam your subscribers or send them viruses.

Payment for your services should be half the total fee when you accept the job and half when each campaign is complete. In every case possible, try to get clients to sign a six-month to one-year contract, allowing you to manage their newsletters for a prolonged amount of time.

ONLINE MARKETING TECHNIQUES

- Develop your own newsletter and send it out to prospective clients outlining your services and the benefits of having theirs developed remotely by you.

- Develop a sponsored listings campaign to bid on appropriate keyword phrases with the popular search engines.

- Get listed and linked from directories and meta-indexes related to mail lists, newsletters, and Internet marketing services.

- Include your clickable logo at the bottom of all newsletters you develop for clients, if possible.

- Participate in newsgroups and discussion forums related to online advertising or the industries to which your newsletter services would appeal.

- Organize a strategic reciprocal linking and advertising strategy between your site and all the businesses that currently use your services.

For a more detailed description of these techniques, along with many other effective online marketing methods, I recommend the companion book *101 Ways to Promote Your Web Site*. You can also find tons of free resources at *http://www.susansweeney.com/resources.html.*

ADDITIONAL INCOME

Additional income can come from creating a newsletter development business that broadens the scope of services by integrating the newsletter with other online marketing techniques that cooperate with ad networks, marketing research groups, and mail list buyers.

ONLINE EXAMPLES

The Lisa Company
http://www.thelisaco.com/newsletters.html
The Lisa Company provides writing, editing, and research services for newsletters and e-newsletters.

The Newsletter Factory
http://www.nlf.com

The Newsletter Factory provides a full range of services—proofreading, editing, writing, newsletter design, custom newsletters, magazines, brochures, Web sites, and e-mail newsletter design.

57. Online Coach

OVERVIEW OF BUSINESS MODEL

Traditional coaching can now happen online. If you have experience or expertise in consulting or coaching, this could be the business for you. Currently there are many industry experts and professionals offering online coaching services. This doesn't mean that competition is fierce, however. The number of potential clients for this service is enormous, as everyone needs some form of coaching. Whether you offer spiritual coaching, business coaching, family coaching, and so on, there will be a market for your services.

How does it work? You simply design a Web site to effectively promote your coaching services, market it all over the Web, and business should come your way. Your coaching services can be delivered as personal consultation, over the telephone, or via e-mail.

SKILLS NEEDED

You should have in-depth knowledge in your area of expertise, together with the skill to motivate others and give fair, constructive feedback. You will need to be available through e-mail, instant messenger service, and perhaps telephone in some cases. You should possess basic Web publishing skills to update and administer your Web site.

COST TO START THIS BUSINESS

Since you are providing a service that has no inventory, your initial costs will be minimal. You will have to pay for the design, hosting, and marketing of your Web site. Estimated cost to start up is $1,000 to $5,000.

NUMBER OF EMPLOYEES NEEDED TO START

You can start this business single-handedly from your home office.

INTERNATIONAL POTENTIAL

This business has strong international potential. Depending on the type of coaching you offer and the languages you speak, the global opportunity is abundant.

E-Business Model/Payment Processing Method

E-business level 1 is most appropriate for this type of business. For more information, see Part 1.

Important Business Issues To Be Addressed

You will have to carefully plan how to charge for your services. There are options. You can charge a monthly retainer for a decided number of hours, or you can charge by the hour. How you communicate with your clients is also an issue to be considered. Make sure your budget includes telecommunications expenses and try to cut back on these as much as possible by using other online communication methods such as e-mail, live voice chat, online meeting facilities, and MSN.

Online Marketing Techniques

- Develop a coaching tips and tools archive and feature lead-ins to it in an online newsletter or e-zine.

- Participate in newsgroups and discussion forums related to coaching and consulting or in your area of expertise.

- Develop a sponsored listings campaign to bid on appropriate keyword phrases with the popular search engines.

- Write articles or be a contributing editor to e-zines that focus on your area of expertise.

- Develop a few podcasts available from your site that profile your expertise.

- Get testimonials from clients whom you've helped already and send articles about the benefits of online coaching to e-zines that focus on such topics.

For a more detailed description of these techniques, along with many other effective online marketing methods, I recommend the companion book *101 Ways to Promote Your Web Site*. You can also find tons of free resources at *http://www.susansweeney.com/resources.html*.

Additional Income

You could generate additional income for your online coaching business by providing ad space on your site for associated products that your client base might be interested in buying. Another idea is creating and selling e-books that outline your coaching strategies within your field of expertise.

ONLINE EXAMPLES

Cool Running
http://www.coolrunning.com
This site offers online coaching that allows a real-life coach to interact with athletes via the Internet and electronic mail.

Your Natural Edge
http://www.yournaturaledge.com
This site facilitates enduring, positive change within organizations using simple strategies that focus on individuals' specific needs rather than on corporate systems.

58. Online Flower Store

OVERVIEW OF BUSINESS MODEL

Who doesn't like to be sent flowers? This business is as much about helping people stay connected as it is about selling flowers. You will often be marketing your flowers to busy executives whose work schedule doesn't allow them to shop in a more conventional store. It is very important that the service you provide is easy to use and reliable.

There are several methods of selling flowers online, and you must decide which one you wish to use. The easiest method is to affiliate with a major supplier like FTD. Your Web site will market and sell the flowers, but when customers make a purchase you send the order to FTD and they take care of the order fulfillment and delivery. You make your revenue by generating a small commission on all sales you send to FTD. A second and more complex method of selling flowers online is to handle the fulfillment yourself through your own store or through your affiliate network. This type of business is usually restricted to larger stores with an offline as well as an online store. When people purchase from you online, you send their order directly (if they are in your geographic order) or forward the order to an offline store in the location where the order is to be delivered. This can be done through FTD or by setting up your own affiliate network.

SKILLS NEEDED

You will need to set up your online storefront and handle the order distribution. If you are also providing the order fulfillment, then you will need to become familiar with that aspect of the business as well as being part of a national and international network for handling orders outside your geographic area.

COST TO START THIS BUSINESS

To start this business you need a computer, the appropriate software, and a printer. You will also need a dynamite Web site designed, developed, and hosted, as you have a lot of competition online. Your Web site will include an online storefront. You will need to become part of the FTD or some other flower distribution network. The setup will cost between $4,000 and $20,000.

If you have an offline presence to handle order fulfillment, you will have to consider the costs of physical space, inventory, furniture, and equipment, as well as staff-related costs.

In addition to these expenses, you will need to allow for online and offline advertising, cybermall participation, or paid directory listings. These costs depend on your budget and your aggressiveness. At a minimum you should allow another $5,000 to $10,000.

NUMBER OF EMPLOYEES NEEDED TO START

This type of business can be started as a one-person part-time venture if you are using FTD or are affiliated with real-world stores and are doing none of the order fulfillment yourself. However, if you are handling the order fulfillment side of things as well, your staffing requirements will depend on your hours of operation, the size of your store, and the volume of business you handle.

INTERNATIONAL POTENTIAL

This type of business has significant international potential as long as you belong to a network to handle the order fulfillment outside your geographic area.

E-BUSINESS MODEL/PAYMENT PROCESSING METHOD

E-business level 3 is most appropriate for this type of business. For more information, see Part 1.

IMPORTANT BUSINESS ISSUES TO BE ADDRESSED

It is important to belong to an international network for order fulfillment.

ONLINE MARKETING TECHNIQUES

- Join a number of cybermalls that target the same customers you do.

- Include on your Web site a spot asking if your customers would like to be notified when a certain service or type of flower arrangement gets updated or changed.

- You may want to have an area to advertise deals and discounts. These should change on a regular basis. Ask your visitors if they would like to be notified via e-mail of specials.

- Develop a reminder service as part of your Web site where people can register and be reminded of special occasions (e.g., anniversaries, birthdays, Valentine's Day, Secretary's Day, etc.) when flowers may be appropriate.

- Develop a sponsored listings campaign to bid on appropriate keyword phrases with the popular search engines.

- Develop a comprehensive link strategy, getting linked from appropriate cybermalls, directories, meta-indexes, and gift sites.

For a more detailed description of these techniques, along with many other effective online marketing methods, I recommend the companion book *101 Ways to Promote Your Web Site*. You can also find tons of free resources at *http://www.susansweeney.com/resources.html*.

ADDITIONAL INCOME
To generate additional income, you could include additional products on your Web site that your customers might find interesting:

- Small gifts or gift baskets to be sent with or in lieu of fresh flowers.

- Silk plants and flower arrangements.

- Special-occasion balloons, cookies, or other products.

ONLINE EXAMPLES

FTD.com
http://www.ftd.com
One of the most famous online flower stores, FTD.com redefined the way flowers are sold online.

Flower.com
http://www.flower.com

Figure 2.10. Buying flowers online is an easy and convenient solution for the busy person.

A good example of an average site (Figure 2.10) that uses many different methods to sell its flowers.

59. Online Modeling Agency

OVERVIEW OF BUSINESS MODEL

This is a business that is easy to start, requires little capital investment, and has no inventory, but has the potential for a high profit margin. This business would be perfect for someone with experience in the modeling industry. It would help greatly if you had contacts in the photography and marketing industries as well.

The basic business is finding models to represent, putting their portfolios on the Web site, and using this medium to promote their services. Revenue can come from commissions made from the jobs that the models on your Web site get and from the fee for putting their portfolio online.

SKILLS NEEDED

To run this business, you will need basic Web publishing skills to update and maintain your Web site. You should have an eye for talent. To get referrals and grow your business, a personable manner with clients in person and over the phone is a must. Your customers will include fashion designers, trade shows, event organizers, exhibitions, local stores, and malls. You will have to communicate with them in the traditional ways—face to face, direct mail, and telephone—as well as over the Web.

COST TO START THIS BUSINESS

The cost to start this business will include the design, development, and hosting of your Web site as well as a computer, appropriate software, a printer, a digital camera, and a scanner. You can start this venture from home and on a part-time basis. The approximate start-up cost ranges between $3,000 and $4,000.

NUMBER OF EMPLOYEES NEEDED

One experienced and competent individual can start this business single-handedly, but remember that you will need a collection of models to be featured on your site to get any business.

INTERNATIONAL POTENTIAL

There is some international potential of this business, but for the most part the market will be local and national.

E-BUSINESS MODEL/PAYMENT PROCESSING METHOD

E-business level 1 is most appropriate for this type of business. The models featured in your virtual modeling agency will likely be in touch personally when you put their portfolios online, and they can pay you in person when this happens. The clients who find your models over the Web will also likely be in direct contact with you and the models, so they can pay you directly for each job. For more information, see Part 1.

IMPORTANT BUSINESS ISSUES TO BE ADDRESSED

The important issues to be addressed are the proper representation of the models and making sure that the clients understand the parameters of what the models are comfortable with. Perhaps they are comfortable with fashion photo shoots but not with trade shows, where dialogue with show visitors is involved.

Payment for the model's services and your commission should be clearly stated in a contract that you, the client, and the model all sign to ensure that there is no confusion when the revenues come in for each job.

ONLINE MARKETING TECHNIQUES

- Register with all the major search engines, focusing on the region in which you and the models reside and on the marketing/modeling industry.

- Participate in local chat rooms and discussion forums related to marketing and modeling to create awareness of your current models and attract new ones.

- Get linked from online modeling directories and meta-indexes.

- Contribute articles to modeling-related e-zines. Make sure you provide your contact information and a link to your Web site.

- Organize a reciprocal linking arrangement with regional ad agencies, publications, and marketing businesses to align your business with their client base.

- Send press releases to online e-zines and offline magazines that relate to fashion, local general interest, and trade.

For a more detailed description of these techniques, along with many other effective online marketing methods, I recommend the companion book *101 Ways to Promote Your Web Site*. You can also find tons of free resources at *http://www.susansweeney.com/resources.html*.

ADDITIONAL INCOME

Additional income can be made in this business in several ways. You could be a talent scout for various acting and talent agencies. It's possible to be the photographer for online portfolios if you are able to master the art of digital photography, and you could be the Web master for other modeling agencies that have operated solely in print and video but now wish to mirror their business online.

ONLINE EXAMPLES

New Faces Models and Talent
http://www.newfaces.com
This site (Figure 2.11) is a good example of an online modeling agency. They focus on both modeling and acting. You can contact the models directly from the site via e-mail.

Paradise Models
http://www.paradisemodels.com
This site features fitness and glamour models who live in the North Carolina area. It is an example of a niche modeling site. Clients can book the models online using a credit card.

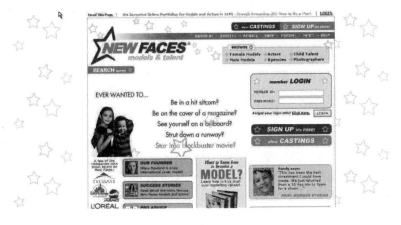

Figure 2.11. New Faces is a very popular online modeling agency.

60. Online Promotion Company

OVERVIEW OF BUSINESS MODEL

An online promotion company organizes online promotional efforts for out-sourcing businesses. Different forms of online promotions include banner advertising, direct e-mail campaigns, search engine submissions, contests, games, live interactive chat sessions, message boards, live Web cams, real audio, news-group marketing, link strategy promotion, and mobile marketing; and the list goes on. The idea is to *promote* something or someone on the Internet. The number of businesses willing to outsource their online promotional activities is enormous. This high demand provides you with an excellent business opportunity.

How can you generate revenue for your online promotion company? Initially you will have to perfect various online marketing techniques to ensure that you are an online marketing expert. You can do this during the initial promotion of your online promotion company. Once you have gained exposure, potential clients will visit your site to find out more about your services. You can then charge your clients based on each promotional activity that you fulfill for their business (e.g., banner ad campaign, e-mail campaign, etc.). Since you can't withdraw your services once they have been completed, it is important to always have a signed contract with your clients before implementing a promotional campaign. This will ensure that you receive payment for your efforts.

SKILLS NEEDED

Knowledge of online advertising and promotion techniques is necessary to run this type of business. If you decide to offer banner ad design services, knowledge of graphic design would benefit your business and eliminate the costs associated with outsourcing to a graphic designer. You will need Web publishing skills to update your Web site.

COST TO START THIS BUSINESS

Initially you will have to pay for the design and hosting of your Web site, computer hardware, computer software, a scanner, and a printer. If you currently have some of these items, your initial start-up costs will be considerably lower. If you plan to set up a mailing list, you will have ongoing fees to your ASP or Application Service Provider of choice for the use of the mailing list software to help you organize and maintain your mail lists. You should also purchase comprehensive Web traffic analysis and Web metrics software to track the results of your online marketing efforts. This information can be great for future marketing opportunities. Other costs that you will incur are related to the promotion of your Web site. Estimated cost is $10,000 to $40,000 to start.

NUMBER OF EMPLOYEES NEEDED TO START

The number of employees needed to run this type of business is one dedicated individual, and you can start this venture while keeping your regular job.

INTERNATIONAL POTENTIAL

This business has strong international potential. More and more businesses around the globe are recognizing the need to use the Internet as a communication and promotional medium with their target market.

E-BUSINESS MODEL/PAYMENT PROCESSING METHOD

E-business level 1 or 2 would be appropriate for this type of business. For more information, see Part 1.

IMPORTANT BUSINESS ISSUES TO BE ADDRESSED

You should ensure that your prices are competitive and that the promotional campaigns that your business develops for your clients are targeted to their correct target market segment. If you target the wrong audience, your campaign will prove to be useless. Situations like this will hinder the professionalism of your business. To gain a competitive advantage, you should not only offer promotional services similar to those of your competition, you should also differentiate your business by offering unique services. For example, you might consider offering geographically targeted e-mail campaigns. This would not only differentiate your services from those offering general e-mail marketing campaigns, it would also enhance the professionalism of your business.

Since you can't withdraw the effects of a promotional campaign once it has been implemented, it is very important that you take the time to plan all of your campaigns to avoid possible mishaps. Negative or unprofessional exposure for your client's business not only affects that business, it also affects the professionalism of your own business. On the same note, it is also important that you have a signed contract with your client before you launch a promotional campaign for their business. This will ensure that you will receive payment for your services. You might also consider collecting a 30 to 50 percent deposit for your services before the campaign is launched. This will provide a cushion for your business in case clients default on their payment.

ONLINE MARKETING TECHNIQUES

- Developing a comprehensive affiliate/associate program would not only increase the awareness of your promotions and traffic-generation strategies, it would also send referral business to your site.

- Participate in newsgroups and discussion forums related to online advertising or the industries that your clients are targeting.

- Launch a strategic banner advertising campaign on Web sites frequented by your target markets. Web sites that would be appropriate include sites concentrating on online advertising or the industries that you are targeting.

- Participating in mailing lists related to online advertising would be a great way to generate exposure for your online promotion business. Remember to use a cleverly designed signature file including a catchy tagline in all messages that you send to the mail lists. Your signature file will act as an advertisement for your online promotion business. A possible tagline for your signature file is "Ask Us about Our Online Promotion Services," or some variation of this phrase. This will be a great way to encourage traffic to your Web site.

- Develop a sponsored listings campaign to bid on appropriate keyword phrases with the popular search engines.

- Get listed and linked from the Internet marketing services directories and meta-indexes.

- Contribute articles that profile your expertise in e-zines related to marketing online. Make sure to include your complete contact information and a link to your Web site.

- Do some free promotions for charity organizations and the like.

For a more detailed description of these techniques, along with many other effective online marketing methods, I recommend the companion book *101 Ways to Promote Your Web Site*. You can also find tons of free resources at *http://www.susansweeney.com/resources.html*.

ADDITIONAL INCOME

You could generate additional income for your online promotion business by selling products on your site related to online advertising—things such as online advertising educational materials and online promotional training kits. You could even become a reseller for another business and sell various promotional software tools (e.g., search engine submission software, mailing list software, etc.). This would be a great way to generate revenue for your business.

ONLINE EXAMPLES

VERB Interactive
http://www.verbinteractive.com
VERB provides a complete range of Web development, Internet marketing consulting, and campaign execution.

Grantastic Designs
http://www.grantasticdesigns.com/marketing.html
This print graphic design firm includes Web site design and online promotion, logo design, illustration, presentation design, and Web image design utilizing traditional and electronic art production methods.

61. Online Resort Directory

OVERVIEW OF BUSINESS MODEL

If vacationers know where they want to go or what they want to do, the best way for them to get information to plan their trip is through a resort directory.

As the entire travel vacation industry makes its rapid transition to online service, so too are resort directories. A resort directory is a collection of Web sites and information about various resorts in a given region or by type of vacation. For example, if you wanted to go to Florida you would look for a Florida resort directory. However, if you wanted to go hiking in the Rockies you would look for a Rocky Mountain or a hiking resort guide.

Your Web site will generate income through banner advertisements, through affiliate program revenue, by taking a small percentage of online reservations, or by making hotels pay to be members. An affiliate program pays you money whenever someone uses your Web site and then visits one of the resorts affiliated with you.

SKILLS NEEDED

A broad familiarity with the resort industry by region or by type would be of benefit. However, you could pick up this knowledge as your business progresses. Since your Web site will need to be updated fairly frequently, you will need someone who can take care of this function.

COST TO START THIS BUSINESS

The cost to initially set up your resort directory will range from $10,000 to over $50,000. These costs include a high-end computer, appropriate software, a printer, a scanner, and a digital camera. You will need to have a Web site designed, developed, and hosted. You will also want a special searchable database researched, designed, and integrated into your Web site. However, you could use a much less sophisticated Web site to start if you wish.

NUMBER OF EMPLOYEES NEEDED TO START

Your business will require one or more part-time employees. These include one part-time computer programmer to write and maintain your Web site and the database. You will also need someone to contact all the resorts in the directory and plug your services. Then, depending on how your site will generate money, you must try to gain advertisements, affiliate with the resort, arrange an online reservation system, or get resorts to join your site.

INTERNATIONAL POTENTIAL

You can easily access the international market by contacting foreign resorts that fit your theme and integrating them into your Web site. Obviously, if you are advertising resorts in California, then you couldn't really exploit this, but if your directory was a beach resort directory, then you could include resorts from all over the world. Your only restriction is the language barrier.

E-Business Model/Payment Processing Method

Your e-business model depends on how you are set up. If you generate income through advertising, then you need use only e-business level 1. However, if you are offering online reservations, you will need to use level 4 for complete integration. For more information, see Part 1.

Important Business Issues to Be Addressed

You must carefully select what type of resorts or which niche your directory will cover. Review your competition online before you start to ensure that there is an opportunity.

Online Marketing Techniques

- Launching a strategic banner advertising campaign on Web sites frequented by your target market would be a great way to increase traffic to your site. Sites that you could place banner ads on include noncompeting travel and resort sites, and other Web sites that would be of interest to your target market.

- You could hold a weekly or monthly contest on your site for a free weekend at a resort, which would be provided by your clients. You could ask people if they would like to be notified of the winner via e-mail. This would encourage them to return to your site and re-enter your contest, thus re-exposing them to your site.

- Develop as many links as possible from appropriate Web sites, directories, meta-indexes, and Web rings frequented by your target market.

- You could develop a Featured Resort page on your site. You could change this every week. People will continue to return to your site to see what the featured resort is. You could even ask people if they would like to be notified of updates to your Featured Resort section via e-mail. This would be a great way to encourage repeat traffic.

- Develop a sponsored listings campaign to bid on appropriate keyword phrases with the popular search engines.

- A mail list or newsletter can also be used to advertise your deals and keep consumers interested in your site.

- Develop articles for travel-related e-zines. Perhaps be a contributing editor with a featured resort for e-zines and magazines related to travel and tourism. Make sure to provide your Web address in the resources box.

For a more detailed description of these techniques, along with many other effective online marketing methods, I recommend the companion book *101 Ways to Promote Your Web Site*. You can also find tons of free resources at *http://www.susansweeney.com/resources.html*.

ADDITIONAL INCOME

Additional income can be generated by using more than one of these methods for setting up your resort directory. You could also sell equipment related to the vacation type you represent. If your directory is for scuba resorts, for example, you could sell scuba gear.

ONLINE EXAMPLES

Colorado Resort Net
http://www.toski.com
A listing of resorts and lodgings in Colorado for ski vacations.

RSN.com
http://www.rsn.com
A nice Web site that offers information on several skiing resorts. It also offers complete ski vacation planning, though you can't order online.

62. Party Planning and Supplies

OVERVIEW OF BUSINESS MODEL

Planning and finding supplies for a large party is a lot of work. Often the hosts cannot find the time to organize or track down the supplies they will need. More and more corporations are turning to party planners to organize their annual parties and events. With the advent of the Internet, you can now offer party planning services and party supplies online.

You will make your money through consulting fees for the party planning as well as through selling party products online. Often, when you do the party planning, you will be responsible for choosing the supplies for the party as well. These party products include balloons, confetti, musical instruments, paper products, decorations, food, drinks, and so on.

SKILLS NEEDED

You will need to have a great imagination. When people use a party planner they expect something out of the ordinary. You will also need to have some familiarity with Web site maintenance, as you will need to update your Web site periodically.

COST TO START THIS BUSINESS

Costs will range from $3,000 to over $10,000. This includes the purchase of a computer, appropriate software, a printer, a scanner, and a digital camera. You will need your initial inventory. You will also need to have your Web site designed, developed, and hosted. The business's initial costs can be quite high because some party supplies are very expensive and they often are bought in bulk.

NUMBER OF EMPLOYEES NEEDED TO START

This business can fairly easily be started with only one employee.

INTERNATIONAL POTENTIAL

Selling on an international level can become quite difficult. Since you will be shipping a large number of party items to your customers, overseas shipping costs will have a major impact on your international viability. If the overseas shipping costs are too great, then it would be much more cost effective for your customer to shop locally.

E-BUSINESS MODEL/PAYMENT PROCESSING METHOD

E-business level 2 or 3 is most appropriate for this type of business. For more information, see Part 1.

IMPORTANT BUSINESS ISSUES TO BE ADDRESSED

It is important to discuss and have a contract relative to the services you are to perform in the party planning. It is also important that your contract itemize the party supplies, entertainment, food and drink, and so on, that your client wants and that you have agreed to supply. Once the party is over, you don't want any surprises! You should collect up front the budgeted amount for the expenses and then provide your client with an itemized account of your allocation of those funds.

ONLINE MARKETING TECHNIQUES

- Develop a comprehensive link strategy. Develop as many links as possible from Web sites, directories, meta-indexes, and Web rings frequented by your target market.

- Launching a strategic banner advertising campaign on Web sites frequented by your target market would be a great way to increase traffic to your site. Sites that you could place banner ads on include noncompeting party planning sites, business service sites, party product directories, and other Web sites that would be of interest to your target market.

- You could post client testimonials on your Web site.

- Develop a sponsored listings campaign to bid on appropriate keyword phrases with the popular search engines.

- You could have a gallery of pictures of parties you have planned as long as you have the client's permission. If you can include photos of some great theme parties along with the client's testimonial, it could go a long way to building your reputation and credibility online.

For a more detailed description of these techniques, along with many other effective online marketing methods, I recommend the companion book *101 Ways to Promote Your Web Site*. You can also find tons of free resources at *http://www.susansweeney.com/resources.html*.

ADDITIONAL INCOME

If you are ambitious, you could expand your services to include event planning. (See the entry about event planning earlier in this book.) Otherwise, you could offer your customers photographic services or offer hosting for their parties.

ONLINE EXAMPLES

iParty
http://www.iparty.com
A huge party supplies Web site with something for just about every type of party—and they ship worldwide.

Vieco Balloons
http://viecoballoons.com
A Web site that provides specialty balloons. They ship anywhere in the world.

63. Photo Display Site

OVERVIEW OF BUSINESS MODEL

There are a number of approaches you can take to setting up an online photo display site. You can focus on artists, photographers, or the general public. If you focus on artists, you would generate revenue by charging them a fee to have their work displayed on your site. This would assist them in selling their original pieces of work.

Alternatively, if you focus on photographers, you can earn revenue on a commission basis or by a flat fee. You could allow photographers to submit images to your site. In turn, you would sell access to your site to the consumer market. People would pay for the license rights to the image and in turn you would pay the photographer and retain a percentage.

The third option is to open a photo display site to the general public where people could create their own folders and upload their own images for free. Revenue would come from complementary products and services. Photopoint.com is one such example. They sell cameras, printers, postcards, photo prints, and so on.

SKILLS NEEDED

Knowledge of online advertising techniques is an asset to run this type of business. If you decide to launch a photo display site, you are going to have to ensure that you are generating as much traffic as possible to your site to make it appealing to photographers or artists looking to use your site as a sales vehicle. Likewise, you will need a large amount of traffic to increase your opportunity to achieve success with a consumer photo gallery. To do this, you are going to have to dedicate a lot of time implementing various Internet marketing techniques to create a constant flow of traffic to your site.

COST TO START THIS BUSINESS

Initially you will have to pay for the design, development, and hosting of your Web site, computer hardware, computer software, a scanner, and a printer. If you currently have some of these items, your initial start-up costs will be considerably lower. Other costs that you will incur are related to the promotion of your Web site. Photographic images can take up a lot of storage space and you will also need a lot of bandwidth to ensure that your site loads quickly—this can be relatively expensive. Estimated cost is $5,000 to $15,000 to start.

NUMBER OF EMPLOYEES NEEDED TO START
This business can be started by one individual.

INTERNATIONAL POTENTIAL
This business has significant international potential. Artists and photographers from around the world will be interested in using your site as a sales or promotional vehicle. In addition, if you approach the photo display site from the general consumer's angle, the concept has mass appeal.

E-BUSINESS MODEL/PAYMENT PROCESSING METHOD
E-business level 1 or 2 would be appropriate for this type of business if you are following the artist and photographer photo display sites. If you take the more general approach and sell related merchandise, then e-business level 3 will be more appropriate. For more information, see Part 1.

IMPORTANT BUSINESS ISSUES TO BE ADDRESSED
There is a lot of competition for the general consumer category, some of which is backed by large corporations. You will need to be able to differentiate yourself from the pack.

You will want to have high bandwidth to ensure that visitors to your site do not experience delays with downloads.

ONLINE MARKETING TECHNIQUES

- Develop a viral marketing strategy where people can "Tell a Friend about This Site" via a link on your site. This will spread the word about your site and encourage others to visit.

- Develop a comprehensive link strategy. You will want to generate as many links as possible from Web sites, directories, and meta-indexes related to your target market. There are many relevant sites pertaining to photographic pieces and original artwork that would be appropriate. Likewise, there are many sites that would appeal to the general consumer.

- Develop a sponsored listings campaign to bid on appropriate keyword phrases with the popular search engines.

- Promotion through appropriate mail lists, e-zines, and newsletters is important. You could even develop your own newsletter or mail list to stay close to your target market.

- You should consider developing an affiliate program. This can increase your sales force dramatically if you sell products, such as cameras, relating to your site content.

For a more detailed description of these techniques, along with many other effective online marketing methods, I recommend the companion book *101 Ways to Promote Your Web Site*. You can also find tons of free resources at *http://www.susansweeney.com/resources.html*.

ADDITIONAL INCOME

Additional advertising can be earned by selling advertising spots on your site. If you have your own newsletter, you can earn additional revenue by allowing companies to sponsor it.

ONLINE EXAMPLES

World Photo Gallery
http://www.worldphotogallery.com
This is a site where photographers from around the world gather to exhibit their work. If you require a photographer or would just like to know how to contact one for an assignment or to purchase their work, you can go to the photographers' directory to see some of their work and profiles.

The Stock Solution
http://www.tssphoto.com/tssphoto.html
The Stock Solution (TSS) is a stock photo agency, representing the images of approximately 100 photographers. Their copyrighted images can be licensed for a variety of uses including brochures, newsletters, magazines, multimedia, display, and Web pages.

64. Podcasts and Podcast Directory

OVERVIEW OF BUSINESS MODEL

A Podcast is an audio broadcast saved as an MP3 file. The MP3 file can be downloaded to a computer and then to an iPod or any other type of MP3 player. There are all kinds of music-related podcasts available online already.

There is always an opportunity for more as long as you focus on a niche or do a great job of marketing to get your name out there. There are lots of opportunities for educational podcasts as people like to learn about things of interest at their convenience—why not listen to an hour on Search Engine Optimization while working out on the treadmill!

There are podcasts where the visitor can listen to the broadcast live, or download it into an MP3 player such as an iPod, or even a cell phone, and listen to it at a later time. Usually a podcast will feature one type of broadcast, or "show," and will add new episodes daily, weekly, or monthly.

A podcast is receivable to anyone at any time. It is much more intimate and interactive than a traditional blog.

You can offer your podcasts through your own site or podcast directories. You can also consider developing a podcast directory to provide access to a broad range of podcasts. With this you could charge a fee to host the podcast, or include it for free with a view to making your money with affiliate programs, banner advertising, sponsorship, and subscription opportunities.

SKILLS NEEDED

A podcast is a great idea for someone who loves to write and speak passionately about any given topic of shared interest. If you have a great voice, you can provide podcasting services for various industries.

COST TO START THIS BUSINESS

You will need a computer. Most computers these days come complete with all the appropriate software you will need. Start-up costs will also include the design, development, and hosting of your Web site. The start-up costs for this type of business will generally run between $1,000 and $5,000.

NUMBER OF EMPLOYEES NEEDED TO START

Starting off, you need only one employee, not even full-time if that's not what you can fit into your schedule.

INTERNATIONAL POTENTIAL

This business's international potential increases if it's translated into the major languages of the globe. English is widely accepted, however.

E-BUSINESS MODEL/PAYMENT PROCESSING METHOD

If you are going to charge for the podcast downloads, you will want to use e-business level 2. See Part 1 for more details.

IMPORTANT BUSINESS ISSUES TO BE ADDRESSED

Podcasts are pretty simple. Make sure to keep your broadcasts clear and remember the audience the whole time you are composing podcasts; make sure you continue to appeal to the same niche of listeners; and watch for other sites encroaching on your content. It happens all the time.

Have a detailed Web traffic analysis package on the server on which your site is hosted so that you can show advertisers accurate information about your site traffic.

If you are providing educational content in your podcast, there is opportunity to charge a fee. For example if I developed podcasts of different Internet marketing techniques, I would charge a fee for people to download the podcasts.

ONLINE MARKETING TECHNIQUES

- Participating in newsgroups and discussion forums related to your target audience would be a great way to increase exposure of your podcast and the traffic to your Web site.

- Launching a strategic banner advertising campaign on topic-specific Web sites would generate targeted exposure for your podcast.

- Develop as many links as possible from potential Web sites, directories, and meta-indexes related to the topic of your podcast, or podcast directory.

- Develop a sponsored listings campaign to bid on appropriate keyword phrases with the popular search engines.

- Participating in publicly accessible opt-in mail lists related to the topic of your podcast would be a great way to communicate with your target market.

For a more detailed description of these techniques, along with many other effective online marketing methods, I recommend the companion book *101 Ways to Promote Your Web Site*. You can also find tons of free resources at *http://www.susansweeney.com/resources.html*.

ONLINE EXAMPLES

Podcast.net
http://www.podcast.net
A large online podcast directory with many different topics from which to choose.

Urban Coffee
http://www.urbancoffee.net
Poscast focused on current events, political discussions and technology.

65. Photography

OVERVIEW OF BUSINESS MODEL

If you enjoy taking pictures and exercising your creativity, then setting up your own photography business may be for you. You could offer your services on a contract basis. Some areas of concentration to consider include weddings, architecture, portraits, and commercial, underwater, and graduation photography. You would bill for your services accordingly. Final work could be provided to clients digitally on disk or CD, regular photographic prints, or framed pictures. You could earn additional money for framing the pictures or placing the images on a CD.

SKILLS NEEDED

Photography skills are a must. Your clients will be looking for highly professional photography. Some knowledge of digital imaging to make enhancements to pictures, add customized phrases, and so on, would also be an asset.

COST TO START THIS BUSINESS

Initially you will have to pay for the design, development, and hosting of your Web site, computer hardware, computer software, a scanner, a CD burner, photographic equipment (e.g., a digital camera), and a printer. You will also need to purchase relevant packaging materials, blank CDs, and a variety of picture frames. If you currently have some of these items, your initial start-up costs will be considerably lower. Other costs that you will incur are related to the promotion of your Web site. Estimated cost is $6,000 to $8,000 to start.

NUMBER OF EMPLOYEES NEEDED TO START

This business can be started by one individual and can be started as a part-time endeavor.

INTERNATIONAL POTENTIAL

This business will focus mainly on your immediate geographic region, as you will need to be able to travel to the appropriate locations to perform your services.

E-BUSINESS MODEL/PAYMENT PROCESSING METHOD

E-business level 1 would be appropriate for this type of business. You could have an online form so that people can request pricing and inquire about your availability. See Part 1 for more information.

IMPORTANT BUSINESS ISSUES TO BE ADDRESSED

Your biggest challenge is making yourself visible to your target market. You will need to ensure that you implement and monitor appropriate online marketing techniques. If your area has relevant local sites, such as a coupon site, then you should consider participating. Although this discounts your services, it is an excellent way to attract business.

Online Marketing Techniques

- Include a Photo Gallery or a Virtual Postcard section on your site. Allow people to send sample images or virtual postcards to friends. The images used would be from your own work and would act to build credibility for your talent as well as to increase traffic to your site.

- Develop a viral marketing strategy where people can "Tell a Friend about This Site" via a link on your site. This will spread the word about your site and encourage others to visit.

- Develop a comprehensive link strategy. You want to generate as many links as possible from appropriate Web sites, directories, Web rings, and meta-indexes related to your target market. Ensure that you get listed in sites that target your local area as well as your area of expertise.

- Develop a sponsored listings campaign to bid on appropriate keyword phrases with the popular search engines.

- Ensure that you submit your site to the search engines and directories.

For a more detailed description of these techniques, along with many other effective online marketing methods, I recommend the companion book *101 Ways to Promote Your Web Site*. You can also find tons of free resources at *http://www.susansweeney.com/resources.html*.

Additional Income

Other services you can offer to earn additional income include digital imaging, photo manipulation, and selling your own stock work on your site via CD, as screen savers, or as postcards. This can attract the large tourism market if your images pertain to historic sites or sites of interest in your area. You can provide custom framing services from your site as well. Gift certificates always provide an additional revenue source.

Online Examples

World Photo Gallery
http://www.webshots.com

The Webshots site is a place where photographers from around the world gather to exhibit their work, share their passion for photography, and learn from one another.

Colleen Dagnall Photography
http://www.shooterbug.com
A corporate, wedding, lifestyle, and promotional photographer. Also offered is Web page design and photo manipulation.

66. Press Release Developer

OVERVIEW OF BUSINESS MODEL

A press release is a statement or article about a particular company, its products and services, or a significant event involving that company that is considered newsworthy. It provides the press with the background information needed to develop a formal story. Positive coverage by the press is like free advertising. In fact, it can be more effective than advertising because press coverage is seen as unbiased by consumers.

Many companies do not have the internal capability or personnel capacity to develop appropriate press releases on a regular basis and look to outside firms or individuals to develop them. If you have an interest in writing and earning extra money from home, then this may be the ideal job for you. You can gather all necessary information from the client company to write a press release for them. You would earn your revenue by charging a fee per press release. A common fee falls between $200 and $250.

SKILLS NEEDED

Press releases have a standard format. Experience in developing press releases according to this format is essential. Press release distribution experience would be an asset. Prior journalism knowledge or experience would also be an asset. Some knowledge of HTML would be of benefit to you. Companies may want their press release to be designed as an interactive press release that they can include on their site with active hypertext links—this could give you a competitive edge over those press release developers without this skill set.

COST TO START THIS BUSINESS

Initially you will have to pay for the design, development, and hosting of your Web site, computer hardware, computer software, a scanner, and a printer. If you currently have some of these items, your initial start-up costs will be reduced accordingly. Other costs that you will incur are related to the promotion of your Web site. Estimated cost is $3,000 to $5,000 to start.

NUMBER OF EMPLOYEES NEEDED TO START

When starting a business of this nature, you would not need to hire additional employees. You could very easily operate this business on your own.

INTERNATIONAL POTENTIAL

This business offers some international potential. However, a majority of your clients will be based in your immediate area or within the same country.

E-BUSINESS MODEL/PAYMENT PROCESSING METHOD

E-business level 1 or 2 would be appropriate for this type of business, depending on whether or not you want to directly accept payment for your services online. For more information, see Part 1.

IMPORTANT BUSINESS ISSUES TO BE ADDRESSED

Presentation is very important, so you must follow standard press release formatting procedures. Also, the timeliness and newsworthiness of the information being presented is important. To write an effective press release, you must understand the product or company you are writing about.

ONLINE MARKETING TECHNIQUES

- Develop a viral marketing strategy where people can "Tell a Colleague about This Service" via a link on your site. This will spread the word about your site.

- Develop as many links as possible from appropriate Web sites, directories, Web rings, and meta-indexes related to your target market. There are many business services-related sites that would be appropriate link sites.

- Ensure that you submit your site to the search engines and directories. Companies looking to have press releases developed will often refer to the search engines to find the sites that provide the services they're looking for.

- Promotion through related mail lists and newsletters is important. You could even develop your own newsletter or mail list to stay close to your target market.

- Participation in cybermalls related to business services in your geographic area would be very appropriate.

For a more detailed description of these techniques, along with many other effective online marketing methods, I recommend the companion book *101 Ways to Promote Your Web Site*. You can also find tons of free resources at *http://www.susansweeney.com/resources.html*.

ADDITIONAL INCOME

In addition to your press release writing service, the next logical step to extend your range of services and to earn additional income would be to submit the press releases you write for your client to the appropriate media.

An additional way to generate revenue is to offer clipping and monitoring services. These services help companies keep track of what the online and offline press is saying about their company—valuable information for any company to have.

ONLINE EXAMPLES

Press-Release-Writing.com
http://www.press-release-writing.com/options-writing.htm
This company offers press release writing services as well as distribution services.

Xpress Press
http://www.xpresspress.com/Writing_Service.html
This company offers press release writing, information on how to write a news release, and public relations resources.

67. Press Release Distribution Service

OVERVIEW OF BUSINESS MODEL

Distributing press releases to the right media contacts poses a significant challenge for many companies. They often do not have the expertise within their organization to perform this function. This service is very important to ensure that their press releases reach the appropriate media and have the best chance of getting attention.

Setting up an online press release distribution service, also known as a wire service, is an excellent opportunity to earn additional income from home. Wire services use electronic means such as the Web, e-mail, and fax to distribute press releases to journalists, publications, and related media contacts. You can focus on industry-specific press releases in an area in which you have extensive knowledge, or you can focus on broad press release distribution. Companies would pay you to oversee their press release distribution.

You will need to develop a comprehensive list of media contacts or subscribe to one of the online services like Media Map or Press Access. If you develop your own media list, it is imperative that you keep it up to date, as there is much movement in this industry.

SKILLS NEEDED

Experience with press release distribution is important. Knowledge of the Internet and how to navigate it is vital. Also, you should have some journalism experience and should understand the industry lingo and how the industry works in order to effectively distribute press releases.

COST TO START THIS BUSINESS

Initially you will have to pay for the design, development, and hosting of your Web site, computer hardware, computer software, a scanner, a fax machine, and a printer. Other costs that you will incur are related to the promotion of your Web site. You will incur additional costs in the form of media contact databases, editorial calendars, media research, and related studies as well as services. You need to keep this information up to date. Trying to locate all of the appropriate media contacts and maintaining accuracy on your own would be very time-consuming. This information can run upwards of $11,000. Your start-up costs will be in the range of $5,000 if you develop your own media database to $25,000 if you use a media contact service.

NUMBER OF EMPLOYEES NEEDED TO START

This business can be started by one individual.

INTERNATIONAL POTENTIAL

Some international potential exists. Companies may be interested in outsourcing a company to distribute press releases to contacts outside of their immediate target area as a form of test marketing or because they cannot handle the distribution efficiently in-house. However, most business will come from companies in your immediate area and across your country.

E-BUSINESS MODEL/PAYMENT PROCESSING METHOD

E-business level 1 or 2 would be appropriate for this type of business. See Part 1 for additional details.

IMPORTANT BUSINESS ISSUES TO BE ADDRESSED

The accuracy of your media contact information is a big issue. Members of the media tend to move around a lot, so you will want to ensure that you always have the latest contact information to keep your press releases from being disregarded. Another issue to consider is that you must be able to select and send your press releases to appropriate media contacts, depending on the information contained within the press release. You do not want to risk annoying the recipients of your press release distributions to the point that they disregard everything you send.

ONLINE MARKETING TECHNIQUES

- Develop a viral marketing strategy where people can "Tell a Colleague about This Service" via a link within your site. This will spread the word about your site.

- Develop a comprehensive link strategy. You want to generate as many links as possible from appropriate Web sites, directories, and meta-indexes related to your target market. There are many press release resource sites and business services sites that would be appropriate for this type of business.

- Ensure that you submit your site to the search engines and directories. Companies looking to have press releases distributed will often refer to the search engines to find the information and service providers they're looking for.

- Promotion through related mail lists, e-zines, and newsletters is important. This could include your own press release distribution, article contributions, or advertising sponsorships. You could even develop your own newsletter or mail list to stay close to your target market.

For a more detailed description of these techniques, along with many other effective online marketing methods, I recommend the companion book *101 Ways to Promote Your Web Site*. You can also find tons of free resources at *http://www.susansweeney.com/resources.html*.

ADDITIONAL INCOME

The most logical extension of your service offerings would be to offer to develop and track press releases, and to provide feedback to your clients. This information would be useful to them in planning future campaigns and to measure the success of recent campaigns. You could charge an additional fee to monitor this information for your clients.

ONLINE EXAMPLES

Send 2 Press
http://www.send2press.com/PRservices/press_release.shtml
This company offers target press release distribution services.

Press Flash
http://www.pressflash.com
Press Flash is a press release distribution company that focuses on the Internet and areas related to high tech.

68. Printing Service

OVERVIEW OF BUSINESS MODEL

Every business at some time or another will need printing services. These services include business cards, letterhead, envelopes, mail-outs, posters, flyers, and occasionally huge banners for use at trade shows or special events. Your online printing service business will provide these services, but your customers will have the added benefit of being able to order their products online and receive an instant quote for your services. With the huge growth in home-based businesses, there is an increasing need for printing suppliers for this market.

You will be generating your income through printing orders you receive through your Web site. You will create the printed products to your customers' exact specifications, and then you will ship the products to your customer wherever they may be. Many customers will allow a reasonable lead time, but you should be aware that occasionally you will need to be able to complete a job in 24 or 48 hours or less.

SKILLS NEEDED

You must have graphic design skills as well as a familiarity with a broad range of layout software such as Adobe Acrobat, Quark, and PageMaker. You will also need to know how to operate industrial printing equipment.

COST TO START THIS BUSINESS

The cost to initially set up your printing service will range from $20,000 to $100,000. These costs include a high-end computer, appropriate administrative software, a printer, a scanner, a digital camera, and the specialized software you will need. You will also need to buy special industrial printing equipment. This equipment will account for approximately half of your initial expense if not more. Finally, you will have to have your Web site designed, developed, and hosted. Other initial costs to consider include your inventory of printing supplies and some advertising for your Web site.

NUMBER OF EMPLOYEES NEEDED TO START

It is possible to run this business with one person. However, due to the nature of industrial print jobs, you will find it much more efficient to have at least two full-time employees.

INTERNATIONAL POTENTIAL

The Internet opens up your business to the international market; however, shipping large print jobs overseas will eliminate any competitive pricing edge, making it much more likely that those customers will order from a local store.

E-BUSINESS MODEL/PAYMENT PROCESSING METHOD

E-business level 2 is most appropriate for this type of business. For more information, see Part 1.

IMPORTANT BUSINESS ISSUES TO BE ADDRESSED

The high cost of printing equipment means you'll have to be as cost-conscious as possible. You need to generate as much repeat business as possible. This is done through both high quality and high customer service.

ONLINE MARKETING TECHNIQUES

- Develop a comprehensive link strategy. You want to get as many links as possible from appropriate Web sites, directories, and meta-indexes related to your target market. There are thousands of business-related Web sites on the Internet that would provide a great linking opportunity for your site. You should also attempt to develop links from business service Web sites and directories. These sites will provide highly targeted traffic to your site.

- Launching a strategic banner advertising campaign on Web sites frequented by your target market would be a great way to increase traffic to your site. Sites that you could place banner ads on include noncompeting business service sites, business-related cybermalls, local high-traffic sites, and other Web sites that would be of interest to your target market.

- You could hold a weekly or monthly contest on your site for a free print job with a maximum dollar value. You could ask people if they would like to be notified of the winner via e-mail. This would encourage them to return to your site and re-enter your contest, thus re-exposing them to your products and services.

- Develop a sponsored listings campaign to bid on appropriate keyword phrases with the popular search engines.

- Participate in newsgroups and discussion forums related to business services. Remember to use a cleverly designed signature file with a catchy tagline and hypertext link that will send readers to your site.

- Providing valuable contributions to business services-related mail lists would be a great way to create exposure for your business. Again, a cleverly designed signature file with a catchy tagline would be a great way to send traffic to your site.

For a more detailed description of these techniques, along with many other effective online marketing methods, I recommend the companion book *101 Ways to Promote Your Web Site*. You can also find tons of free resources at *http://www.susansweeney.com/resources.html*.

ADDITIONAL INCOME

To generate additional income, you can include graphic design or Web development services. You might also consider providing personalized promotional printed products like corporate calendars.

ONLINE EXAMPLES

Anchor Imaging
http://www.anchorimaging.com
A solid Internet-based print job company. They take jobs online and files through e-mail and FTP, plus they have a two-day turnaround time.

Miranza.com
http://www.miranza.com
With their array of specialty printing equipment, they can handle even exotic print jobs.

69. Private Investigator/People Finder

OVERVIEW OF BUSINESS MODEL

As people age over the years, they meet many people, make many friends, and in turn grow apart from other friends. Sometimes friends grow so far apart that they no longer know what each friend is doing or where each friend lives. Quite often, friends want to reunite with other friends from school or their childhood, parents want to reunite with their children or another family member, or people need to locate individuals for criminal or monetary reasons. This provides you with an excellent opportunity to launch a private investigator/people finder business. Since the Internet connects the world internationally, you can easily promote your private investigator/people finder services to people all over the world.

How does this type of business generate revenue? Private investigator/people finder businesses make money from locating information about the whereabouts of an individual or by specifically locating an individual for a client. Clients can range from families to businesses (insurance companies often use private investigators to locate individuals who don't fulfill financial responsibilities) to missing-people organizations. If you promote your business appropriately and you have a good reputation as a private investigator, you should be able to earn a significant amount of revenue. Offering your services via the Internet also gives you a wide geographic reach. The Internet will enable people who are located out of your native region to contact you to perform a job in your region. This greatly expands your customer base.

SKILLS NEEDED

You will need to be a licensed private investigator. Being bonded and insured would be an additional benefit. There are several other certificates that private investigators can hold to prove their credibility. An example of this would be the fraudulent claim investigator certificate, which proves that you are well versed in solving fraudulent claims.

COST TO START THIS BUSINESS

Initially you will have to pay for the development, design, and hosting of your Web site, a computer, computer software, and possibly a printer. If you currently have some of these items, your initial start-up costs will be considerably lower. You will also have to pay to be certified as a private investigator. You may also want to earn additional certificates to enhance your career as a private investigator. Other costs that you will incur are related to the promotion of your Web site. Estimated cost is $10,000 to 20,000 to start.

NUMBER OF EMPLOYEES NEEDED TO START

Approximately one or two employees will be needed to operate this type of business. One employee will be responsible for fulfilling service requests (i.e., finding people, information, etc.), while the other employee will be responsible for all administrative tasks involved with running day-to-day business operations.

INTERNATIONAL POTENTIAL

This business has strong international potential. People from all over the world may be looking for someone in your geographic area; thus they would be able to hire your business to fulfill their need. Also, people may hire you to travel to another country to locate individuals. This gives this business opportunity strong international potential.

E-BUSINESS MODEL/PAYMENT PROCESSING METHOD

E-business level 1 would be most appropriate for this type of business. For more information, see Part 1.

IMPORTANT BUSINESS ISSUES TO BE ADDRESSED

To prove your credibility, you will have to take several courses and get yourself licensed as a private investigator. Once you have achieved this goal, there are several other certifications you could try to obtain to enhance your career as a private investigator. Although it will take quite a bit of time to obtain these certifications, they will add credibility to your business. The more credibility your organization has, the better the chances are that clients will turn to your business when they desire private investigation/people locator services.

As a private investigator, it is important that you do not violate any laws or regulations that would invade an individual's right to privacy. Since your job typically entails "snooping" around, you should be aware of the legal limits to your job. This is especially true when dealing in an international environment. If a client hires you to locate an individual in another country, you should review all legal policies that may affect how you conduct your investigation. If at any time you invade a person's legal rights and a charge is brought against your business, you could seriously damage the professional image of your business.

ONLINE MARKETING TECHNIQUES

- Participate in newsgroups and discussion forums related to missing people, investigation work, locator services, and other topics related to your target market.

- Participating in mailing lists related to missing people/children or locator services would be a great way to generate exposure for your business. Remember to use a cleverly designed signature file including a catchy tagline in all messages that you send to the mail lists. Your signature file will act as an advertisement for your business. A possible tagline for your signature file is "Find a Missing Loved One Today! Click Here!" or some variation of this phrase. This is a great way to encourage traffic to your Web site.

- Do some free promotions for charity organizations related to missing children or missing people. This would be a great way to generate exposure for your private investigation/people finder business.

- Develop a sponsored listings campaign to bid on appropriate keyword phrases with the popular search engines.

- Develop as many links as possible from Web sites, directories, and meta-indexes related to missing people, private investigators, and locator services. These links will send highly targeted traffic to your Web site.

For a more detailed description of these techniques, along with many other effective online marketing methods, I recommend the companion book *101 Ways to Promote Your Web Site*. You can also find tons of free resources at *http://www.susansweeney.com/resources.html*.

ADDITIONAL INCOME

In addition to earning revenue from your private investigator/people finder business, you could earn additional income by investigating computer-related crimes. Internet crimes happen daily. Computer-related crimes range from credit card fraud to child pornography, so there is plenty of business in investigating such crimes. This would be an excellent way to earn additional income for your business.

ONLINE EXAMPLES

Kale Investigation

http://www.kaleinvestigation.com

A small private investigation firm making good use of the Internet to generate additional contracts.

Digdirt.com

http://www.digdirt.com

A huge international group of private investigators. Their operations span seven countries, and they will handle any job.

70. Professional Organizer

OVERVIEW OF BUSINESS MODEL

Organization comes naturally to few and not at all to the rest of us. Today's average homes and offices are in dire need of order. Our time is precious, and it too needs to be planned out. If you are a gifted organizer and enjoy helping others enjoy ordered existence, this is the operation for you.

A professional organizer can provide ideas, information, structure, solutions, and systems that could increase productivity, reduce stress, and lead to more control over time, space, and activities. The Internet is an ideal place to market and communicate with clients in this business.

The revenue is made from charging your clients for professional consulting services. You may charge by the hour and guage the hourly rate by specifying the value of your advice. For example, helping to organize someone's closet is not as valuable as coaching a client to operate a desktop organizer software program. Rates for specific services should be reflected in your hourly billing. You may alternatively elect to charge on a contract fee basis where you set the price for the project.

SKILLS NEEDED

To operate the professional organizer business, you must of course be very organized in your own life. This form of consulting involves a lot of specifics and troubleshooting. You will need creative and practical solutions to complicated issues in order to provide quality advice to your clients, who will always seem to be in a chaotic state. You will need basic Web publishing skills and computer skills to update your Web site, communicate with clients, and teach them how to integrate the computer into their lives to save time and create order.

COST TO START THIS BUSINESS

Since you are providing a service that has no inventory, your initial costs will be minimal. The cost to start this type of business will include a computer, appropriate software, and a printer as well as the costs involved with developing and hosting your Web site. Start-up costs range from $2,000 to $5,000. This type of business can be run out of your home, which eliminates the overhead costs of setting up an office for your professional organizing business.

NUMBER OF EMPLOYEES NEEDED TO START

One highly organized person can run this business part-time in the beginning stages. This is a perfect idea for someone working from home.

INTERNATIONAL POTENTIAL

This business does not have strong international potential due to the nature of the service provided. Common tasks include on-site consulting. This will require your business to be located near your clients, so this business has a more local or regional appeal.

E-BUSINESS MODEL/PAYMENT PROCESSING METHOD

E-business level 1 is most appropriate for this type of business. You will be accepting orders and payment directly from your clients. For more information, see Part 1.

IMPORTANT BUSINESS ISSUES TO BE ADDRESSED

Your services are often needed only once by a client. After you have organized their life, your job is done. Not so fast! Try to operate your business in such a way that you continue relationships with your clients and create repeat business. For example, establish a pro-organizer "report card" and have them fill it out each month after your consultation is over to see the effectiveness of your strategy. Stay in touch with clients to get referrals and recommendations. Make sure to get paid up front for your services, and carefully research the pricing of other professional organizers so you remain competitive and aware of what is expected within your industry. In this business, your time equals money, so plan out the time you spend on each job and make sure you spend more time on the higher-priced services.

ONLINE MARKETING TECHNIQUES

- Participate in online chats, message boards, and Web rings that target individuals who are seeking more organization in their lives. This will draw an audience and increase the traffic to your Web site.

- Establish a reciprocal linking program with Web sites frequented by your target market. Some suggestions are online organizational software sites, organizing tips sites, and so on.

- Become a solid part of the online community in your regional area by putting links to your site in the professional directories.

- Design your site to be search engine friendly. Consider participating in pay-per-click sponsored listings programs with the popular search engines.

- Participating in mail lists and discussion groups related to organizational methods and techniques with a cleverly designed signature file would be a great way to generate awareness for your services.

For a more detailed description of these techniques, along with many other effective online marketing methods, I recommend the companion book *101 Ways to Promote Your Web Site*. You can also find tons of free resources at *http://www.susansweeney.com/resources.html*.

ADDITIONAL INCOME

Extra income in the professional organizing business can come from various special services that you can provide to clients with certain needs. You will be helping people organize their lives. This means that they will look to you for assistance in many daily tasks—finding a dog walker, for example. Your willingness, resources, and capabilities in helping them solve a variety of life's glitches will strengthen your value and increase the amount of time you dedicate and, therefore, your income.

ONLINE EXAMPLES

The Zen of Organization—Professional Organizer
http://home.earthlink.net/~ecarleton/gallery.html
This business provides all types of organizing services including management consulting, Web site design, space and time organization, and so on.

Chaos Cancelled
http://www.chaoscancelled.com
This site describes the benefits of hiring a professional organizer and is also a marketing tool for the book *Chaos Cancelled*.

71. Public Relations Specialist

OVERVIEW OF BUSINESS MODEL

Many small and medium-sized companies do not have an internal public relations department and cannot handle their own online public relations activities. Other companies choose not to because they feel their time is better served doing what they're good at and that other activities should be outsourced to specialized companies.

As an online public relations specialist, you would help companies that want to promote their company and their Web site online. Your goal is to build or maintain a positive image of your clients in the eyes of their target market. This would be done through various search engines and Web media such as e-zines, e-mail, newsletters, blogs, online radio stations, streaming video sites, and mail lists. Additionally, you would use familiar traditional media and electronic media.

As a public relations specialist, you may be required to take on additional duties such as responding to media queries, developing media events and promotions, arranging interviews, and arranging press conferences.

Payment would be based on your services and would be either on a contractual or an hourly basis.

SKILLS NEEDED

Your business is based on your ability to successfully communicate your message, and as such, excellent oral and written skills are necessary. A background in traditional public relations strategies as well as Netiquette is a great asset to have. Imagination and creativity will help you in this business. A bachelor's degree in a relevant field, such as public relations, marketing, advertising, journalism, or communications, is required.

COST TO START THIS BUSINESS

Initially you will have to pay for the design, development, and hosting of your Web site, computer hardware, computer software, a scanner, a fax machine, and a printer. If you plan to do any image editing work, then you will need to purchase some image editing software (e.g., Adobe PhotoShop, Jasc Paint Shop Pro). If you currently have some of these items, your initial start-up costs will be considerably lower. Other costs that you will incur are related to the promotion of your Web site. Estimated cost is $3,500 to $6,000 to start.

NUMBER OF EMPLOYEES NEEDED TO START

When starting a business of this nature, you would not need to hire additional employees. You would operate this business on your own.

INTERNATIONAL POTENTIAL

This business has some international potential. A majority of your clients will be based in your immediate geographic area or within your country; however, some companies outside of your country may contact you to handle public relations-related activities in your area or culture.

E-BUSINESS MODEL/PAYMENT PROCESSING METHOD

E-business level 1 would be appropriate for this type of business. The needs of the client would be discussed and a proposal for your services would be based on this. For more information, see Part 1.

IMPORTANT BUSINESS ISSUES TO BE ADDRESSED

Do not take on more work than you can handle. You do not want to have to explain to your clients that you are a couple of weeks behind because you took on too much. Limit yourself to what you can comfortably handle. Another major issue is that there is a perception that this is an easy business to get into. As a result, individuals and companies that are the most qualified will face competition from those who are inexperienced.

ONLINE MARKETING TECHNIQUES

- Develop a comprehensive link strategy. You want to generate as many links as possible from Web sites, directories, and meta-indexes related to your target market. Many marketing and promotional-related sites are ideal for promoting this type of business.

- Promotion through related mail lists and newsletters is important. You could even develop your own newsletter or mail list to stay close to your target market.

- Ensure that you submit your site to the search engines and directories. Before you submit, make sure your site has been optimized for search engine friendliness. You might also consider participating in the pay-per-click campaigns of some of the more popular search engines.

- Because many of your clients will likely be regional, be sure to get yourself listed in any regional online business directories that your target market may frequent.

- Develop a viral marketing strategy where people can "Tell a Colleague about This Service" via your site. This will spread the word about your site.

For a more detailed description of these techniques, along with many other effective online marketing methods, I recommend the companion book *101 Ways to Promote Your Web Site*. You can also find tons of free resources at *http://www.susansweeney.com/resources.html*.

ADDITIONAL INCOME

Additional income can be earned by cross-promoting your existing services to clients. If you implemented an e-mail marketing campaign for a client, then the next logical step would be to try to sell the client on a related service. Many businesses now realize that maximizing the dollar amount captured from an existing customer can significantly boost revenue. Additional services you could offer include annual report development, customer surveys, and product evaluations.

ONLINE EXAMPLES

Abel Associates, Inc.
http://abelpr.com
This full-service marketing and communications firm specializes in public relations, media relations, and marketing communications both offline and online.

Technopolis
http://www.technopolis.com
This company provides public relations, marketing communications, and marketing services to computer hardware and software companies, Internet-based companies, and so on.

72. Real Estate Site

OVERVIEW OF BUSINESS

The Internet has revolutionized the way real estate agents are doing business. Traditionally, real estate agents would publish their listings in home buyer publications, on television, and in monthly newsletters that they may distribute throughout the area that they represent. Now real estate agents can easily post their listings online to attract a more global audience. Having an online real estate Web site can benefit you in two ways: (1) increased exposure for your real estate listing, and (2) increased exposure for your services.

There are two ways that you can approach this type of business. If you are a real estate agent, you can launch your site to target potential clients in a specific geographic location. This is the most common approach taken by many real estate agents. Your second option is to offer your services to a larger geographic location such as the United States or North America. As a real estate agent, you cannot possibly represent the interests of homebuyers on a national level, but you can provide other real estate agents with the opportunity to publish their real estate listings on your site. You can then earn a commission from each sale that resulted from a referral from your site. This is an easy way to earn additional income from your real estate business.

SKILLS NEEDED

Similar to an offline real estate agent, in order to sell real estate online you will have to be licensed to do so by the area that you represent. Knowledge of various online advertising techniques would also be an asset.

COST TO START THIS BUSINESS

Initially you will have to pay for the development, design, and hosting of your Web site, computer hardware, computer software, a printer, a scanner, and a digital camera. If you currently have some of these items, your initial start-up costs will be considerably lower. A major cost that you will incur is associated with the development of the database that will contain your real estate listings. If you are going to include only your own listings, this will not be that expensive; however, if you are planning to offer your services to agents across a wide geographic span, it will cost significantly more. You will also have to design some sort of tracking system to track your referrals to the agents that you represent. You might consider purchasing comprehensive Web traffic analysis software, which will enable you to track where your Web site visitors are coming from. This information can be quite beneficial for future marketing purposes. Other costs that you will incur are related to the promotion of your Web site. Estimated cost is $10,000 to $60,000 to start.

NUMBER OF EMPLOYEES NEEDED TO START

The approach you take to operating this business determines how many employees will be needed. If you are going to represent only your own real estate listings online, you will need one employee—yourself. If you are targeting a wide geographic span, one to three employees will be needed. They will handle the offline and online promotion, fulfill service requests, and take care of all administrative tasks involved with running the day-to-day business operation.

INTERNATIONAL POTENTIAL

This type of business has very high international potential, as people planning to relocate to the area(s) that you represent may be interested in your real estate listings.

E-BUSINESS MODEL/PAYMENT PROCESSING METHOD

A hybrid of e-business 4 would be appropriate for this type of business. Since you will not be taking any payments online, there is no need for online payment processing capabilities; however, if you are enabling real estate agents to update their listings on your site, you will need a fully integrated database of real estate listings. For more information, see Part 1.

IMPORTANT BUSINESS ISSUES TO BE ADDRESSED

There are several business issues to be addressed when operating this type of business. Like a traditional offline real estate listing, you should ensure that all listings you place on your Web site are accurate and are not misleading. If anything changes with the listing (e.g., the price changes, features change, it is no longer for sale or is sold), you should update your site immediately with the new information. For example, if you sell a house but don't update your listing with this new information, potential buyers may contact you. When you tell them that the sale has been made, they may be discouraged from ever visiting your site again.

If you enable real estate agents to post their listings on your site, you are going to have to develop a system to track and monitor who is posting what on your site. First, you should make sure that you don't allow people to post listings on your site if they are not licensed real estate agents. Since agents will be able to update their listings on your site with images and text, you are going to have to set up a password-protected area where they will be able to enter your database to manipulate information. To easily track your clients, you might consider using their real estate license number as their unique ID. This would make it easy for you to reference them when searching through your database.

Each listing on your site should have a unique listing number. If visitors are interested in a listing on your site, they can choose to have a real estate agent contact them about the listing by filling out a simple form that will integrate with their selection to include the listing number. Once you receive the request, it is your responsibility to contact the agent to inform him or her of the interest in their listing. This will be an easy way to keep track of your referrals.

ONLINE MARKETING TECHNIQUES

- Launch a strategic banner advertising campaign on Web sites frequented by your target market. These sites could include relocation and moving sites, real estate sites, home buyer sites, and sites targeted toward particular geographic locations. These are the types of Web sites that will be viewed by your target market.

- Develop as many links as possible from Web sites, directories, and meta-indexes related to moving, real estate, and home buying. You should also try to develop links from sites targeted to the geographic locations that you represent.

- Participating in newsgroups and discussion forums related to real estate or the geographic area that you represent would be quite effective. Through providing valuable contributions, you will be able to exercise your professionalism and capture the attention of your target audience. Make sure you include a cleverly designed signature file in all of your postings. This will act as an advertisement for your services.

- Participating in mailing lists related to your target market would be a great way to encourage people to visit your site. Make sure you provide a valuable contribution and include your signature file.

- Develop a sponsored listings campaign to bid on appropriate keyword phrases with the popular search engines.

- Develop a viral marketing strategy where people can "Tell a Friend about This Listing" via your site. This will spread the word about your site.

- You could have a featured real estate listing on your site. If you represent multiple locations, you could have a featured listing for each location. People will return to your site repeatedly to view the featured listing. You could ask people if they would like to be notified via e-mail whenever you update your featured listing. This would be a great way to encourage visitors to return to your site.

- You could ask new homebuyers if they would like to be notified via e-mail whenever a new listing is posted to your site for a specific town or city that you represent. For example, if a couple were interested in buying a home in Houston, Texas, you could notify them via e-mail whenever a new listing is added for the Houston area. This would be a great way to stay in touch with your target market.

For a more detailed description of these techniques, along with many other effective online marketing methods, I recommend the companion book *101 Ways to Promote Your Web Site*. You can also find tons of free resources at *http://www.susansweeney.com/resources.html*.

ADDITIONAL INCOME

In addition to displaying real estate listings on your site, you could also sell advertising space to noncompeting businesses that target the same audience. This is a great way to earn additional income for your site.

ONLINE EXAMPLES

Realtor.com
http://www.realtor.com
This is a dynamite site that targets a North American audience. They have a huge integrated database of real estate listings, which is easily traced using individual number IDs for each listing.

HomeSeekers.com
http://www.homeseekers.com
This is a great site that has listings for residential and commercial real estate. They host a contest for a vacation getaway directly on their site. This is a great way to encourage repeat traffic to their Web site.

73. Resume Writing Service

OVERVIEW OF BUSINESS MODEL

The key to catching the attention of a potential employer and securing an interview for a job is to have a well-written and well-designed resume. Although this may not seem that complicated, many people don't know how to effectively write a resume, a cover letter, or a thank you letter. If you have good writing skills and know how to write effective resumes and business letters, this business opportunity could be perfect for you.

How do you operate this type of business? You can easily accept service requests via the Internet. In order for you to write a resume for a client, you will have to have accurate information regarding past education, work experience, and interests. You could obtain this information via e-mail, telephone, or a personal interview. You could develop a generic questionnaire that you send to your clients, asking them to provide you with all of the information that you need. It's as easy as that.

To speed up the process, you could develop a database of resume design templates that you could easily complete with your client's information. Similarly, you could develop a database of templates for cover letters and thank you letters. This would enable you to customize and complete a project for your client within hours.

SKILLS NEEDED

Excellent writing skills and knowledge of effective resume writing techniques are necessary assets for operating this type of business.

COST TO START THIS BUSINESS

Initially you will have to pay for the design, development, and hosting of your Web site, computer hardware, computer software, a scanner, and a printer. If you currently have some of these items, your initial start-up costs will be adjusted accordingly. You will also have to purchase quality resume paper to print your finished product. Although this cost is not significant, it will be more than traditional overhead. Other costs that you will incur are related to the promotion of your Web site. Estimated cost is $3,000 to $5,000 to start.

NUMBER OF EMPLOYEES NEEDED TO START

The number of employees needed to run this type of business is one part-time employee. You can work at this business in your spare time while working at your current job.

INTERNATIONAL POTENTIAL

This business has strong international potential. People from all over the world would be interested in your resume-writing services, with the exception of countries that communicate using a different language than you do.

E-BUSINESS MODEL/PAYMENT PROCESSING METHOD

E-business level 1 would be appropriate for this type of business. For more information, see Part 1.

IMPORTANT BUSINESS ISSUES TO BE ADDRESSED

When you accept a service request from a client and you complete a project, it is recommended that you receive payment at the time you deliver the finished product. If you provide digital copies, you might want to receive payment before delivery is made electronically.

If you are shipping your completed resume product to your clients, you should ensure that the resumes are packaged appropriately. Postal carriers are not always cautious with their packages, and having a resume with wrinkled paper would not be effective, no matter how well it is written. To ensure that your resumes and cover letters are not damaged during the shipping process, it is recommended that you package them in a file folder or a protective device of some kind.

ONLINE MARKETING TECHNIQUES

- Develop a comprehensive link strategy. You want to generate as many links as possible from Web sites, directories, Web rings, and meta-indexes related to your target market. These sites should relate to employment opportunities, job seeking, and business/consumer services. It would also be effective to have your services listed on college and university Web sites, as graduating students could benefit from your services.

- Participating in newsgroups and discussion forums related to employment, job seeking, or business/consumer services would be a great way to generate traffic to your Web site. Make sure you use a cleverly designed signature file with a catchy tagline. A potential tagline could be "Learn more about our resume writing services. Click Here!" You would be surprised how many people will do what they are told.

- You could have your services listed in cybermalls related to your target market. Many cybermalls have a section dedicated to employment opportunities, or business/consumer services. Having your site listed in a popular cybermall would provide targeted exposure for your service.

- You could develop a strategic banner advertising campaign on Web sites frequented by college or university graduates and job seekers. These are the people who would be interested in your services, so a strategic banner advertising campaign would provide your business with targeted exposure.

- Develop a sponsored listings campaign to bid on appropriate keyword phrases with the popular search engines.

- You could launch a job advice column where you could provide visitors with advice on everything from body language with potential employers to how to conduct yourself during the interview process. You could also ask visitors if they would like to be notified via e-mail when you update your advice column. This would be a great way to encourage repeat traffic to your site.

For a more detailed description of these techniques, along with many other effective online marketing methods, I recommend the companion book *101 Ways to Promote Your Web Site*. You can also find tons of free resources at *http://www.susansweeney.com/resources.html*.

ADDITIONAL INCOME

You could develop additional income for your resume writing business by selling advertising to employers on your site. You could have an employment opportunities section on your site where businesses could pay a fee to have their employment listings posted. This would be a great way to generate additional income.

ONLINE EXAMPLES

Resume.com
http://www.resume.com
Resume.com guarantees that their resumes will get their clients an interview within 30 days or they'll rewrite it for free! Resume.com makes their resumes stand above the rest by providing clients with the edge that they need to compete in today's job market.

A+ Career & Resume Design
http://www.successfulresumes.com
A+ Career & Resume Design (Figure 2.12) is a dynamite business that offers career assessment, skills development, career planning and implementation, resume writing, and interview assistance services.

74. Rubber Stamp Business

OVERVIEW OF BUSINESS MODEL

Self-inking stamps have been used for business and personal use for years, and the demand is still strong today. If you currently have the equipment and skills

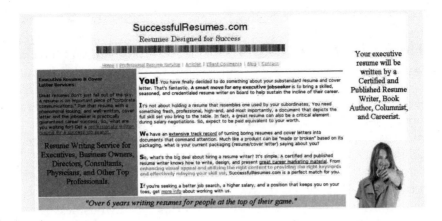

Figure 2.12.   SuccessfulResumes.com is a dynamite professional resume writing business.

necessary to operate this type of business, you can dramatically increase your business via the Internet. The Internet provides you with a unique and efficient way to take orders for rubber stamps.

So how does it work? You can display the various styles and sizes of rubber stamps that you offer directly on your Web site. Visitors should be able to view your entire catalogue of stamps, allowing them to select the ones that they are interested in. Once they have selected a particular stamp, they should be prompted to personalize the stamp to suit their needs via a template form, which will be available for each style of stamp. The form will ask for information such as the name (business or personal), address, tagline, and other pertinent information. Once visitors are happy with the rubber stamp design, they will be prompted to place an order that will provide you with all necessary contact and credit card information to complete the purchase. Once the order has been submitted, you receive the request and design the stamp to the user's specifications. This type of business runs very smoothly and can generate maximum exposure for your offline rubber stamp business.

SKILLS NEEDED

Knowledge of how to develop, design, and produce self-inking rubber stamps would be an asset when operating this type of business.

COST TO START THIS BUSINESS

Initially you will have to pay for the design, development, and hosting of your Web site, computer hardware, computer software, a scanner, and a printer. If you currently have some of these items, your initial start-up costs will be reduced accordingly. If you don't have any of the equipment needed to produce rubber stamps, you will have to purchase it. Either you will have to purchase storefront software, equipped with electronic shopping cart features, or you will be responsible for developing this in-house. You will also have to pay for the design and development of the rubber stamp template system. This is a more advanced Web site feature; therefore, it may be more costly. Other costs that you will incur are related to the promotion of your Web site. Estimated cost is $10,000 to $60,000 to start.

Number of Employees Needed to Start

The number of employees needed to run this type of business is one full-time individual and potentially one part-time employee depending on the number of product requests that your business receives.

International Potential

This business has limited international potential due to the cost of shipping your products overseas. It may be more economical for international clients to purchase rubber stamps from businesses in their local area due to the added costs of shipping, duties, and tariffs.

E-Business Model/Payment Processing Method

E-business level 3 would be appropriate for this type of business. For more information, see Part 1.

Important Business Issues to Be Addressed

It is important that you don't offer a specific rubber stamp design on your Web site that you don't have in stock. If a client purchases a specific stamp and you can't provide them with what they want in a timely fashion, you could damage the reputation of your business. In order to avoid this, it is suggested that you monitor your inventory closely and update your online catalogue accordingly.

When a customer designs a stamp on your site, you should do whatever you can to ensure that they are completely satisfied with the design before you produce the end product. To avoid displeasing your customer, you should have a two-stage review process before any order is submitted—one before the order processing takes place and then another before the order is finalized. You should also place a disclaimer on your site that states that customers understand and take full responsibility for the design of the stamp. This will protect you if you design a stamp to user specifications and they say that that is not what they ordered. It is in your best interest to go through this process to avoid producing multiple stamps for customers.

ONLINE MARKETING TECHNIQUES

- Develop as many links as possible from Web sites, directories, and meta-indexes related to your target market. These sites should be related to business products, stationery, or rubber stamps. It would surprise you how many rubber stamp-related sites there are on the Internet. Many people collect self-inking rubber stamps.

- Participating in newsgroups and discussion forums related to business products, rubber stamps, and just business in general would be a great way to generate traffic to your Web site. Make sure you use a cleverly designed signature file with a catchy tagline. A potential tagline could be "Check Out Our Rubber Stamps Today!" You would be surprised how many people will do what they are told.

- You could have your services listed in cybermalls related to your target market. Many cybermalls have categories related to business products, office supplies, and stamps. Having your site listed in a popular cybermall would provide targeted exposure for your service.

- Develop a viral marketing strategy where people can "Tell a Friend about This Stamp Design" via a link on your site. This will spread the word about your site.

- Develop a sponsored listings campaign to bid on appropriate keyword phrases with the popular search engines.

- You could hold a weekly or monthly contest on your Web site for a free rubber stamp. You could ask people if they would like to be notified of the winner via e-mail. This e-mail will encourage them to return to your site to reenter your contest, thus reexposing them to your site.

For a more detailed description of these techniques, along with many other effective online marketing methods, I recommend the companion book *101 Ways to Promote Your Web Site*. You can also find tons of free resources at *http://www.susansweeney.com/resources.html*.

ADDITIONAL INCOME

In addition to designing stamps, you could also produce stationery and embossers, and offer engraving services. These services would complement your rubber stamp business and could generate additional revenue for your business.

Online Examples

Riverside Rubber Stamp & Engraving
http://www.rrse.com
Riverside Rubber Stamp & Engraving is a rubber stamp manufacturer located in California. They also sell embossers and daters, which complement their rubber stamp business.

JLS Rubber Stamp Co., Inc.
http://www.jlsrubberstamp.com
JLS Rubber Stamp Co. is a rubber stamp manufacturer offering complete marking device services including engraving, pre-inked stamps, self-inked stamps, and personalized engraved gifts.

75. Search Engine Optimization Service

Overview of Business Model
Getting their site to appear in the top ten results is worth big bucks to any company marketing online. If you know how to optimize sites to get top search engine ranking, your services will be very valuable and of great interest to many online companies.

Skills Needed
You will have to be very knowledgeable about search engines, their ranking algorithms, and the keyword phrase selection and allocation process.

Cost to Start This Business
If you decide to launch this type of business, you will have to pay for the design, development, and hosting of your Web site, a high-speed Internet connection, computer hardware, computer software, and a printer. Other costs that you will incur are related to the promotion of your Web site. Estimated cost is $5,000 to $10,000 to start.

Number of Employees Needed to Start
At first you may be able to work at this type of business part-time, but as your service requests increase, you might have to work with this business venture full-time.

INTERNATIONAL POTENTIAL

Since businesses from around the world are all competing for the number one position in the search engines, this type of business has strong international potential.

E-BUSINESS MODEL/PAYMENT PROCESSING METHOD

E-business level 1 is most appropriate for this type of business. For more information, see Part 1.

IMPORTANT BUSINESS ISSUES TO BE ADDRESSED

The search engine ranking criteria, their weighting, and elements included in their algorithms change on a regular basis. It will be extremely important to stay current. You're only as good as your last search engine optimization job!

ONLINE MARKETING TECHNIQUES

- Optimize your own site to appear at the top of the results when someone does a search on "search engine optimization services." You may also want to participate in the pay-to-play sponsored listings programs with the popular search engines.

- Develop as many links as possible from Web sites, directories, and meta-indexes related to your target market. There are thousands of Internet marketing and business service-related sites on the Internet that would provide a great linking opportunity for your site. These sites can provide highly targeted traffic to your site.

- Participate in newsgroups and discussion forums related to Internet marketing and online business. Remember to use a cleverly designed signature file with a catchy tagline and hypertext link that will send newsgroup readers to your site.

- Providing valuable contributions to Internet marketing and online business-related mail lists and e-zines would be a great way to create exposure for your business. This will allow you to display your professionalism and generate awareness for your services.

- Launching a monthly Search Engine Submission Tips newsletter or e-zine would be a great way for you to stay in touch with your current clients and potential customers. You can also offer this via e-mail or

RSS. Offering sound advice is a great way to enhance your corporate image. When your newsletter readers implement your suggested submission techniques, they will want to check their results. This provides you with an opportunity to offer your search engine submission reporter services.

For a more detailed description of these techniques, along with many other effective online marketing methods, I recommend the companion book *101 Ways to Promote Your Web Site*. You can also find tons of free resources at *http://www.susansweeney.com/resources.html*.

ADDITIONAL INCOME

One way to earn additional income for your business is by offering a search engine submission service. This service would complement your current business practice. Because link popularity is becoming such a strong element in the ranking criteria of a number of the search engines, you might also consider providing an online marketing service that includes generating links to the client's site.

ONLINE EXAMPLES

VerbInteractive.com
http://www.verbinteractive.com
This is a company in which I am a partner. Check out the term "tourism Internet marketing" to see how we fare.

Elixir Systems
http://www.elixirsystems.com
Elixir Systems provides search engine optimization services as well as other Internet marketing services.

76. Search Engine Submission and Monitoring Service

OVERVIEW OF BUSINESS MODEL

Marketing research has revealed that when researching online, approximately 85 percent of Internet users find what they are looking for through search engines. It is also a well-known fact that users rarely go beyond the first three screens of search results. Because of this, it is highly important that businesses have their Web sites appropriately submitted to the major search engines. There currently are hundreds of search engine submission services online that promise results, but many never come through on their end of the bargain. They typically do one mass submission of a business's URL to the search engines using a submission tool and choose to ignore proper submission techniques. This provides you with an opportunity to offer services that surpass those of many of the competition.

Since this business's sole purpose is to submit a client's URL to the search engines and directories, this will be the main source of revenue. You have to know the various search engines' ranking criteria and ensure that your client's site is conducive to high ranking before you submit. A Web site has to have appropriate keywords in its meta-tags, Alt-tags, and page titles, and throughout the text on its site, as well as having a significant number of links to its site. As an additional service, you could develop these for your clients as a value-added service (see Search Engine Optimization Service). This will not only generate additional revenue and add to the overall professionalism of your business, it will also increase the chances that your clients will receive high search engine rankings.

SKILLS NEEDED

You should know how to submit appropriately to the various search engines and directories. You should be knowledgeable about the Web site ranking criteria of the major search engines.

COST TO START THIS BUSINESS

If you decide to launch this type of business, you will have to pay for the development, design, and hosting of your Web site, a high-speed Internet connection, computer hardware, computer software, and a printer. If you currently have some of these items, your initial start-up costs will be considerably lower. Other costs that you will incur are related to the promotion of your Web site. Estimated cost is $10,000 to 20,000 to start.

NUMBER OF EMPLOYEES NEEDED TO START

At first you may need to work at this type of business part-time, but as your service requests increase, you might have to work with this business venture full-time.

INTERNATIONAL POTENTIAL

Since businesses from around the world are outsourcing this activity to professionals, this business venture has strong international potential.

E-Business Model/Payment Processing Method

E-business level 2 is most appropriate for this type of business. For more information, see Part 1.

Important Business Issues to Be Addressed

Since search engines change their ranking criteria constantly, it is very important that you stay up-to-date on the latest advancements in search engine technology. Not knowing what a search engine is using to rank the sites in its index could seriously hinder the success of your search engine submission service. Being knowledgeable about the latest advancements in search engine technology will not only enhance the professionalism of your business, but will also increase the chances that you will receive repeat business from your clients as you will develop a strong, trusting relationship.

You should inform your clients that many things factor into receiving high search engine rankings—things such as an effective Web site design, proper meta-tags, keyword prominence throughout the site, page titles, Alt-tags, and, most important, link popularity. Many of the major search engines are now using link popularity—that is, the amount of incoming links to your site—as one of their ranking criteria. If your clients are unwilling to outsource the development of these to your business, it is essential that you inform them how important they are to receiving high rankings. Once you submit their URL to the search engines, if your clients don't receive high rankings, you can again inform them that it was because they didn't comply with all of the requirements of the search engines' ranking criteria. This will save the professionalism of your organization and will ultimately result in the sale of your additional search engine optimization services.

Online Marketing Techniques

- Participate in newsgroups and discussion forums related to Internet marketing and online business. Remember to use a cleverly designed signature file with a catchy tagline and hypertext link that will send newsgroup readers to your site. Potential taglines could include "Ask Us about Our Search Engine Submission Services" or some variation of this phrase.

- Develop as many links as possible from Web sites, directories, and meta-indexes related to your target market. There are thousands of Internet marketing- and business services-related sites on the Internet that would provide a great linking opportunity for your site. These sites will provide highly targeted traffic to your site.

- Providing valuable contributions to Internet marketing and online business-related mail lists and e-zines would be a great way to create exposure for your business. This will allow you to display your professionalism and generate awareness for your services.

- Launching a monthly search engine news newsletter or e-zine would be a great way for you to stay in touch with your current clients and potential customers. This could be offered via e-mail or an RSS feed. Offering sound advice is a great way to enhance your corporate image. When your newsletter readers implement your suggested submission techniques, they will want to check their results. This provides you with an opportunity to offer your search engine submission optimization services.

- You could have your search engine submission services listed in cybermalls related to your target market. You could list your site in industry-specific cybermalls related to technology or doing business online, or you could simply have your site listed in categories related to business services.

For a more detailed description of these techniques, along with many other effective online marketing methods, I recommend the companion book *101 Ways to Promote Your Web Site*. You can also find tons of free resources at *http://www.susansweeney.com/resources.html*.

ADDITIONAL INCOME

One way to earn additional income for your business is by offering a search engine reporting service. Many people regularly submit their URL to the search engines but never take the time to actually know where their Web site is ranking. This service would complement your current submission service and would be a great way to earn additional income for your business.

ONLINE EXAMPLES

Hand Submit
http://www.handsubmit.com
Hand Submit provides manual search engine submission services.

Surf Promote
http://www.manual-search-engine-submission.co.uk
Surf Promote (see Figure 2.13) provides manual search engine submission services.

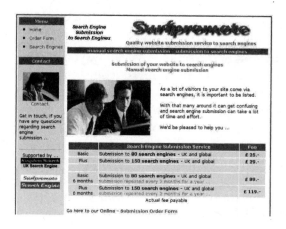

Figure 2.13. Surf Promote offers a great search engine submission service.

77. Seminars Online

OVERVIEW OF BUSINESS

If you are an educator, public speaker, industry specialist, or software salesperson, this could be your winning ticket!

Online seminars are becoming very common, with many online training sites now available. They are a perfect way to deliver a multimedia message that holds the user's full attention until the points are clearly communicated. The monitor screen is a cold and inhuman medium, but with the new online seminar software and associated technology, we can deliver a human voice accompanied by moving images and presentation slides, thus delivering an engaging educational experience that is available to users 24/7. Some software available today requires a relatively small download in order to receive the message, and some is directly available through the browser interface.

Many meeting and event planners are turning to the Internet to research and book a speaker or trainer for their next event. For many speakers' Web sites, it's a great idea to have an online demo for event coordinators to sample. This lessens the associated costs and time consumed by sending out videos and brochures.

The online seminar Web site should host a comprehensive amount of information pertaining to the topics discussed in the seminars, as well as feature bios about the speakers or educators and technical support FAQ files for users to refer to if they have any questions about the associated technologies being used. There should be a clear schedule of past and upcoming seminars posted on the site. All the past seminars should be available via download for a fee to maximize revenue potential for this business.

The online seminar provides a perfect opportunity to upsell books, training kits, and in-person speaking engagements or classes, providing you with an excellent opportunity to generate additional income for your business.

SKILLS NEEDED

You will need working knowledge of the software programs and hardware used to create the online seminar files and store them on servers, making them available for download via the Web. You will need Web publishing skills and must be able to manage the automated online payment processing function that takes place when users download a seminar.

COST TO START THIS BUSINESS

Initially you will have to pay for the development, design, and hosting of your Web site, computer hardware, computer software, a printer, and a digital video camera. You will have to pay for the online seminar software. If you currently have some of these items, your initial start-up costs will be considerably lower. If you are selling books or related training materials and are considering taking online payments, you will have to pay for the development of your storefront or purchase storefront software. You will also incur all costs associated with setting up your merchant account, which enables you to take online payments. Other costs that you will incur are related to the promotion of your Web site. Estimated cost is $3,000 to $10,000 to start.

NUMBER OF EMPLOYEES NEEDED

Only one employee is needed to run this operation. If your service requests exceed what you can handle, you may have to hire an additional employee to handle all administrative duties associated with the daily operations of the business.

INTERNATIONAL POTENTIAL

The software that was created to make online seminars possible was designed with global potential in mind. It bridges the gap between experts and the people who want to learn from these experts but cannot meet them in person. Therefore, the only barrier is language, and this can be overcome with professional translation services.

E-Business Model/Payment Processing Method

E-business level 2 or 3 would be appropriate for this type of business. You will be providing an automated payment processing function associated with the download of seminars from your site and possibly selling related products such as books, training kits, and bookings in your e-store. For more information, see Part 1.

Important Business Issues to Be Addressed

The technology involved is new and still being perfected, so be careful when you choose the seminar software and hardware. Make sure you research the file types, streaming techniques, browser compatibility, and user-friendliness of the options available. In addition, keep on top of the breaking multimedia technology and change with it as it improves to maintain the long-term viability of your business. Keep your prices competitive and offer some samples for free. There already are many free seminars available on the Web today. Your pricing should reflect the nature and value of the seminars you provide.

Online Marketing Techniques

- Launch a strategic banner advertising campaign on Web sites frequented by your target market. These sites could relate to the specific industry or educational subject that your seminars target, or be targeted toward universities or meeting and event planners. These are the Web sites that your target market will visit on a regular basis.

- Develop as many links as possible from Web sites, directories, and meta-indexes related to your target market. These sites should relate to the industry that you target, such as student resource sites, meeting and event planning sites, or sites dedicated to professional speakers and trainers.

- Participating in newsgroups and discussion forums related to your area of expertise would be quite effective. Provide valuable demonstrations of the power of online seminars by inviting chat room acquaintances to visit your site and test it out for free.

- Make sure you include a cleverly designed signature file in all of your postings. This will act as an advertisement for your services.

- Develop a sponsored listings campaign to bid on appropriate keyword phrases with the popular search engines.

- Participating in mailing lists related to online seminars or your area of expertise is a useful way of encouraging people to visit your site.

- You could hold a weekly or monthly contest on your Web site for products in your e-store. This creates loyalty, spurs viral marketing, and ensures repeat traffic generation.

For a more detailed description of these techniques, along with many other effective online marketing methods, I recommend the companion book *101 Ways to Promote Your Web Site*. You can also find tons of free resources at *http://www.susansweeney.com/resources.html.*

ADDITIONAL INCOME

If your primary focus is selling your online seminars via download or online seminar publishing services, you could earn additional income from banner advertising because chances are you will have a tremendous "stickiness" factor to your site, and this allows for significant banner exposure time. You could also be a useful reseller for the online seminar software product you choose and earn a commission for all the packages you sell.

ONLINE EXAMPLES

Susan Sweeney

http://www.susansweeney.com/tele_seminars.html
On my site I offer a full range of Internet marketing online seminars. These can be taken live with a question and answer at the end of each session; they can be purchased as a CD; or they can be taken immediately as a prerecorded training program.

Seybold Seminars

http://www.key3media.com/seyboldseminars
This site provides comprehensive, in-depth online seminars directed toward cutting-edge notions within the publishing industry.

Virtual Seminars for Teaching Literature

http://info.ox.ac.uk/jtap/tutorials
This site has online tutorials (seminars) about poetry, history, and other topics with fantastic user-friendliness in the tech support department, and it explains exactly how to benefit from the tutorials by doing background reading and other preparatory activities. The software used on this site works in Netscape.

78. Senior Services

OVERVIEW OF BUSINESS MODEL

The number of seniors who are online is increasing every day. Many retired seniors spend hours on the Internet daily—learning, doing research, purchasing products, and planning the rest of their retirement. This provides you with an excellent opportunity to capitalize on this trend. You can launch a senior services Web site where senior citizens can learn about health, eating, fitness, travel, literature, money, entertainment, and many other things that are of interest to senior citizens.

How does this business generate revenue? You can generate revenue from selling online advertising. The senior citizen market is quite appealing to many businesses; this can provide a key advertising opportunity for businesses whose products and services would be of interest to seniors. You could sell advertisements for different vitamins and health products, or you could sell advertisements promoting senior trips to Las Vegas. There are many advertising opportunities for this type of site. You could also generate revenue by participating in the affiliate programs of companies providing goods and services of interest to seniors.

SKILLS NEEDED

Knowledge of online advertising techniques would be a benefit if you are operating this type of business. You can't promote to a specific market segment unless you understand that segment; therefore, you should have knowledge of different interests of senior citizens.

COST TO START THIS BUSINESS

Initially you will have to pay for the development, design, and hosting of your Web site, computer hardware, computer software, a scanner, and a printer. If you plan to set up a mailing list, you will also have to purchase mailing list software to help you organize and maintain it. It would probably be in your best interest to purchase comprehensive Web traffic analysis software to track where your Web site visitors are coming from. This information can be great for future marketing opportunities. Other costs that you will incur are related to the promotion of your Web site. Estimated cost is $4,000 to $10,000 to start.

NUMBER OF EMPLOYEES NEEDED TO START

This business could be started by one individual on a part-time basis. To take this to the next level, you will want one or two full-time employees. One person will be responsible for the daily promotion of your Web site online. The other employee will handle advertising sales, accounting, and all administrative tasks associated with operating the business.

INTERNATIONAL POTENTIAL

This business has strong international potential. Your services will be of interest to senior citizens all over the world.

E-BUSINESS MODEL/PAYMENT PROCESSING METHOD

E-business level 1 would be appropriate for this type of business. For more information, see Part 1.

IMPORTANT BUSINESS ISSUES TO BE ADDRESSED

Since your main source of revenue is going to be generated from the sale of online advertising, it is very important that you ensure that the server hosting your site has high-speed access. You don't want to have a slow-loading site, because this won't be attractive to advertisers. If it takes a long time to download a page of your site, both visitors and advertisers will be dissatisfied.

You should ensure that your Web site has an attractive interface with consistent navigation throughout your site. Since your advertisers will be posting their ads on your site linking out to their site, you should develop the interface so that the visitor doesn't actually leave your site. What you can do is have your advertiser's site appear in a pop-up window. This enables the visitor to continue to navigate throughout your site without having to click back in his or her browser.

Since your target market is senior citizens, you should remember not to make your Web site design too complex. You should use fonts that are larger than your typical font size. You should also ensure that navigating throughout your site is easy. Any complications may cause a senior citizen to leave your site due to confusion.

You should update your Web site constantly. Perhaps you could have a What's New page that is continuously updated with recent site additions or information that would be of interest to seniors. You could ask visitors if they would like to be notified via e-mail of any updates that you make to your What's New page. This would be a great way to encourage repeat traffic, and seniors would definitely appreciate hearing from you.

ONLINE MARKETING TECHNIQUES

- Develop a viral marketing strategy where seniors can "Tell a Friend about This Site" via your site. This will spread the word about your site.

- Develop as many links as possible from appropriate Web sites, directories, Web rings, and meta-indexes related to your target market. These sites could relate to travel, health and fitness, money, entertainment, growing older, or anything related to senior citizens.

- You could hold a weekly or monthly contest on your Web site for a free product offered by one of your advertisers. You could ask people if they would like to be notified of the winner via e-mail. This e-mail will encourage them to return to your site to re-enter your contest, thus re-exposing them to your site.

- Have a What's New page where visitors can view recent changes to your site and new things that would be of interest to seniors. You could ask people if they would like to be notified of additions to your What's New page via e-mail. This would encourage them to return to your Web site.

- Participating in mailing lists related to the interests of senior citizens would be a great way to encourage repeat traffic to your Web site. Remember to include a signature file in all of your messages. This will be your online advertisement for your senior services site.

- Develop a sponsored listings campaign to bid on appropriate keyword phrases with the popular search engines.

- You could purchase banner advertising on Web sites that are frequented by your target market. Sites related to health and fitness or travel, or sites that target senior citizens, would generate targeted exposure for your business.

For a more detailed description of these techniques, along with many other effective online marketing methods, I recommend the companion book *101 Ways to Promote Your Web Site*. You can also find tons of free resources at *http://www.susansweeney.com/resources.html*.

Additional Income

You can generate additional revenue by participating in affiliate programs of suppliers of products and services that are of interest to seniors. You can have sponsors of appropriate sections of your Web site or your mail list.

Online Examples

Seniors.com
http://www.seniors.com

Figure 2.14. Seniors.com is a great place for seniors to find information about health, investments, news, and much more!

Seniors.com is a great site (Figure 2.14) that provides senior citizens with multitudes of information on health, news, family, fitness, travel, finance, Medicare, and more.

ThirdAge!
http://www.thirdage.com
This is a dynamite site that offers health, money, fitness, and travel advice to mature adults.

79. Sign-Making Service

OVERVIEW OF BUSINESS MODEL

A sign-making service is a great way to earn additional income from home. You can design and manufacture signs for companies that reflect their corporate image, or you can develop custom signs for other clientele. How involved you get during the design process is up to you. You may choose to operate only on the production end of things. Some opportunities for you to consider are:

- Carved signs

- Banners

- Neon or electronic signs

- Slate signs

- Truck and trailer lettering

- Magnetic signs

- Site signs

- Decorative pinstriping

- Real estate signs.

Skills Needed

Graphic design and computer skills as well as additional technical skills are important; however, no postsecondary education is necessary. Other skills will reflect the path you take. If you are going to make carved signs, then woodworking knowledge would be a valuable asset. If you are going to paint signs on vehicles, then past experience with airbrushes and vinyl/hand lettering would be important.

Cost to Start This Business

Initially you will have to pay for the design, development, and hosting of your Web site, computer hardware, sign-making computer software, a scanner, photographic equipment (e.g., a digital camera), sign-making machinery, and a printer. If you currently have some of these items, your initial start-up costs will be considerably lower. Other costs that you will incur are related to the promotion of your Web site. Estimated cost is $18,000 to $20,000 to start.

Number of Employees Needed to Start

One additional employee may be needed to run this business. You may choose to focus on the sign design aspect of the business and have an additional employee handle the fabrication and installation.

International Potential

This business will focus on your immediate geographic region, as you will need to be able to travel to the appropriate locations to deliver and install your signage cost effectively. On the other hand, you may get some business requests from outside of your area. In these cases, you would courier the end product to the customer.

E-BUSINESS MODEL/PAYMENT PROCESSING METHOD

E-business level 1 would be appropriate for this type of business. You could have a form so that people can request price estimates and inquire about your services. See Part 1 for more information.

IMPORTANT BUSINESS ISSUES TO BE ADDRESSED

Your biggest challenge is making yourself visible to your target market. You will need to ensure that you implement and monitor appropriate online marketing techniques. If your area has relevant local sites, such as a coupon site, then you should consider participating. Although this discounts your services, it is an excellent way to attract business.

ONLINE MARKETING TECHNIQUES

- Develop as many links as possible from appropriate Web sites, directories, and meta-indexes related to your target market. Ensure that you get listed in sites that target your local area as well as your area of expertise.

- Develop a viral marketing strategy where people can "Tell a Friend about This Site" via a link on your site. This will spread the word about your site and will encourage others to visit.

- Advertising in business-related e-zines will encourage people to visit your site.

- Develop a sponsored listings campaign to bid on appropriate keyword phrases with the popular search engines.

- Develop a section of your site to display your more impressive signs.

For a more detailed description of these techniques, along with many other effective online marketing methods, I recommend the companion book *101 Ways to Promote Your Web Site*. You can also find tons of free resources at *http://www.susansweeney.com/resources.html*.

ADDITIONAL INCOME

Extending your product line is an excellent opportunity to earn additional income. For example, you could take up actual logo design or develop your own bumper stickers. Both are natural extensions that flow from your existing capabilities. You may also want to consider sign-restoration services.

ONLINE EXAMPLES

A Sign 4 U
http://www.asign4u.com
A company that makes a wide range of graphical business products.

SignMaker1.com
http://www.signmaker1.com
A sign company offering custom design, fabrication, and installation of all types of advertising signage.

80. Small Business Resource Center

OVERVIEW OF BUSINESS

This type of business can be established to assist entrepreneurs who are interested in starting a business or to help existing businesses enhance their current business operation. You can provide entrepreneurs with information on how to register a business, different tax issues that need to be addressed when running a business, and other information that can help them set up and run their business. This information will be easy for you to provide to your visitors, as it will be accessible from your local government offices. These government offices will also be able to supply you with any forms, brochures, or pamphlets that you will want to make available to your visitors. This will help you cut down on high overhead costs.

You can also provide current business operators with resources that will help them run their businesses more efficiently. You could develop a directory of various consultants, accountants, financial advisors, office equipment suppliers, and so on, that would be accessible from your Web site. Current business operators could easily reference your site when trying to outsource activities to a specialized organization or purchase new materials for their business operation. This directory would be a great asset to all business operators.

To generate revenue for your business, you can set up a referral system with business service providers that target entrepreneurs and business operators. For example, you could receive a referral fee for every business person you send to a financial planner, an accountant, or a lawyer in a specific area. You could also develop an alliance between office equipment suppliers, print houses, and other businesses that would benefit from receiving business from your Web site's visitors. After developing these alliances, you would be surprised how much money you could make from referrals. You can also sell banner advertising to business service-oriented companies. They would benefit from the targeted advertising exposure that could be generated from your Web site.

Skills Needed

Knowledge of how to operate a business, business rules and regulations, and online marketing skills would be an asset when operating this type of business.

Cost to Start This Business

Initially you will have to pay for the development, design, and hosting of your Web site, computer hardware, computer software, and a printer. If you currently have some of these items, your initial start-up costs will be considerably lower. You will also have to design some sort of tracking system to track your referrals to the businesses that you are promoting on your site. If you are planning to launch a mailing list, you will have to purchase mailing list software. This will help you maintain, manage, and distribute your mail list. Other costs that you will incur are related to the promotion of your Web site. Estimated cost is $10,000 to $30,000 to start.

Number of Employees Needed to Start

Generally, one full-time employee will be needed to run the day-to-day operation of this business.

International Potential

Although people from other countries may use this service if they are moving to the country, city, or state that you represent, this business generally has national or regional appeal.

E-Business Model/Payment Processing Method

E-business level 1 would be most appropriate for this type of business. For more information, see Part 1.

Important Business Issues to Be Addressed

Since the majority of the information on your site will remain the same (i.e., business forms, laws, and regulations), you should continuously update your site to encourage repeat traffic to your Web site. Ideas you may want to include on your site are a What's New page or an Emerging Business page that entrepreneurs can read for inspiration. This would be a great way to encourage repeat traffic.

Since revenue will be based upon generating referrals to other business service providers, you are going to have to develop a system to track your referrals. To do this, you should assign a unique ID to each business that you have listed on your site. If visitors are interested in a particular business's service, they can request that a representative from that business contact them by filling out a simple form that will integrate with their selection to include the unique ID number. Once you receive the request, it is your responsibility to contact the business to inform them about the potential client or customer. This will be an easy way to keep track of your referrals.

Businesses are going to want to purchase advertising on your site for one reason—the potential traffic that you will send to their sites. To ensure that this happens, you are going to have to do whatever you can to promote your business online and offline.

ONLINE MARKETING TECHNIQUES

- Develop as many links as possible from Web sites, directories, and meta-indexes related to entrepreneurship, starting a business, or business services. There are hundreds of business services-related Web sites and meta-indexes online. You should attempt to receive links from as many of these as possible.

- Participating in newsgroups and discussion forums related to business, entrepreneurship, starting a business, or the geographic area that you represent would be quite effective. Through providing valuable contributions, you will be able to exercise your professionalism and capture the attention of your target audience. Make sure you include a cleverly designed signature file in all of your postings. This will act as an advertisement for your services.

- Participating in mailing lists related to your target market would be a great way to encourage people to visit your site. Make sure you provide a valuable contribution and include your signature file. This will encourage people to visit your Web site.

- Develop a sponsored listings campaign to bid on appropriate keyword phrases with the popular search engines.

- You could have a What's New section on your site. You could ask people if they would like to be notified via e-mail whenever you update your What's New page. This would be a great way to encourage visitors to return to your site.

For a more detailed description of these techniques, along with many other effective online marketing methods, I recommend the companion book *101 Ways to Promote Your Web Site*. You can also find tons of free resources at *http://www.susansweeney.com/resources.html*.

ADDITIONAL INCOME

In addition to generating revenue from business referrals, you could also promote upcoming business-related conferences and seminars on your Web site. You could promote the event, take online registrations, and earn a commission for every registration that you take. This would be a great way to earn additional income.

ONLINE EXAMPLES

MoreBusiness.com
http://www.morebusiness.com
MoreBusiness.com is a dynamite resource site for entrepreneurs. Their site offers advice on everything from starting a business to building a Web site for that business.

BusinessCity.com
http://www.businesscity.com
This is a huge business resource site offering all kinds of advice to business start-ups and already established businesses.

81. Software Download Site

OVERVIEW OF BUSINESS MODEL

Everyone loves free shareware. The increase in Web sites offering free software downloads proves this. These sites allow up-and-coming software designers to display their programs to the public. They also allow established businesses to offer trial copies of their software. Usually these trial versions are limited either in their functionality or by the number of days you can use them. Since these sites offer free programs, they typically receive high volumes of traffic.

How do you generate revenue with this type of business? Since these sites receive such high volumes of traffic, you provide businesses with an excellent online advertising opportunity. You can sell banner advertisements on pages throughout your site. If you decide to launch a mailing list, you can also sell advertisements in the body of the mailing list message. Since your site will receive so many visitors, you will be able to generate maximum exposure for your advertisers' products and services; thus you will be able to generate a tremendous amount of revenue for your business.

SKILLS NEEDED

Knowledge of online advertising techniques is an asset to run this type of business. Since you will have to evaluate all of the software that you allow people to submit to your site, it is recommended that you have some knowledge of software design.

COST TO START THIS BUSINESS

Initially you will have to pay for the development, design, and hosting of your Web site. You will have to purchase computer hardware, computer software, a scanner, and a printer. If you currently have some of these items, your initial start-up costs will be considerably lower. You should expect the cost for Web hosting to be considerably larger than that for a typical online business due to the high volumes of traffic that your site is going to receive and the space needed to store the various programs that your visitors will be able to download. You will also need high bandwidth because of all the files that will be downloaded. If you plan to set up a mailing list, you will also have to purchase mailing list software to help you organize and maintain it. It would probably be in your best interest to purchase comprehensive Web traffic analysis software to track where your Web site visitors are coming from. This information can be great for future marketing opportunities. Other costs that you will incur are related to the promotion of your Web site. Estimated cost is $10,000 to $50,000 to start.

NUMBER OF EMPLOYEES NEEDED TO START

The number of employees needed to run this type of business is one full-time individual and potentially one part-time employee. Initially you are going to be responsible for the mass promotion of your software download site through various online media. This is going to be a very time-consuming task, as a high volume of traffic is imperative to the success of this business.

INTERNATIONAL POTENTIAL

This business has strong international potential. Since you are representing software developers from all over the world, your software download site will appeal to everyone.

E-BUSINESS MODEL/PAYMENT PROCESSING METHOD

E-business level 1 would be appropriate for this type of business. For more information, see Part 1.

IMPORTANT BUSINESS ISSUES TO BE ADDRESSED

There are several things that you have to remember when launching a software download site. It is very important that you ensure that the server that you're hosting your site on has high-speed access. If it takes a long time to download software from your site, visitors will be dissatisfied. This will also turn away potential advertisers from your Web site. This can be avoided if your host has a state-of-the-art server with lots of capacity and a high-speed connection.

To keep your software download site fresh, you should try to update your site on a regular basis. Consider having a What's New page on your site. You could ask visitors if they would like to be notified via e-mail when you have made updates to your site. This would be a great way to generate repeat traffic to your site.

Advertisers are going to want to purchase ads on your site for one reason—exposure. This can't happen unless your site receives high volumes of traffic. To ensure that this happens, you are going to have to do whatever you can to promote your business online and offline.

ONLINE MARKETING TECHNIQUES

- Launch a strategic banner advertising campaign on Web sites frequented by your target market. These sites should relate to software, programming, or technology in general.

- You could hold a weekly or monthly contest on your Web site for a free full version of a product offered by one of your regular program providers. The programmer or business donating the product could be your Featured Designer. You could ask people if they would like to be notified of the winner via e-mail. This e-mail will encourage them to return to your site to re-enter your contest, thus re-exposing them to your site.

- Develop a viral marketing strategy where people can "Tell a Friend about This Program" via your site. This will spread the word about your site.

- Develop as many links as possible from Web sites, directories, and meta-indexes related to your target market. These sites should relate to software design, development, programming, or technology in general. There are also thousands of "free stuff" sites online. It would be very appropriate for your site to be listed on all of these sites.

- Develop a sponsored listings campaign to bid on appropriate keyword phrases with the popular search engines.

- You should develop a What's New page for your site. Here you could feature the newest software uploaded to your site. You could ask people if they would like to be notified via e-mail when you update your What's New page. This will encourage them to return to your site.

For a more detailed description of these techniques, along with many other effective online marketing methods, I recommend the companion book *101 Ways to Promote Your Web Site*. You can also find tons of free resources at *http://www.susansweeney.com/resources.html.*

ADDITIONAL INCOME
You could develop additional income for your site by selling software from your site or launching a referral business, where you receive a commission on all software sales resulting from a referral from your site. This would be a great way for you to earn additional income from this type of business.

ONLINE EXAMPLES

TUCOWS
http://www.tucows.com
One of the first sites of its kind, TUCOWS is a great software download site. They offer tons of programs on their site including music editors, HTML editors, games, and screen savers.

DOWNLOAD.com
http://www.download.com
This is a great site brought to you by CNET.com. They have a huge database of various software downloads.

82. Sports Equipment, New and Used

OVERVIEW OF BUSINESS MODEL
The sports industry generates billions of dollar a year. With that much interest, it was inevitable that online sports stores would appear in force. There are an

insane number of sports stores online already; however, because of the diversity in sports, there is still a lot of room for those with unique interests. If you can correctly combine the proper sports niche with the global Internet community, you will still have a huge customer base—this is one of the primary strengths of the Internet. You can run this business a number of ways:

1. You could provide classified ad space for a fee to those interested in selling new or used sports equipment.

2. You could be an online storefront and carry an inventory of new and used sports equipment.

3. You could belong to a number of sports-related stores' affiliate programs and provide recommendations and links to their sports products.

Your main source of income will depend on the business model you choose.

SKILLS NEEDED

Some familiarity with sports and sports equipment is suggested, as people may ask you questions about the merchandise. Also, some familiarity with Web site programming would be an asset, though it is not required.

COST TO START THIS BUSINESS

The expenses to start an online new and used sporting goods store will depend on the business model you choose. The costs can be separated into several key areas.

Hardware

You will need a computer, appropriate software, a scanner, and a printer. This will cost around $2,000 to $4,000.

Web Site

You will need to have your Web site designed, developed, and hosted. The cost to set up your basic Web site is highly variable, and it will range from $3,000 to $10,000. If you choose the classified ad business model, your Web site development costs will have to allow for the development of a searchable database and also classified ad input forms and online payment forms. This will add $2,000 to $5,000 to your basic Web site costs. If you choose the online storefront model, you will have to develop your storefront and all you need for online payment. This will add $50 to $100 per month to your basic Web site costs. If you choose the affiliate program model, no additional Web development costs will be incurred.

Other

If you choose to have an online storefront and keep inventory, building up your inventory will be one of your largest expenses. Though highly variable, you should expect it to start at $5,000, and it could go much higher depending on your inventory size and the types of items you are selling.

NUMBER OF EMPLOYEES NEEDED TO START

The number of employees needed to start depends on the business model you choose and the volume of business you expect to handle. The degree of automation incorporated into your online presence will also be a factor. Should you choose the classified ad model or the affiliate program model, you can start with one employee as a part-time venture. If you choose to use the online store model, at a minimum you'll need several people to handle your customer service and shipping.

INTERNATIONAL POTENTIAL

Sports is a universal pastime, and the market for sports equipment is huge, so the international potential for this business is excellent. The language barrier will be the only major hindrance to total international access.

E-BUSINESS MODEL/PAYMENT PROCESSING METHOD

For the classified ad business model, e-business level 2 is most appropriate. For the online storefront, you will want to use e-business level 3 or level 4 if you have an offline presence as well. For the affiliate program business model, e-business level 1 is appropriate. For more information, see Part 1.

IMPORTANT BUSINESS ISSUES TO BE ADDRESSED

A major issue to be addressed is the competition on the Internet. All the major sporting goods stores are on the Internet, and they all probably will be able to sell products cheaper than you. It is important then that you niche your market. This carries several significant advantages, such as being able to narrow your target market, and it also keeps down your inventory.

ONLINE MARKETING TECHNIQUES

- Develop a comprehensive link strategy. Generating links from sports sites that are related to your products could be a great way of reaching a targeted market.

- Use permission marketing by asking customers if they would like to be notified when you update or expand your product line.

- On your site, include a Special of the Week (or Month) section where the customer will get a discount on big-ticket items. Again, ask visitors if they would like to be notified via e-mail when you introduce new specials.

- If your site is dedicated to one sort of sport, then you can use publicly accessible opt-in mailing lists to market your site. The mailing list should contain key items of information about the sport and maybe a few small plugs for your store.

- Develop a sponsored listings campaign to bid on appropriate keyword phrases with the popular search engines.

- You might want to consider a targeted banner advertising campaign.

For a more detailed description of these techniques, along with many other effective online marketing methods, I recommend the companion book *101 Ways to Promote Your Web Site*. You can also find tons of free resources at *http://www.susansweeney.com/resources.html*.

ADDITIONAL INCOME
To increase your income, you could also include a section of your Web site dedicated to sports memorabilia. Sports memorabilia items have significant sentimental value attached to them due to a significant past event or a particular owner. Sports memorabilia is a huge subsection of the sports industry.

ONLINE EXAMPLES

Fogdog Sports
http://www.fogdog.com
The largest online sports store. Many other sport sites that sell sporting goods online are actually using Fogdog's affiliate program.

Sports.com
http://www.sports.com
One of the largest sports sites on the Web, in five languages, and covering all the major sports. Its store is divided into European and American divisions.

83. Survey Service

OVERVIEW OF BUSINESS MODEL

In business, it pays to know what your customers are thinking. This allows you to change your marketing strategy or target a more receptive audience. In a survey service, businesses pay you to find out what people are thinking. A survey service organizes polls and arranges questionnaires on topics the client chooses. In fact, the better survey services create questionnaires and polls from criteria that their clients give them. As an online survey service, most of your services will be targeted at an online market.

Your business will generate income by attracting clients who need to have online surveys performed. You will create an online survey, poll, or questionnaire based on criteria that your clients provide you. You will arrange to have the surveys introduced to the targeted market segment and have people answer it. You will then correlate the results and provide them to your client, at which point you collect your fee.

SKILLS NEEDED

You will need experience in developing appropriate survey questions and developing a campaign.

COST TO START THIS BUSINESS

The cost to initially set up your survey service will range from $7,000 to over $20,000. These costs include at least one high-end computer, appropriate administrative and Web-enabled survey software, and a printer. You will need to have your Web site designed, developed, and hosted.

NUMBER OF EMPLOYEES NEEDED TO START

Your business can be started with one knowledgeable employee.

INTERNATIONAL POTENTIAL

Information services have none of the restrictions that so often apply to Internet retail businesses. There is nothing preventing your services from being used by anyone online. Your only restrictions are the language barriers. For this reason, you may wish to include in your Web site several language options.

E-BUSINESS MODEL/PAYMENT PROCESSING METHOD

E-business level 1 is most appropriate for this type of business. For more information, see Part 1.

Important Business Issues to Be Addressed

Getting people to fill out your surveys may be difficult, so it might be necessary to offer some sort of reward or incentive, such as the chance to win a prize.

Online Marketing Techniques

- Develop a comprehensive link strategy. You should generate as many links from appropriate business services Web sites, directories, Web rings, meta-indexes, and business-related cybermalls as possible.

- Develop a sponsored listings campaign to bid on appropriate keyword phrases with the popular search engines.

- Participate in business services-related opt-in mail lists, discussion groups, and forums. Be sure to utilize your signature file and have a catchy tagline.

For a more detailed description of these techniques, along with many other effective online marketing methods, I recommend the companion book *101 Ways to Promote Your Web Site*. You can also find tons of free resources at *http://www.susansweeney.com/resources.html*.

Additional Income

Additional income can be generated by expanding your online marketing services. This is suggested only after you have established yourself. However, there is a great need for market research services, and marketing advice online at the present time would be a logical expansion of your business.

Online Examples

Surveysite.com
http://www.surveysite.com
The main Web site for a large corporate marketing firm. Several survey sites on the Internet are actually generated by Surveysite.

HostedSurvey.com
http://www.hostedsurvey.com/home.html
A nicely laid out corporate site (Figure 2.15) that lets you perform rapid online marketing surveys, feedback forms, and evaluations so that customers can get the information quickly.

Figure 2.15.   HostedSurvey.com provides extensive online survey services.

84. Tourist Information Center

OVERVIEW OF BUSINESS MODEL

A tourist information center is a Web Site that provides prospective travelers with information about popular tourist locations. It provides the user with common weather conditions, sites to see, places to go, things to do, or anything else someone might want to know about their travel destination.

Your site should be designed so that the average user can easily access accurate information about a travel destination. Accuracy is of the utmost importance as people will be relying on your information to plan their vacation. It is suggested that you choose a niche, a small area, or a single travel topic to cover. You will need to cover a lot of information even when covering a small area.

Your main source of income will be generated by banner ads or commercial listings with links to Web sites that are related to tourism in the area you cover. Thus, if you cover the state of New York, for example, you can offer your service to New York's bed and breakfasts, amusement parks, restaurants, hotels, RV parks, car rental agencies, and other related sites.

SKILLS NEEDED

Since you are an information service, it is of the utmost importance that the information you provide be highly accurate since people will be depending on you. Another skill that may prove to be helpful is a familiarity with Web site design and maintenance. If you are not familiar with this, you will need to hire someone who is, or outsource this activity to someone who can perform changes to your Web site regularly.

Cost to Start This Business

The costs associated with setting up this business have been divided into three categories: hardware and software purchases, accumulating information for your business, and setting up your Web site.

You will need a computer, administrative and database software, a printer, a scanner, a digital camera, and graphics software. You will need to pay to have your Web site designed, developed, and hosted unless you are capable of doing this yourself. Most importantly, you will need to do a lot of research and information gathering. The amount of money you spend on this will depend on your familiarity with the area or travel topics you are covering.

The final cost to set up and run this type of business will range from $5,000 to $40,000 depending on what you believe you need to run it most efficiently. The Web site and database will usually account for at least half of your initial expenses. Once you are set up, you should expect additional costs that are associated with promoting your business online and offline.

Number of Employees Needed to Start

The number of employees needed to start your tourist center depends on how much information you will be managing. This type of business can be started with one person.

International Potential

Although your site visitors will be international, it is likely that your clientele will be local or national depending on the niche you choose to develop.

E-business Model/Payment Processing Method

E-business levels 1 and 2 are most appropriate for this type of business. For more information, see Part 1.

Important Business Issues to Be Addressed

The key to your success in this business is high-quality information and a well laid out Web site.

Since you need to provide a lot of detailed information on various travel destinations, it is necessary that you choose a niche, an area, or a type of travel to cover. Unless you have a huge staff, you won't be able to provide enough up-to-date, quality information for worldwide or even nationwide coverage. By limiting your information coverage, you also gain the advantage of avoiding competing with the larger tourist Web sites.

You might consider giving the tourism locations in your database access to their record for updating purposes. You would provide them with password-controlled access to their record only. This will require additional programming on the front end but will shift some of the maintenance of the records outside your organization.

ONLINE MARKETING TECHNIQUES

Some of the online marketing techniques that would be most effective for promoting this type of business include:

- Develop a comprehensive link strategy. Linking to a wide variety of tourism sites and especially tourism service sites will be a definite benefit for your business. You will also want to generate links to your site from tourism cybermalls directories, meta-indexes, and Web rings.

- Participate in news and discussion groups related to tourism. Remember to include your signature file and a great tagline.

- Providing a section of your site for coupons and discounts for various travel services such as car rentals or hotels could also increase repeat traffic and customer loyalty. You might ask your visitors if they'd like to receive your coupons and discount information as the site is updated.

- Develop a sponsored listings campaign to bid on appropriate keyword phrases with the popular search engines.

- Another good idea to increase customer loyalty is to develop an advice column, travel articles, pictures, or video. High-quality information is guaranteed to draw customers back to your site.

For a more detailed description of these techniques, along with many other effective online marketing methods, I recommend the companion book *101 Ways to Promote Your Web Site*. You can also find tons of free resources at *http://www.susansweeney.com/resources.html*.

ADDITIONAL INCOME

If your Web site is dedicated to a specific type of travel such as adventure tours or hunting, you could sell items related to that type of tourism. For example, you could sell mountain gear for adventure tours or hunting gear for hunting trips. It is important to note that the cost to develop your Web site will increase slightly since you will need to incorporate an e-commerce service. This will also change your e-commerce model from level 1 to level 3.

ONLINE EXAMPLES

Beachcomber.com
http://www.beachcomber.com
A site that contains tourism and travel information for a wide selection of beaches worldwide.

Townnet
http://www.townnet.com
A global list of tourist information with a wide selection of towns and cities.

85. Trade Show Directory

OVERVIEW OF BUSINESS

The trade show industry is a huge business these days. Facilitating the quest for information and providing up-to-date industry news is a great opportunity for you to capitalize on and increase your annual income. If you decide to start this type of business, you can take two approaches. You can tackle the trade show directory in general, listing trade shows and conferences from various industries; or you can take a more targeted approach, focusing on individuals in a specific industry.

You can generate revenue for this type of business in more ways than one. Most important, you can sell advertising on your site for upcoming conferences or to businesses selling products or services related to the various industries that your site might represent. You can sell advertising both via banner advertisements and in a weekly or monthly mail list. You can also consider offering users the ability to register for different trade shows and conferences via your Web site. As a directory, you can also charge conference organizers a fee to have their conference or trade show listed on your site. This type of business provides multiple ways for you to increase your overall revenue.

SKILLS NEEDED

You will need top-notch research skills if you plan to keep on top of everything that's going on in the industry. If you are targeting a specific section of the industry, such as medical trade shows or travel conferences, then it would be extremely appropriate to have a background in that field. Knowledge of various online advertising techniques would also be an asset, as this type of business requires a large number of Web site visitors.

COST TO START THIS BUSINESS

If you decide to launch this type of business, you will have to pay for the development, design, and hosting of your Web site, a high-speed Internet connection, computer hardware, computer software for administration as well as Web-enabled database software, and a printer. If you currently have some of these items, your initial start-up costs will be considerably lower.

Since you will be gathering information about different trade shows and conferences that you will be listing on your site, you can purchase lists of trade shows per sector (often $100 or more per guide) or you can perform the research yourself online. Depending on how extensive a directory you plan to develop, your costs can vary significantly. For example, if you plan to accept online conference registration and provide streaming audio/video Webcasting samples, you will need some e-commerce capabilities as well as additional Web storage and bandwidth. If you plan to set up a mailing list offering different search engine submission techniques, you will have to purchase mailing list software to help you organize and maintain it. You might also want to purchase comprehensive Web traffic analysis software to track the visitors that are coming to your Web site. This information can be used to help encourage potential advertisers to buy advertising on your site and for future marketing purposes. Other costs that you will incur are related to the promotion of your Web site. Estimated cost is $10,000 to $100,000 to start.

NUMBER OF EMPLOYEES NEEDED

You could start this business as a one-person operation.

INTERNATIONAL POTENTIAL

This type of business has more of a national appeal as opposed to international unless your site encompasses a global listing of upcoming conferences and trade shows. Although people from other countries may visit the site to identify upcoming conferences, the site will most likely be of interest to the national market.

E-BUSINESS MODEL/PAYMENT PROCESSING METHOD

E-business level 2 is most appropriate for this type of business. For more information, see Part 1.

IMPORTANT BUSINESS ISSUES TO BE ADDRESSED

You should ensure that your home page has an attractive interface with consistent navigation throughout your site. Also, if some of your trade show listings provide a link out to their site, you should develop the interface so that the visitor doesn't actually leave your site. What you can do is have your advertiser's site appear within a pop-up frame from your site. This enables the visitor to continue to navigate throughout your site without having to click back in his or her browser.

It is important that you constantly look for upcoming conferences, conventions, and trade shows to be listed on your site. Remember that conferences are very time sensitive, so people are not going to want to be listed two weeks before their event. You should try to contact planners six months to a year before their event. This will allow you to provide them with maximum exposure for their event.

People are going to want to have their event listed on your site for one reason—exposure for their event. To ensure that this happens, you are going to have to do whatever you can to promote your business online and offline.

ONLINE MARKETING TECHNIQUES

- Develop links from Web sites, directories, and meta-indexes related to your target market. If you are focusing on a particular industry, you should develop links from as many sites related to that industry as possible. If you are taking a more general approach, you should still do the same, but for each industry. You can also develop links from conference, trade show, and convention directories and link sites.

- Participate in newsgroups and discussion forums related to the industry (or industries) that you are targeting. You can also participate in newsgroups and discussion forums related to convention planning and upcoming event listings. The participants of these newsgroups would be your potential clients and may be interested in having their event listed on your site. Remember to use a cleverly designed signature file with a catchy tagline and a hypertext link that will send newsgroup readers to your site.

- Develop a sponsored listings campaign to bid on appropriate keyword phrases with the popular search engines.

- Launching a monthly newsletter would be a great way for you to stay in touch with your target market. You could send recipients a listing of upcoming conferences pertaining to a particular industry or geographic area, or just upcoming conferences in general. You can also encourage people to visit your site and register for an upcoming trade show. This is a great way to encourage people to visit your site.

For a more detailed description of these techniques, along with many other effective online marketing methods, I recommend the companion book *101 Ways to Promote Your Web Site*. You can also find tons of free resources at *http://www.susansweeney.com/resources.html*.

ADDITIONAL INCOME

To earn additional income for your business, you might consider selling books and other publications related to particular industries. Since potential registrants will be visiting your site because of their interest in a particular topic, they will also be interested in books related to that topic. You can list books for each industry that you are targeting. This would be a great way to earn additional income for your site.

ONLINE EXAMPLES

Tradeshowweek.com
http://www.tradeshowweek.com
A leading online trade show, conference, and training information resource.

TSNN.com
http://www.tsnn.com
A database for the trade show industry, containing data on more than 15,000 trade shows and conferences. They also have data on more than 30,000 seminars.

86. Training/Speaking

OVERVIEW OF BUSINESS

The number of professional speakers and trainers developing an online presence is growing rapidly. Many meeting and event planners are turning to the Internet to research and book a speaker or trainer for their next event. Many business professionals are also looking for professional coaches and trainers to teach them specific trades or skills. Therefore, if you are a professional trainer or speaker, the Internet provides an excellent opportunity for you to generate more income for your business.

There are multiple ways in which you can generate revenue if you are operating this type of online business. If you are a professional speaker or trainer, you can easily promote your services and take bookings online. The latest advancements in Webcasting technology enable speakers to convert traditional videotapings of their offline seminars so that people can easily download and view them on their desktop—for a fee, of course. This is growing in popularity among many trainers and speakers, as it provides a self-generating stream of revenue once the files have been developed and uploaded to your site.

Many speakers and trainers also develop and sell products at their various speaking engagements. Things such as books, video- and audiotapes, and training kits are typically sold at conferences, training seminars, and conventions. These same products can also be sold online directly from your Web site. This provides you with an excellent opportunity to generate additional income for your business.

SKILLS NEEDED

Excellent training or speaking skills are a must for operating this type of business. Professional designations would also be a benefit, as they would enhance the professionalism and credibility of your services.

COST TO START THIS BUSINESS

Initially you will have to pay for the development, design, and hosting of your Web site, computer hardware, computer software, a printer, and a digital camera. If you currently have some of these items, your initial start-up costs will be considerably lower. If you are selling books or related training materials and are considering taking online payments, you will have to pay for the development of your storefront or purchase storefront software. You will also incur all costs associated with setting up your merchant account, which enables you to take online payments. If you decide to offer online training seminars, you will have to pay for their development. Other costs that you will incur are related to the promotion of your Web site. Estimated cost is $10,000 to $60,000 to start.

NUMBER OF EMPLOYEES NEEDED

Approximately one employee is needed to run this operation. If your service requests exceed what you can handle, you may want to hire an additional employee to handle all administrative duties associated with the day-to-day operation of the business.

INTERNATIONAL POTENTIAL

This type of business has very high international potential, as people from all over the world can hire you to come speak at their event or to their employees. Also, if you are offering downloadable training sessions, people can easily download them to their computer to learn from the comfort of their home no matter where they live.

E-BUSINESS MODEL/PAYMENT PROCESSING METHOD

E-business level 3 or 4 would be appropriate for this type of business. For more information, see Part 1.

IMPORTANT BUSINESS ISSUES TO BE ADDRESSED

Since you will be promoting your speaking or training services both offline and online, you should remember to keep your marketing strategies consistent with each other. This means that you should use consistent colors, images, logos, and overall creative strategy when developing all of your marketing pieces. This will create a consistent visual atmosphere for your business. If people read one of your offline brochures and later visit your Web site, they will remember the brochure, and vice versa. This is a great way to keep your business fresh in the minds of your potential customers.

Since clients will be interested in purchasing your services, you should try to do whatever you can to assist them with their decision-making process. Provide them with background on your career, including past training or speaking seminars that you may have delivered, what you currently do, and even a listing of your upcoming training sessions and seminars. All of this information should be accompanied with positive testimonials from past sessions. This will encourage your potential clients to book you for their next event.

ONLINE MARKETING TECHNIQUES

- Launch a strategic banner advertising campaign on Web sites frequented by your target market. These sites could relate to the specific industry that your services target or Web sites targeted toward meeting and event planners. These are the Web sites that your target market will visit on a regular basis.

- Develop as many links as possible from Web sites, directories, and meta-indexes related to your target market. These sites should relate to the industry that you target, meeting and event planning sites, or sites dedicated to professional speakers and trainers.

- Participating in newsgroups and discussion forums related to your area of expertise would be quite effective. Through providing valuable contributions, you will be able to demonstrate your expertise and capture the attention of your target audience. Make sure you include a cleverly designed signature file in all of your postings. This will act as an advertisement for your services.

- Participating in mailing lists related to your target market would be a great way to encourage people to visit your site. Make sure you provide a valuable contribution and include your signature file.

- Develop a sponsored listings campaign to bid on appropriate keyword phrases with the popular search engines.

- You could hold a weekly or monthly contest on your Web site for one of your speaking or training products. You could ask people if they would like to be notified of the winner via e-mail. This e-mail will encourage them to return to your site to re-enter your contest, thus re-exposing them to your site.

For a more detailed description of these techniques, along with many other effective online marketing methods, I recommend the companion book *101 Ways to Promote Your Web Site*. You can also find tons of free resources at *http://www.susansweeney.com/resources.html*.

ADDITIONAL INCOME

If your primary focus is selling your speaking and training services, you could earn additional income from the sale of related products and services. This could include books, audio- and videotapes, and training kits. You could also set up a referral business with businesses offering products or services related to your area of expertise. For example, if you spoke about database management, you could partner with Oracle to promote their database products. You could then receive a percentage of all sales made as a result of your referral.

ONLINE EXAMPLES

Susan Sweeney
http://www.susansweeney.com
A little shameless self-promotion here.

Robin Sharma
http://www.robinsharma.com
This is a dynamite site that has many features including audio and video feeds and online training seminars.

87. Transcript Service

OVERVIEW OF BUSINESS

Transcripts are in high demand, and they are not always easy to obtain. Did you ever listen to a talk radio show, TV news, TV talk show, or important public meeting and notice that at the end they announce that written transcripts of the event are available? Then they tell you how to order. The big national networks and organizations use national transcript services, but who transcribes the smaller, yet not less important, local events? In most locales, the answer is *no one!*

There is a huge opportunity available here—especially for an Internet transcript service. You could make your services open to local radio and TV stations, and political, educational, business, and not-for-profit organizations that would offer a written transcript if they had such a service available to them. Because you are local, you can transcribe these programs and distribute them quickly and efficiently at a low price.

Most of your partners will provide the transcripts for free or at a very low cost in return for your service of handling all the requests and organizational duties associated with making them available—which they are required to do by law.

The cash comes in like this: When orders come in from the Web site, you simply send a copy of the transcript to the customer, who has already included payment with the order. You keep a master copy of each transcript on file to fill future orders. Organizations frequently get calls weeks or months after an event has occurred to inquire about transcript availability.

You can even advertise and offer Internet e-mail service to speed delivery. The opportunities within the media industry are limitless if you employ a little imagination and market your services well to the right market.

SKILLS NEEDED

The transcript service business requires four key ingredients to be successful: excellent keyboard (typing) skills, a good-quality printer, access to a copy machine (or Kinko's or a clone), and a firm connection with organizations that hold transcripts of speeches, meetings, records, and documents that are of value to many people.

Cost to Start This Business

Initially you will have to pay for the development, design, and hosting of your Web site, computer hardware, necessary software, and a high-quality printer. You need desk space, a small table for paper handling, a telephone, and a good filing system. If you currently have some of these items, your initial start-up costs will be considerably lower. You will also incur all costs associated with setting up your merchant account, which enables you to take online payments. Other costs that you will incur are related to the promotion of your Web site. Estimated cost is $5,000 to $12,000 to start.

Number of Employees Needed

One employee is needed to run this operation. If your transcript requests exceed what you can handle, you may want to hire an additional employee to handle all administrative duties associated with the daily operations of the business.

International Potential

The global potential of the transcript service is somewhat limited because there are already large databases of national and international public records available, and these are primarily of interest to the international community. There are chances, however, that people doing research from remote or foreign areas may have a need for the transcripts you provide. Your online marketing reach will determine the international scope of your business.

E-Business Model/Payment Processing Method

E-business level 2 or 3 would be appropriate for this type of business. You will be providing an automated payment processing function associated with the order of transcripts from your site. For more information, see Part 1.

Important Business Issues to Be Addressed

The benefits of this business are small start-up and operational cost, you can work the number of hours and days per week that you choose, there is little competition, there are no employees needed until growth is beyond your capacity, and the business has easy operation with few of the usual start-up headaches.

ONLINE MARKETING TECHNIQUES

- Develop as many links as possible from Web sites, directories, and meta-indexes related to your target market. These sites should relate to the industries to which your transcripts pertain.

- Participating in newsgroups and discussion forums related to the specific issues that are discussed in the transcripts would be quite effective.

- Make sure you include a cleverly designed signature file in all of your postings. This will act as an advertisement for your services.

- Develop and grow a mailing list of all your clients and send out weekly newsletters including highlights of the latest events or minutes that are of interest to them.

- Optimize your site for organic search results. Consider participating in the pay-per-click programs of the popular search engines.

For a more detailed description of these techniques, along with many other effective online marketing methods, I recommend the companion book *101 Ways to Promote Your Web Site*. You can also find tons of free resources at *http://www.susansweeney.com/resources.html*.

ADDITIONAL INCOME

Additional income could come from offering an e-mail reminder service to clients who need to keep informed about certain information, letting them know when important events happen or are about to happen. You could also have banner advertising on your site and offer discounted booklets of transcripts that are fashioned in a linear format and focus on one issue.

ONLINE EXAMPLES

FNS Transcript Search
http://www.fnsg.com/searchfnsx.html
This site is a search tool with several options divided by governmental department. Users may use this site to search for various transcripts that are available to the public and can download or receive them via mail or e-mail.

Datalyst
http://www.datalystcorp.com/services.html
You may search this site for the transcripts you choose and have them mailed to you for a fee.

88. Translation Services

OVERVIEW OF BUSINESS

Are you fluent in two or more languages? Then setting up an online translation business may be appropriate for you. Many people are not fluent in multiple languages, so they have no choice but to outsource their translation activities to an outside firm. This can provide you with an excellent money-making opportunity.

This type of business generates revenue by taking requests for translation services via the Web and receiving a fee for providing the services. The translation software on the Web today is typically a one-time sale, which can offer a word-by-word translation but cannot get the meaning across as well as a human translator can. This means your personal translation services will be in high demand for businesses that want to present themselves professionally and are not afraid to pay for it. It will not be difficult to stress the added benefits of having a personal translator to quality clients.

It is said that the Internet language is English, but this is not entirely true. To globalize any online business, operators must consider the languages of their target markets and make their site understandable to the whole array to ensure success. Providing translation services is a promising venture.

SKILLS NEEDED

The capability to effectively communicate orally and in written format in two or more languages is essential to operate this type of business. You will need basic Web publishing skills to update and maintain your Web site.

COST TO START THIS BUSINESS

Initially you will have to pay for the development, design, and hosting of your Web site, computer hardware, computer software (including any translation software that you might need to assist you), and a printer. If you currently have some of these items, your initial start-up costs will be considerably lower. Other costs that you will incur are related to the promotion of your Web site. Estimated cost is $3,000 to $5,000 to start.

NUMBER OF EMPLOYEES NEEDED TO START

Approximately one talented and organized employee is needed to run this operation. If your service requests exceed what you can handle, you may want to hire an additional translator.

INTERNATIONAL POTENTIAL

This type of business has very high international potential. In most cases, companies need information translated for international reasons.

E-BUSINESS MODEL/PAYMENT PROCESSING METHOD

E-business level 1 would be appropriate for this type of business. For more information, see Part 1.

IMPORTANT BUSINESS ISSUES TO BE ADDRESSED

The main issues you need to be concerned with are reinforcing the privacy and security of materials entrusted to you by your client and how delivery of pre-translated and translated materials will be dealt with. How can you make your clients comfortable with entrusting sensitive materials with you? Do you want to transfer materials back and forth electronically by e-mail? By CD? All formats? Or do you want to stick to traditional hardcopy distribution? Whatever you decide, you should ensure that it is in the best interest of your client's privacy.

Since mainly businesses will be interested in your services, you should attempt to have your business listed on as many business services-oriented Web sites as possible. These are the sites that people are going to visit if they are interested in your services. There are thousands of service directories online. You should attempt to develop links from as many of these sites as possible.

ONLINE MARKETING TECHNIQUES

- Launch a strategic banner advertising campaign on Web sites frequented by your target market. These sites could relate to international business or business services where visitors would be interested in your target market.

- Develop as many links as possible from Web sites, directories, and meta-indexes related to your target market. These sites should relate to international business, business services, or just business in general.

- Develop a sponsored listings campaign to bid on appropriate keyword phrases with the popular search engines.

- Make sure your site is optimized for organic search engine placement.

- Participating in newsgroups and discussion forums related to business would be quite effective. Make sure that any message postings that you make provide a valuable contribution to the group. To generate traffic to your site, include a cleverly designed signature file with a catchy tagline in all of your postings. An "Ask Us about Our Translation Services" tag line could be quite effective.

For a more detailed description of these techniques, along with many other effective online marketing methods, I recommend the companion book *101 Ways to Promote Your Web Site*. You can also find tons of free resources at *http://www.susansweeney.com/resources.html*.

ADDITIONAL INCOME

If your primary focus is providing translation services, then your additional income could come from the software or related tools you sell. You could also consider offering bilingual copy-writing services to firms looking to advertise in foreign countries. This would be a great way to earn additional income.

ONLINE EXAMPLES

Click2Translate.com
http://www.click2translate.com
This is a dynamite translation services business. They offer a "translation tips" section, which is a great repeat traffic builder for their site (Figure 2.16).

The Language Bank, Inc
http://www.language-bank.com
A full-service document translation and interpretation company, they offer full translation services including basic translations, e-mail translations, Web design, and voiceover translations for audio and video.

Figure 2.16. Click2Translate.com is an online translation service business.

89. Travel Consultant

OVERVIEW OF BUSINESS MODEL

The nature of the travel consulting industry is ideally suited to the Internet. In every country, many people are interested in traveling to foreign destinations. With the Internet's widespread reputation for information and international access, it is only natural that tourists will look first to the Internet for information. Many individuals enjoy working with a travel consultant to plan their vacation. Also, many travel agencies today are hiring consultants who work from home to complete research, planning, and reservation tasks via e-mail. This business has a low cost of entry and a high profit potential.

Online travel consultants provide a wide variety of services for their customers. Usually you will be providing clients with an organized travel plan including travel arrangements, car rental reservations at the destination, and accommodation reservations. Occasionally, customers will also want a completely planned itinerary with a list of things to do, tour companies, and popular sites to see in the area. Your reports or itineraries should have competitive rates for all expenses involved due to the highly competitive environment of the online travel market. The information should be comprehensive and full of choices so that your clients understand the value of your service as an online travel expert. Revenue is usually generated from a commission that comes from the hotels and car rental agencies you work with, the travel agencies you are affiliated with, and the tour operators.

SKILLS NEEDED

Familiarity with the travel industry naturally is required to start this business. You will also need clear communication skills, telephone skills, e-mail skills, and basic Web publishing skills to update your Web site.

COST TO START THIS BUSINESS

If you already have a "real-world" travel consultant business, then your main cost will be to design, develop, and host your Web site. This will cost you between $2,000 and $10,000 depending on the functions of the site and the service you want to provide. You will need software programs and a T1 or cable connection to join the main travel intranets and booking networks. This will increase the initial cost by $5,000 to $10,000.

NUMBER OF EMPLOYEES NEEDED TO START

The online travel consulting business can be operated by one experienced person from home.

INTERNATIONAL POTENTIAL

Generating international business is an integral part of this business concept. International travel has always been a multi-billion-dollar industry. It's only natural, given the international marketing potential of the Internet, that the tourism industry would have a strong online presence. Language and the specialty of your travel knowledge are the only foreseeable barriers.

E-BUSINESS MODEL/PAYMENT PROCESSING METHOD

E-business level 1 is most appropriate for this type of business; however, if you are going to be taking online reservations or selling travel merchandise online, then you will need to use a level 3 or level 4 business model. For more information, see Part 1.

IMPORTANT BUSINESS ISSUES TO BE ADDRESSED

Since the Internet is such a natural step for a travel consulting business, competition is fierce. It is very important to have a well-executed set of services and a robust Web site with plenty of resources, testimonials, and content. Your service should be timely and reliable, with competitive pricing.

Having an expertise in a particular type of travel experience or area is a good idea at this stage in the online travel business. For example, if you became an expert on planning outdoor adventures in the highlands of Mexico, you have targeted a niche and you become more valuable to travel agencies who get this request and do not have the information or expertise to produce the itinerary that the client desires.

ONLINE MARKETING TECHNIQUES

- Develop a comprehensive link strategy. Generate as many links as possible from appropriate travel-related Web sites, cybermalls, directories, Web rings, and meta-indexes.

- Develop a contest area of your site where a winner is drawn weekly. By sending a winner notification e-mail to all contestants, you get your name in front of their eyes on a regular basis. Companies you recommend from your site or suppliers you use on a regular basis can supply the prizes. In the notification e-mail, you can also encourage visitors to enter this week's contest. This will bring them back to your site.

- Reward or loyalty programs could be used to generate repeat customers. This is especially useful for frequent flyers.

- Viral marketing can be an excellent way to draw in a satisfied customer's family and friends. Using the "Tell a Friend about This Site" or "This Contest" or "This Special" techniques all would be effective in having others spread the word about your site.

- Publish articles about travel experiences that you have planned in travel e-zines that appeal to your target market, with links to your Web site.

- Develop a sponsored listings campaign to bid on appropriate keyword phrases with the popular search engines.

- Have client testimonials with pictures of their vacation included on your Web site.

For a more detailed description of these techniques, along with many other effective online marketing methods, I recommend the companion book *101 Ways to Promote Your Web Site*. You can also find tons of free resources at *http://www.susansweeney.com/resources.html*.

ADDITIONAL INCOME

Should you wish to augment your income, a travel consulting business offers many opportunities. Most governments spend a great deal of money on tourism advertising. With a well-executed banner ad campaign, you could draw in government sponsors.

If your services are targeted toward a type of tourism that requires special equipment (e.g., scuba diving or mountain climbing), then you could sell the equipment through your Web site.

ONLINE EXAMPLES

Onlinetravel.com
http://www.onlinetravel.com
A large travel consultant site that functions in much the same way as its real-world counterparts. The site concentrates on students and young travelers.

InTourNet
http://www.intournet.co.il
Both a travel brochure and a consultant firm for a few Mediterranean countries.

90. T-Shirt Design

OVERVIEW OF BUSINESS

People are always looking for T-shirts for various events, teams, clubs, and associations. If you have a knack for graphic design and are into pulling together artistic pieces of work, then this business may be for you. You might consider doing custom designs, selling designs from a predetermined catalogue, or allowing people to purchase completed T-shirts.

This type of business can generate significant revenue if you offer quality products at competitive prices. There is lots of competition for this type of business; however, if you keep your customers happy, provide something a little different, underpromise and overdeliver, they will generate repeat business for your business. For example, if a baseball team has you design shirts for their team, they will come back to you year after year if you continue to offer them a quality product at a good price. This type of business is extremely customer-oriented, as its growth is highly dependent on customer retention.

SKILLS NEEDED

A strong entrepreneurial background would be a benefit to operating this type of business. Excellent graphic design skills and knowledge of how to screen T-shirts would also be an asset.

COST TO START THIS BUSINESS

Initially you will have to pay for the development, design, and hosting of your Web site, computer hardware, computer software, a scanner, a printer, and possibly a digital camera so that you can take photos of your T-shirts on live models. If you currently have some of these items, your initial start-up costs will be considerably lower. You will also have to purchase T-shirts in bulk and a T-shirt screening machine for the production of your products. If you have a catalogue for the offline promotion of your business, you will have to pay for the design, printing, and distribution of your catalog to potential clients. Other costs that you will incur are related to the promotion of your Web site. Estimated cost is $10,000 to $35,000 to start.

NUMBER OF EMPLOYEES NEEDED

Approximately one dedicated full-time employee is needed to operate this type of business. If requests escalate, you may need to hire an additional employee.

INTERNATIONAL POTENTIAL

There is minimal international potential. The cost to ship T-shirts overseas in the volumes you would likely prefer would make competition against foreign companies difficult. If you are simply selling digital image design, there is some international potential.

E-BUSINESS MODEL/PAYMENT PROCESSING METHOD

E-business level 1 would be most appropriate for this type of business. For more information, see Part 1.

IMPORTANT BUSINESS ISSUES TO BE ADDRESSED

If you decide to print and distribute a catalogue, you should ensure that the catalogue is designed effectively. You may want to outsource a portion of this activity to a professional. The catalogue has to be designed with appropriate layout, colors, contact information, and incentives. You should also ensure that the contact list of potential clients to whom you are sending your information is accurate and up-to-date. If you don't, this could result in the failure of a direct-marketing campaign.

Since this is such a customer-oriented business, you should do whatever you can to make your customers happy. This could be anything from meeting customer demands before they are due to simply calling to thank them for their business. If you are printing T-shirts for a club or team, you should call them two or three months before their season opens to see if they would be interested in having new T-shirts designed. This would be a great way to build loyal relationships with your customers, which in turn will create repeat business for your T-shirt company.

ONLINE MARKETING TECHNIQUES

- Develop a comprehensive link strategy. Generate links to your site from appropriate product-related Web sites, directories, Web rings, and cybermalls.

- Consider a targeted banner advertising campaign on sites that appeal to your target market.

- Participating in newsgroups and discussion forums related to your target market would be a great way to generate traffic to your Web site. These could be association, club, or special-event newsgroups where participants may be interested in your services.

- Develop a viral marketing strategy where people can "Send This T-Shirt Design to a Friend" via your site. This will spread the word about your site.

- You could hold a weekly or monthly contest on your Web site for a free T-shirt, or a discount on the next purchase of a particular quantity of T-shirts. You could ask people if they would like to be notified of the winner via e-mail. This e-mail will encourage them to return to your site to re-enter your contest, thus re-exposing them to your site.

- Develop a sponsored listings campaign to bid on appropriate keyword phrases with the popular search engines.

- You should develop a mail list that features information on your latest T-shirt designs. This would be a great way to keep in touch with your potential and current clients. It would also keep your services fresh in their minds when they decide to have more T-shirts developed.

For a more detailed description of these techniques, along with many other effective online marketing methods, I recommend the companion book *101 Ways to Promote Your Web Site*. You can also find tons of free resources at *http://www.susansweeney.com/resources.html*.

Additional Income

If you enjoy graphic design, you could make additional income by doing other forms of freelance graphic design. You could also sell custom hats, jackets, and so on. This would be a great way to earn additional income for your business.

Online Examples

Custom Ink
http://www.customink.com/services/online-t-shirt-design.htm
Custom Ink gives you an easy way to design your own T-shirts. The online design lab makes it easy to visualize exactly what your custom order will look like.

Djtees.com
http://www.djtees.com/tshop/store/index.asp
A funky full-service site that concentrates on the rock music culture and lets you design your own shirts online.

91. Tutoring Services

OVERVIEW OF BUSINESS MODEL

Online tutors are often sought after in today's high-paced learning environment. If you are a teacher or tutor, taking your services online is an effective way of making extra income or even creating a full-time position from the comfort of your home. You can also provide the tutoring services offline but do your business promotion online.

The Web is a perfect place to showcase and provide this service. Clients can communicate with you through e-mail, telephone, voice chat, or an instant messenger service such as MSN. They can also send their projects, essays, and assignments to you for critique via e-mail attachment, and you can give them timely response and guidance. Your primary source of revenue will come from the hourly rate you charge your clients.

SKILLS NEEDED

You will need experience in tutoring or an expertise in a subject that traditionally requires a tutor, such as calculus. Having clear and concise communication skills is very important, and you should be able to update your business Web site, so basic Web publishing skills are needed.

COST TO START THIS BUSINESS

Your initial setup costs will include a personal computer and the appropriate software programs that students use, a printer, and a fax machine. You will also need to pay for the design, development, and hosting of your Web site. The cost to set up and run this type of business ranges from $2,500 to $5,000.

NUMBER OF EMPLOYEES NEEDED TO START

This business can easily be started with one part-time individual.

INTERNATIONAL POTENTIAL

The international reach of this service is dependent on language and the subject you specialize in. For instance, if you tutor world history students, your global potential is higher than if you specialize in ebonics.

E-BUSINESS MODEL/PAYMENT PROCESSING METHOD

E-business level 1 is most appropriate for this type of business. For more information, see Part 1.

Important Business Issues to Be Addressed

This business has a low cost of entry, and there are a fair number of tutors operating online already. The good news is that most of the sites offer access to a staff of tutors but do not specialize in any one subject. This indicates that there are subjects needing more attention. Before deciding how to diversify your tutoring services, be sure to investigate which subjects are not being provided in an online venue. To ensure that you generate a dedicated audience or client base, you may want to target your services toward a specific niche of people in need of tutelage.

Online Marketing Techniques

- Develop a comprehensive link strategy. Negotiating and reciprocating links from other, related sites is an excellent way to bring targeted business to your Web site. You will want to be linked from sites that cater to your target market. Establish links from educational, university, and college sites, library sites, and academic research directories.

- Register your site throughout the search engines. Make sure your site is designed to be search engine friendly before submission.

- Include a few great testimonials on your site from students you have helped in the past.

- You might also consider using a viral marketing technique like "Tell a Friend." This will allow your clients to easily refer your services to their friends.

- Create a mailing list of all your clients and potential subscribers of your service, and use it to send out regular newsletters with helpful tips on studying, essay writing, and various academic practices.

For a more detailed description of these techniques, along with many other effective online marketing tips, tools, techniques, and resources, I recommend the companion book *101 Ways to Promote Your Web Site*. You can also find tons of free resources at *http://www.susansweeney.com/resources.html*.

Additional Income

Additional income can come from banner advertising if the traffic levels are high on your Web site. There is also an opportunity to become a reseller or

Figure 2.17. Tutor.com is an excellent example of a business offering online tutoring services.

affiliate site for suppliers of products and services that would interest the students who frequent your site.

ONLINE EXAMPLES

Tutor.com
http://www.tutor.com
Tutor.com (Figure 2.17) offers the tools you need to train your employees and students online and employs a staff of tutors to render this service.

Info Math
http://www.infomath.com/html/online-tutor.asp
This business provides one-on-one personalized tutoring services for students in kindergarten through college, with emphasis on developing students' problem-solving skills.

92. Used Computer Sales

OVERVIEW OF BUSINESS MODEL
Many people who cannot afford to purchase a brand-new computer buy second-hand, so why not take advantage of this opportunity? By starting your

own online used-computer store, you can tap into this market and make quite a bit of revenue for your business. You can operate this business in one of two ways: (1) You can purchase used computers and computer parts and sell the refurbished computers directly from your site, or (2) you can allow others to post classified ads on your site. You can decide which business model is most appropriate for you, depending on your knowledge of computers, your budget, and your online marketing objectives.

It is important to remember that if you want to sell computer parts on your site, you are going to have to keep computer components in stock. This means that you will have higher inventory costs. To avoid this, you should look for deals on used computer components all the time. You could even offer to purchase components from consumers directly from your physical location. The better the deals you get on your inventory, the higher your profit margin will be.

SKILLS NEEDED
Knowledge of computer assembly is a must for operating this type of business.

COST TO START THIS BUSINESS
Initially you will have to pay for the development, design, and hosting of your Web site, computer hardware, computer software, a scanner, a printer, and possibly a digital camera so that you can take photos of your computer products. If you currently have some of these items, your initial start-up costs will be considerably lower. If you decide to sell computer products, you will have to keep inventory on hand. If you decide simply to allow others to post ads on your site, you will eliminate the costs of keeping inventory on hand. Other costs that you will incur are related to the promotion of your Web site. Estimated cost is $5,000 to $50,000 to start.

NUMBER OF EMPLOYEES NEEDED
One dedicated full-time employee is needed to operate this type of business.

INTERNATIONAL POTENTIAL
This online business has strong international potential, as its products are of interest to consumers across the globe. However, it might not be worth selling products to consumers in certain countries due to shipping costs, customs regulations, tax regulations, and currency exchange rates.

E-BUSINESS MODEL/PAYMENT PROCESSING METHOD
E-business level 1 would be most appropriate for this type of business if you are simply selling online classified ads to others. However, if you are going to be selling used computers directly from your site, you are going to want to use e-business level 3 or 4. For more information, see Part 1.

Important Business Issues to Be Addressed

When purchasing and selling used computer parts, you should always ensure that the parts work correctly. Nothing will hurt your image more than if you sell faulty computer parts to a customer. To avoid this, test all equipment before you ship it to your customers. Dedicating time to this activity will benefit you in the long run.

Since computers are fragile pieces of equipment, you should package all of your products securely before you ship them to your clients. This will ensure that they are not damaged during the shipping process. If they are, you could be held responsible. This could not only destroy your corporate image, but also hurt your bottom line.

Since you may be shipping your computers across country borders, you should ensure that there are no trade regulations that would make you have to pay more to export your products to another country. Sometimes it is so costly that it isn't beneficial for businesses to offer their products in certain countries.

Online Marketing Techniques

- Develop a comprehensive link strategy. Generate as many links as possible from appropriate Web sites, directories, and meta-indexes frequented by your target market. These sites will include all used-computer and computer sales-related sites online.

- Participating in newsgroups would be a great way to increase the traffic to your Web site. You can participate in newsgroups related to computers and technology. Make sure to use a cleverly designed signature file with a catchy tagline. Perhaps it could say "Check Out Our Latest Sales" or some variation of this phrase.

- Developing a mail list would be a great way to stay in touch with your visitors. You could have a Computer Tips newsletter that could be distributed monthly to all of your subscribers. This would be a great way to encourage visitors to return to your site and would also help enhance the professionalism of your site.

- Develop a sponsored listings campaign to bid on appropriate keyword phrases with the popular search engines.

- You could have a Specials page on your site where you list your monthly computer specials. You could ask people if they would like to be notified via e-mail when you make updates to your site. This will encourage your visitors to come back to your Web site.

For a more detailed description of these techniques, along with many other effective online marketing methods, I recommend the companion book *101 Ways to Promote Your Web Site*. You can also find tons of free resources at *http://www.susansweeney.com/resources.html*.

ADDITIONAL INCOME

In addition to selling computers or computer classifieds on your site, you might also consider selling software to consumers or setting up a referral business with software companies. This would allow you to make a percentage from every referral that these companies receive from your Web site.

ONLINE EXAMPLES

123Compute.com
http://www.123compute.com
This is a dynamite site that sells used computers and notebooks to consumers in Canada and the United States.

Comprenew.com
http://www.comprenew.com
Comprenew.com is a company that specializes in selling used computer parts and systems.

93. Virtual Assistant

OVERVIEW OF BUSINESS MODEL

Hiring a "virtual assistant" is becoming extremely popular in today's workplace environment. Many companies will seek the use of a virtual assistant service when they cannot afford or do not have the workload to sustain a full-time in-house staff member. Other companies look for suppliers of this type of service during the summer, when many people are out on vacation, in order to take care of the workload. Other companies simply have too much work to be done by existing staff from time to time and need the assistance of an off-site assistant to handle some of the workload. As more and more home-based businesses are springing up, the need for this type of service is going to increase.

This is an ideal niche market to penetrate as an online business. There is a huge demand for online virtual assistant services. You will charge for your services by the hour, by contract for the job, or on a monthly retainer basis. This is one of the easiest and least expensive businesses to start online.

Skills Needed

Excellent keyboarding skills are an invaluable asset. Oral and written communications skills are also very important as your clients will demand quality work, and you will be communicating with your clients on a regular basis. In addition, an understanding of today's widely used business applications is a must.

Cost to Start This Business

Initially you will have to pay for the design, development, and hosting of your Web site, computer hardware, computer software, a scanner, a fax machine, and a printer. If you currently have some of these items, your initial start-up costs will be reduced accordingly. Other costs that you will incur are related to the promotion of your business. Estimated cost is $3,000 to $5,000 to start.

Number of Employees Needed to Start

One person can easily start this business on a part-time basis.

International Potential

This business has little international potential. A majority of your clients will be based in your immediate geographic area.

E-Business Model/Payment Processing Method

E-business level 1 or 2 would be appropriate for this type of business, depending on whether or not you want to directly accept payment for your services online. For more information, see Part 1. Your client will likely want a report of the work you have actually completed for him or her prior to submitting payment, making level 1 the more appropriate choice, as payment would be negotiated prior to, and delivered after completion of, the work.

Important Business Issues to Be Addressed

One important issue you need to address is compatibility with the software your client uses. You do not want to put your effort into developing an electronic report only to find out your client cannot open it. Find out what software your client prefers beforehand.

Online Marketing Techniques

- Develop a comprehensive link strategy. You will want to generate as many links as possible from appropriate Web sites, directories, Web rings, and meta-indexes related to your target market. Find all the business service sites for your local market and get linked from as many as possible.

- Promotion through related mail lists and newsletters is important. You may even develop your own newsletter or mail list to stay close to your target market.

- Ensure that you submit your site to the search engines and directories. Because many of your clients will likely be regional, be sure to get yourself listed in any regional online business directories that your target market may frequent.

- Develop a viral marketing strategy where people can "Tell a Colleague about This Service" via your site. This will spread the word about your site.

For a more detailed description of these techniques, along with many other effective online marketing methods, I recommend the companion book *101 Ways to Promote Your Web Site*. You can also find tons of free resources at *http://www.susansweeney.com/resources.html*.

Additional Income

You could earn extra money by performing value-added services such as scanning services or printing services. You could charge a per-page fee for either service. You could provide desktop publishing services, newsletter content development and distribution services, bookkeeping services, telephone answering services, and any other administrative services needed by home-based businesses.

Online Examples

Virtual Assistant
http://www.virtualofficeassistant.com
A number of services are offered including word processing, data processing, publishing, scheduling, and mailings.

Office To-Go
http://www.officeto-go.com
A secretarial, transcription, and office support service. Some of their services include desktop publishing, proofreading, resumes, and fax services.

94. Virtual Makeover

OVERVIEW OF BUSINESS MODEL

This business is ideal for someone with an interest in cosmetics, beauty consulting, and fashion. Today's digital-imaging software and hardware (affordable digital cameras and scanners) allow for exciting makeover previews. Currently some virtual makeover sites are charging a fee for the makeover, whereas others are offering to do the makeover for free if the user sends in a picture via e-mail or a photograph in the mail. There is also a software program made by Cosmopolitan that users can download and try for themselves.

The opportunity for selling your products and beauty services exists once the user has engaged in a dialogue with you through the Web site. While giving thoughtful beauty and fashion advice to your users, you have the perfect opportunity to up-sell the services and the products you advertise on your site. Additional revenue will be generated through banner advertising, sponsorship, and affiliate program revenue.

SKILLS NEEDED

To run this business, you will need computer skills. You should know how to use a digital camera, a scanner, imaging software such as Adobe Photoshop, and the virtual makeover software, which is cutting edge and available now. You will need concise writing skills and experience in beauty and fashion consulting.

COST TO START THIS BUSINESS

The start-up cost of this online venture will include a computer, a scanner, a digital camera, and appropriate software to produce the virtual makeovers. Initial costs will also include the cost of the design, development, and hosting of your Web site. It is projected that the start-up costs will be between $4,500 and $12,000. If you already have a computer and related hardware, then deduct from this price estimate accordingly.

NUMBER OF EMPLOYEES NEEDED TO START

One talented beauty- and fashion-oriented person can start this business on a part-time basis from home.

INTERNATIONAL POTENTIAL

The global potential is high for this venture. You can market your site to the entire Web, and your users can interact with you and buy your products from anywhere in the world.

E-BUSINESS MODEL/PAYMENT PROCESSING METHOD

The initial e-business level recommended for the virtual makeover site is level 1 because it's likely that you will be offering beauty consulting and showcasing products from suppliers that you are affiliated with. For more information, see Part 1. There is significant opportunity for earning commissions from the purchases that your users make once they click off your site onto a beauty or fashion e-store because of the sophisticated affiliate tracking software on the Web today.

IMPORTANT BUSINESS ISSUES TO BE ADDRESSED

The beauty and fashion business is competitive, but there is good news. Women represent 50 percent of overall browsers on the Internet, and reports indicate that not nearly enough satisfying content exists for this demographic. Also, clothing shopping is gaining popularity quickly, especially around Christmas. There is a void to be filled. Your site should be highly interactive and tastefully designed, with many useful resources regarding beauty and fashion issues. You should join the affiliate programs of suppliers of the products you recommend on your site. This will increase the revenue generated from your site.

ONLINE MARKETING TECHNIQUES

To market this business online, you should research your target audience carefully. You will want to access women with an interest in getting a makeover and who have purchasing power. There are various ways to do this, and here are some suggestions:

- You could hold a weekly or monthly contest on your Web site for a free product offered by one of your vendors. The vendor donating the product could be your Featured Vendor. You could ask people if they would like to be notified of the winner via e-mail. This e-mail will encourage them to return to your site to re-enter next month's contest, thus re-exposing them to your site.

- Develop a viral marketing strategy where users can "Tell Your Friends about This Site" via a link on your site. This will spread the word about your virtual makeover site.

- Design your site to be search engine friendly. Consider participating in pay-per-click programs with the popular search engines.

- Develop articles for distribution in fashion and women's e-zines. Be sure to provide full contact information and a link to your site.

- Register your site throughout the major search engines and focus on directory sites that have content and links to sites that are of particular interest to 20- to 50-year-old women and teens.

- Negotiate as many links as possible from Web sites, directories, and meta-indexes related to your target market. These sites should relate to the specific products and interests of teens and beauty- and fashion-conscious women.

For a more detailed description of these techniques, along with many other effective online marketing methods, I recommend the companion book *101 Ways to Promote Your Web Site.* You can also find tons of free resources at *http://www.susansweeney.com/resources.html.*

ADDITIONAL INCOME

Additional income can come from advertising if your virtual makeover site has high traffic and interactivity. If you are interested in providing actual hands-on beauty and fashion consulting services to potential clients within your immediate area, you can initiate your contact with them over the Web by providing the free virtual makeover and consultation, and then offer your personalized services.

ONLINE EXAMPLES

Makeover Solutions
http://www.makeoversolutions.com/makeover/virtualMakeover.jsp
You send in a head shot of yourself in JPEG form or you can use a head shot of one of their models, and they will show you various looks to help you decide on a new do.

Beautyriot.com
http://www.beautyriot.com/instant_makeover.php
This site is designed to give you a chance to see what you would look like with one of your favorite celebrity's hairstyles.

95. Web Design

OVERVIEW OF BUSINESS MODEL

Web designers are considered modern artists, and they are becoming a necessity for the survival of small businesses and large corporations alike. Web designers are the original designers of a Web site.

Web designers are different from Web masters in several important ways. The designer has a creative graphical sense that allows him or her to design an entity that is attractive, useful, and representative of a specific product, service, topic, or idea. The designer is not usually involved in the marketing aspect or traffic generation of a site the way a Web master is.

There are several ways that Web designers create business relationships with clients. They may charge by the hour and price the work by the level of difficulty, they may charge a contract price for specific work, or they may work full-time for one client on a contract basis.

SKILLS NEEDED

Web designers need to know HTML language and how to access virtual servers in order to update clients' Web sites. Graphic design capabilities and knowledge of other multimedia programming languages such as Macromedia Flash and Java are a must in today's designing world. Knowing other programming languages such as Perl, CGI, and database management would greatly increase your value as a Web designer. The truth is that knowing all these languages is extremely time-consuming, and the best idea is to work on building a certain set of skills and keeping on top of the developing technologies within that scope so that you can claim an expertise.

COST TO START THIS BUSINESS

Because you are a Web designer, you shouldn't need to outsource the development and design of your Web site. You will need to pay for the hosting. Software will be the main start-up expense. Programs like Dreamweaver, Front Page, Adobe Photoshop, and so on, are needed. Estimated cost is $3,000 to start.

NUMBER OF EMPLOYEES NEEDED TO START

The number of employees needed to run this type of business is one dedicated Web designer, and you can start this venture while keeping your regular job.

INTERNATIONAL POTENTIAL

This business has strong international potential. Often clients prefer to know their Web designer because there is an element of trust involved when you give out the FTP passwords to your Web site. It's highly possible to work while you travel, however, and meet with your clients from time to time.

E-BUSINESS MODEL/PAYMENT PROCESSING METHOD

E-business level 1 or 2 would be appropriate for this type of business. In the starting phases, it's likely that you will receive payment from your clients in the form of a check, cash, or money order. For more information, see Part 1.

IMPORTANT BUSINESS ISSUES TO BE ADDRESSED

The Web design industry is very competitive. Web designers are chosen based on talent. You should ensure that you have a great portfolio. You should provide links out to sites you have designed and developed, allowing site visitors to judge for themselves the quality of your work.

ONLINE MARKETING TECHNIQUES

- Include a portfolio on your site with all your past projects that show your accomplishments and awards as a Web designer.

- Include testimonials from your clients on your site.

- Develop a comprehensive link strategy. You want to get as many links as possible from appropriate Web sites, directories, and meta-indexes related to your target market. There are thousands of Web site development-related sites on the Internet that would provide a great linking opportunity for your site. You should also attempt to develop links from business service sites and directories. These sites will provide highly targeted traffic to your site.

- Participate in newsgroups and discussion forums related to Web development and business services. Remember to use a cleverly designed signature file, a catchy tagline and hypertext link that will send readers to your site.

- Providing valuable contributions to Web design-related mail lists and e-zines would be a great way to create exposure for your business. Again, a cleverly designed signature file with a catchy tagline would be a great way to send traffic to your site.

- Develop a sponsored listings campaign to bid on appropriate keyword phrases with the popular search engines.

- Hosting your own Web design advice column for up-and-coming Web designers would be a great way to encourage repeat traffic to your site. You could offer advice related to using specific software programs or about different design techniques. You could ask people if they would like to be notified via e-mail whenever you update your advice column. This will encourage people to return to your site to view your latest advice.

For a more detailed description of these techniques, along with many other effective online marketing methods, I recommend the companion book *101 Ways to Promote Your Web Site*. You can also find tons of free resources at *http://www.susansweeney.com/resources.html*.

ADDITIONAL INCOME

Web designers can get into many online pursuits because they create the entities on the Web. There are many avenues for additional income, such as graphic design, project management, and getting hired by a design house.

ONLINE EXAMPLES

Verb Interactive
http://www.verbinteractive.com
A full-service Web development and Internet marketing company.

Compucast Web Design
http://compucast.com
A large design house.

Blue Cat Web Design
http://www.bluecatdesign.com
A funky and small design company.

96. Web Master

OVERVIEW OF BUSINESS MODEL

Web masters are becoming a necessity for the survival of small businesses and large corporations alike. Web masters are sometimes the original designers of the sites they maintain, but the term *Web master* throughout the new media industry also means a person who has the ability to edit and manage several Web sites.

Web masters may be responsible for updating and maintaining a site, or they may be responsible for running specific elements of a Web site such as the affiliate program. Web masters may take a contract to provide Internet marketing services for a particular client to promote its Web site through newsgroups and mail lists. For another client, they may choose to help them achieve higher placement in the search engines.

There are several ways that Web masters define business relationships with clients. You can have a specific contract to provide services for a set fee, you may charge by the hour and price the work by the level of difficulty, or you may be working full-time for one client. The ways in which Web masters operate are still being defined in the industry, but it seems we will see more and more Web masters.

SKILLS NEEDED

Web masters definitely need to know the HTML programming language and how to access virtual servers in order to update clients' Web sites as a benchmark. Graphic design capabilities and knowledge of other multimedia programming languages such as Macromedia Flash, Java, Perl, CGI, and others will increase your value as a Web master. Knowledge of Internet marketing techniques is a must.

COST TO START THIS BUSINESS

Because you are a Web master, you shouldn't need to outsource the development and design of your Web site. You will need to pay for the hosting. Software will be one of the main start-up expenses. Programs like Dreamweaver, Front Page, Adobe Photoshop, and so on, are needed. You will need a computer, a printer, a scanner, and a digital camera. High-speed Internet access is a must. Estimated cost is $3,000 to $15,000 to start.

NUMBER OF EMPLOYEES NEEDED TO START

The number of employees needed to run this type of business is one organized Web master, and you can start off working part-time from home.

INTERNATIONAL POTENTIAL

This business has strong international potential. Most clients prefer to know their Web master because there is an element of trust involved when you work with FTP access to their Web site. It's highly possible to work while you travel, however, and meet with your clients from time to time.

E-BUSINESS MODEL/PAYMENT PROCESSING METHOD

E-business level 1 or 2 would be appropriate for this type of business. For more information, see Part 1.

IMPORTANT BUSINESS ISSUES TO BE ADDRESSED

In the Web master business world, contracts are the top priority within the scope of business issues. The industry is quite competitive because the entry-level skills such as HTML are easy to learn and there are many people calling themselves Web masters who will work for very little.

Make sure you carefully define your responsibilities and pricing with your clients, and be aware of their learning curve while explaining to them the value of your services and the importance of hiring a Web master who delivers quality work for fair prices.

Passwords are the only security a Web site has, so make sure you respect this during and even after your contract is completed.

ONLINE MARKETING TECHNIQUES

- Include a portfolio on your site with all your past projects and include testimonials about your service from your clients.

- Enter your work into design contests online and post any awards you may receive on an awards page.

- Optimize your site for organic search placement. Consider participating in the major search engine pay-per-click campaigns.

- Develop a comprehensive link strategy. Generate as many links to your site from appropriate Web sites, directories, business service cybermalls, and meta-indexes as possible.

- Join online communities and networking groups of other Web masters.

For a more detailed description of these techniques, along with many other effective online marketing methods, I recommend the companion book *101 Ways to Promote Your Web Site*. You can also find tons of free resources at *http://www.susansweeney.com/resources.html*.

ADDITIONAL INCOME

You could generate additional income by expanding your skill set to include graphic design and online marketing techniques. This would increase your value as a Web master, and if your service is professional and fairly priced, you will enjoy longer contracts with your clients.

ONLINE EXAMPLES

Metasphere
http://www.metasphere.net
Offers competitive Web master services.

Clocktower Media
http://www.clocktowermedia.com/webmaster.cfm
Offers a range of expertise in order to satisfy all of your online business needs.

97. Web Radio

OVERVIEW OF BUSINESS MODEL

More and more people are listening to real-time audio streams broadcast over the Internet while they're working or relaxing. This is known as Web radio. Web radio has seen growth due to the falling costs of technology, the wide acceptance of the Internet, and the increase in high-speed access.

Many radio stations now broadcast their signal over the Internet for all to listen to. They combine the power of today's technology, their Web site, and their traditional programming to optimize operations. This increases their geographic reach from a local perspective to worldwide. Web-only radio stations are now becoming extremely popular as well.

Web radio is interactive and global, and it creates a superior, engaging experience allowing heightened communication with users and listeners. Advertising in this case can be extremely effective because it allows oratory discourse and online banner ads as well as content to be presented simultaneously. A majority of your income will come through advertising opportunities on your site and audio broadcast.

SKILLS NEEDED

You will need experience in radio and the technological requirements associated with various media communications. Having clear and concise oral and written communication skills is important, and you should be able to update the Web site, so basic Web publishing skills are needed.

COST TO START THIS BUSINESS

Your initial setup costs will include a personal computer and hardware to broadcast the show on the air and over the Web. Investigate the appropriate software programs that Web radio disk jockeys currently use. You will also need to pay for the design, development, and hosting of your Web site. Remember, sending quality streaming audio over the Internet requires a significant amount of bandwidth. The cost to set up and run this type of business ranges from $3,500 to $20,000. If you already have a computer, then deduct from the amount accordingly.

NUMBER OF EMPLOYEES NEEDED TO START
This business can easily be started with one part-time individual.

INTERNATIONAL POTENTIAL
The international reach of this business is dependent on language and the genre of music or popular discussion featured on your radio station. People all over the world will be able to hear you in real-time audio, and how broad your audience is globally will be dictated by the international appeal of your content. Always remember that content is king on the Internet.

E-BUSINESS MODEL/PAYMENT PROCESSING METHOD
E-business level 1 is most appropriate for this type of business. For more information, see Part 1.

IMPORTANT BUSINESS ISSUES TO BE ADDRESSED
Web radio is heavily dependent on advancements in audio file transfer and compression technology.

While constructing your business plan, make sure to consider the evolution of your Web radio station by programming and designing the site so that you can adapt to changes in the future that could optimize your business. For example, you could implement banner ads that are programmed to relate to the song currently playing or advertisement prompts. Your primary source of revenue is advertising, so make sure that your site delivers a superior and engaging marketing opportunity that integrates visual, content, and audio penetration for each advertiser.

Interact with listeners in real time through chat and e-mail so that they appreciate the tangible quality of the Web radio combined medium.

ONLINE MARKETING TECHNIQUES

- Develop a comprehensive link strategy. Negotiating and reciprocating links from other, related sites is an excellent way to bring targeted business to your Web site. You will want to be linked from sites that cater to your target market. Establish links from Web radio directories and meta-indexes as well as music and entertainment sites.

- Develop a sponsored listings campaign to bid on appropriate keyword phrases with the popular search engines.

- You might also consider using a viral marketing technique like "Tell a Friend about This Web Radio Site." This will allow your listeners to refer your site to their friends.

- Have *constant* promotional activities happening, like contests, raffles, and games.

- Get your site mentioned in e-zines and online publications that are likely to be frequented by your target market. There are many online entertainment magazines.

For a more detailed description of these techniques, along with many other effective online marketing methods I recommend the companion book *101 Ways to Promote Your Web Site*. You can also find tons of free resources at *http://www.susansweeney.com/resources.html*.

ADDITIONAL INCOME

Additional income can come from profiling new artists and their music. You could publish an associated e-zine in which you include articles about the specific genre of music and related news. There is also opportunity to become a reseller or affiliate site for suppliers of products and services that would interest the listeners who frequent your Web radio site. For example, while playing a particular artist's song, you could have your site display their CD with the option to "Click here to buy now."

ONLINE EXAMPLES

Web Talk Radio Show
http://www.webtalkradio.com
Listen to the Web talk guys, formerly on CNET Radio—interesting talk radio and podcasting (Figure 2.18).

Live 365.com Web Radio
http://www.live365.com/index.live
A large web radio broadcaster, offering thousands of stations to listen to.

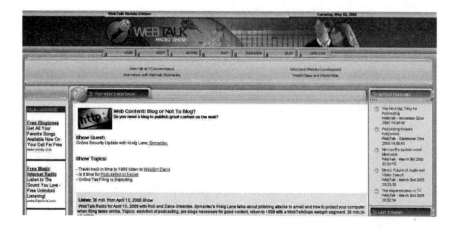

Figure 2.18. Webtalkradio.com offers a large variety of Web radio stations to its visitors.

98. Web Site Review

OVERVIEW OF BUSINESS MODEL

Having a company Web site is a fact of life in the business community today, but what good is having a Web site if no one can find it or if it doesn't meet the expectations of your target market?

Many companies are actively seeking the knowledge of other individuals to evaluate their corporate Web sites. This presents you with an opportunity to launch a business to meet their needs. You can offer your services to perform in-depth Web site analyses. The formal report you hand over to the client should contain information on whether or not the company Web site appeals to its target audience, whether or not the site is easy to use, the extent of search engine friendliness, and so on. Revenue would come directly from Web site review services rendered.

SKILLS NEEDED

A background in Web site design, knowledge of the major search engines and their ranking criteria, and experience in Internet marketing are important. The ability to communicate your observations and recommendations clearly and concisely to your client is a necessity. Your clients generally will not be familiar with the technical jargon surrounding the Internet and will look to you for advice in plain English.

COST TO START THIS BUSINESS

Your initial setup costs will include a personal computer. If you do not have an extensive background in marketing online or a basic understanding of what you need to do during the Web site design process, then you may need to invest additional money in educational materials, such as Internet marketing and Web site design books. Some companies that offer Web site reviews as a service use specific programs to perform part of the Web site analysis process (e.g., HTML review, link verification), and these software packages and services are available to you for a fee; however, this is not a necessity. You will also need to pay for the design, development, and hosting of your Web site. The cost to set up and run this type of business ranges from $3,000 to $10,000.

NUMBER OF EMPLOYEES NEEDED TO START

This business can easily be started with one part-time experienced individual.

INTERNATIONAL POTENTIAL

The international reach of this business is dependent on language. Businesses all over the world need Web site reviews conducted. This business will work well based on referrals, so if your client base has international ties, your services could be solicited from virtually anywhere.

E-BUSINESS MODEL/PAYMENT PROCESSING METHOD

E-business level 1 or 2 is most appropriate for the Web site review business. If you would like to accept payment online for your services, then level 2 makes more sense. For more information, see Part 1.

IMPORTANT BUSINESS ISSUES TO BE ADDRESSED

A Web site review is a critique, and in all critiques the client will question your reasons for having one opinion or another, so to back up all your advice in your reports, use pertinent examples. These examples may come directly from the client's Web site or, when trying to illustrate a suggestion, you may want to reference a competitor's site that is making use of what you're recommending. Remember not to dispense the information until you have collected the amount you are owed for the entire job. Once clients have your report in their possession, your job is essentially done and they no longer need you.

ONLINE MARKETING TECHNIQUES

- Develop a comprehensive link strategy. Negotiating and reciprocating links from other, related sites is an excellent way to bring targeted business to your Web site. You will want to be linked from all content sites and meta-indexes that cater to your target market.

- Develop a sponsored listings campaign to bid on appropriate keyword phrases with the popular search engines.

- You might also consider using a viral marketing technique like "Tell a Friend about This Useful Service." This will allow your clients to refer your site to their friends.

- Get your services mentioned in e-zine articles about online marketing success stories and online publications about advancements and resources within the Internet marketing industry.

For a more detailed description of these techniques, along with many other effective online marketing methods, I recommend the companion book *101 Ways to Promote Your Web Site*. You can also find tons of free resources at *http://www.susansweeney.com/resources.html*.

ADDITIONAL INCOME

Additional income can come from expanding your services to include Web site redevelopment consulting. You could also expand your business to include on-line marketing strategies. The Web site review business puts you in a perfect position to upsell your services to each individual client.

ONLINE EXAMPLES

The Forrester Web & Commerce Site Review
http://www.forrester.com/ER/Products/Advisory/WebSiteReview/.html
This operation provides clients with a targeted, action-oriented assessment of their Web site. Forrester analysts conduct a comprehensive examination of the client's site and corresponding strategies.

KillerSites.com
http://www.killersites.com/websiteReviews/websiteReviews_home.jsp
This is a great way to view a few successful Web sites.

99. Wedding Products

OVERVIEW OF BUSINESS MODEL

People take planning for a wedding seriously. There is a ton of organizing to be done and items to be bought. The many related costs for a wedding can add up, and in an effort to keep the whole lovely event within a budget that doesn't break the bank, many go online searching for the best buys available. It saves them time and money, so putting a wedding products business online is a great idea.

You can generate revenue for the wedding products Web site by selling wedding products directly from your Web site and having them gift-wrapped if need be or delivered to the correct address at the convenience of the customer. You can offer anything from invitations and wine glasses to wedding dresses and veils. You should concentrate on servicing clients within your geographic reach because this will allow you to provide a personalized service with plenty of local resources such as links to all the churches, caterers, halls, hotels, and other related services. You should include a gift registry on the site where guests can check what has already been bought for the happy couple and find suggestions of what they might like or need.

The possibilities for this business can go far if you use your imagination to explore all the services within your power to make a wedding go smoothly and make these services available online on your site!

SKILLS NEEDED

Knowledge of online promotional techniques would be an asset when operating this type of business. The wedding resources within your local area need to be researched and provided on your site. You should know the latest wedding trends and be familiar with different cultural traditions when it comes to marriage. Knowledge of wedding planning would also be a primary benefit. You will need basic Web publishing skills to update and manage your Web site.

COST TO START THIS BUSINESS

If you launch this type of business, you will initially have to pay for the development, design, and hosting of your Web site, computer hardware, computer software, a scanner, a printer, and possibly a digital camera. You will also have to pay for the electronic storefront. This enables you to easily display and sell your wedding paraphernalia. Other costs that you will incur are related to the promotion of your Web site. Estimated cost is $5,000 to $20,000 to start.

NUMBER OF EMPLOYEES NEEDED

One person with wedding product, planning, and organization experience can operate this business at the outset. If you acquire a significant client base and save people money, your business will grow from referrals, so you may want to hire an assistant later on to manage orders and distribution.

INTERNATIONAL POTENTIAL

This business has low international potential. If you are selling wedding products online, chances are the customers will want to do business with someone in the area, and the reason they choose to do it online will be for convenience and discounted pricing.

E-BUSINESS MODEL/PAYMENT PROCESSING METHOD

E-business level 2 or 3 would be most appropriate for this type of business. For more information, see Part 1.

IMPORTANT BUSINESS ISSUES TO BE ADDRESSED

The site must be kept current. When items are discontinued or are out of stock, this must be updated on the Web site. Since you are promoting your products to an online audience, it is extremely important for you to generate as much traffic as possible to your site. There are multiple ways for you to do this; however, it is essential that you allocate a significant amount of time to online promotion of the site.

ONLINE MARKETING TECHNIQUES

- Developing a comprehensive affiliate/associate program would not only increase the awareness of your wedding product site, it would also send referral business to your site.

- Launching a strategic banner advertising campaign on Web sites frequented by your target market would be a great way to increase traffic to your site. Sites that you could place banner ads on include family-oriented sites and noncompeting wedding-related sites. Sites targeted toward party or event planning and sites that particularly target females would also be appropriate.

- You could hold a weekly or monthly contest on your site for a free wedding product. You could ask people if they would like to be notified of the winner via e-mail. This would encourage them to return to your site and re-enter your contest, thus re-exposing them to your wedding products.

- Develop as many links as possible from Web sites, directories, and meta-indexes frequented by your target market. There are thousands of wedding-related Web sites online. These are the sites that your target market will visit if they are planning a wedding; thus it is extremely important that your site generate links from these sites.

- You could develop a Featured Product page on your site. You could change this product every week. People will continue to return to your site to see what the featured product is. You could even ask people if they would like to be notified of your featured product via e-mail. This would be a great way to encourage repeat traffic.

- Optimize your site for organic search engine placement.

- Develop a sponsored listings campaign to bid on appropriate keyword phrases with the popular search engines.

- Develop a wedding registry on your site so brides can inform their wedding guests, via your site, about their preferred gifts. This will increase traffic to your site.

- Develop a viral marketing strategy where people can "Tell a Friend about This Product" via a link on your site. This will spread the word about your site.

For a more detailed description of these techniques, along with many other effective online marketing methods, I recommend the companion book *101 Ways to Promote Your Web Site*. You can also find tons of free resources at *http://www.susansweeney.com/resources.html*.

ADDITIONAL INCOME

You can earn additional income by setting up a referral service with wedding-related businesses such as limousine drivers, DJs, and caterers. If you promote their services on your Web site and they receive business because of it, you can collect referral fees from each person or business that provides their products or services and generates revenue.

Figure 2.19. Wedding Star is a dynamite online wedding planning and gift registry Web site.

ONLINE EXAMPLES

Wedding Star
http://www.weddingstar.com
Wedding Star (Figure 2.19) provides a large database of wedding-related products and services excellent for helping families and friends organize a wedding.

WedNet
http://www.wednet.com
This site is the ultimate resource for planning a successful wedding. Their in-depth database of wedding vendors can help everyone throw a beautiful and successful wedding.

100. Weight Loss Service

OVERVIEW OF BUSINESS MODEL
Weight is an issue for millions of people all over North America. The condition is so widespread that some health professionals have named it an epidemic or

disease. Being overweight is a source of shame for many, and often people feel helpless and not in control of their own bodies. This sounds morbid, but the good news is that it's curable through proper eating habits and exercise.

The advantages of providing a weight loss coaching and resource center on the Internet is that anyone with online access can get help; people do not need to leave their home or take time out from work, but they can consult your Web site 24/7 for most of the information they seek. Also, they can get consulting in private and spare themselves the sometimes embarrassing experience of attending walk-in clinics.

The site should answer many questions that people who want to lose weight need answers to. The content should be motivational and realistic. Your clients who experience success should be featured on the site and mentor others by sharing their strengths and stories of how they gathered the will power to get their weight under control and stay that way.

The way to earn revenue in this business is by charging a fee for one-on-one and group consulting and regime planning, which can happen in various ways online such as e-mail, chat, voice chat, real-time audio, and real-time video sessions. Other ways of consulting are telephone and face-to-face for clients within your geographic reach.

Another way to gain revenue in this business is by joining affiliate programs for weight loss-related products such as fitness wear, books, videos, motivational tapes, exercise equipment, and health foods.

SKILLS NEEDED

To successfully operate a weight loss resource and consulting business online, you should have some credentials as a personal trainer, dietician, health and wellness advisor, or fitness instructor of some kind. You should be active and healthy in your own lifestyle. It could help if you had a personal story of weight loss so that your clients are comfortable with your advice because it comes from experience. You will need clear communication skills and basic Web publishing skills to communicate clearly with your customers and update your Web site.

COST TO START THIS BUSINESS

The cost to initially set up a weight loss center will range from $5,000 to $15,000. These costs include a computer, appropriate software, and a printer. You will need an imaging program such as Adobe Photoshop, and it would help to have a digital camera or scanner so you can put before, after, and "in the process" images on the personalized pages to display the progress and motivate your clients. You will also have to have your Web site designed, developed, and hosted. Other initial costs to consider relate to the advertising of your Web site.

NUMBER OF EMPLOYEES NEEDED TO START

It is possible to run this business with one qualified person, and in the beginning this can be operated on a part-time basis while you keep your regular job.

INTERNATIONAL POTENTIAL

Through your Web site you are providing online counseling and information. Your business will exist primarily in the domain of cyberspace. For many people in today's busy world, the Internet is a new private and anonymous place to access personal services that have never before been available in such a convenient medium. Some clients may prefer to have a weight loss consultant who lives in their geographic area, and some may not care if they know you face-to-face or not. The language barrier is one obstacle to consider if you are interested in running a truly international business; however, there are translation services available to you. If you are selling books, equipment, or medical products, then shipping and tariffs will limit your distribution to an extent.

E-BUSINESS MODEL/PAYMENT PROCESSING METHOD

Depending on what your services are and how many clients you have, the e-business model you choose can upgrade from level 1 to 2 or 3 as the business grows. You may accept payment in the form of check or money order at the outset because you will have a one-on-one relationship with each customer, so the experience will be quite personalized and the need for online credit card payment is not necessary. The option to join affiliate programs and therefore avoid e-store management and simply gain commissions from those sales is also available. If you decide to sell products from your site, you may choose to move to an online storefront and level 3. For more information, see Part 1.

IMPORTANT BUSINESS ISSUES TO BE ADDRESSED

Fierce competition can be expected from bricks-and-mortar operations such as Weight Watchers and Jenny Craig that have established an international presence in the weight loss field. Fortunately, their Web sites are simply marketing and communication outlets to back up their physical locations.

Remember that weight loss consultation is a pseudomedical field, so please do not attempt this business unless you are qualified to provide this kind of advice. The signs you must be aware of are of a serious nature. For example, people could get sick if they lose too much weight too quickly, or they could be diabetic or need emotional counseling due to an eating disorder. Everyone does not lose weight at the same pace or in the same way. You should have a thorough questionnaire and legal agreement for your clients to sign so both of you are protected and understand each other.

Your pricing should be competitive and reflective of the amount of time you dedicate to each customer's individual counseling sessions.

ONLINE MARKETING TECHNIQUES

- Write articles communicating your theories about effective weight loss plans throughout advice columns in weight loss- or health-related e-zines, newsletters, and newsgroups.

- Develop a sponsored listings campaign to bid on appropriate keyword phrases with the popular search engines.

- Get linked from online advertising directories.

- Create a mail list and send out your newsletter or e-zine about weight loss tips, breaking news, and low-calorie recipes for people to try.

- Develop a comprehensive and rewarding permission marketing strategy whereby clients can easily tell a friend about your services and in return receive a discount on a product being sold from or recommended by your site.

For a more detailed description of these techniques, along with many other effective online marketing methods, I recommend the companion book *101 Ways to Promote Your Web Site.* You can also find tons of free resources at *http://www.susansweeney.com/resources.html.*

ADDITIONAL INCOME

Extra income can come from targeted banner advertising if your traffic is high. One way to ensure this is by providing plenty of resources and content on your site for users, making them stick around on your pages and providing more time for banner impressions and rotations.

Another facet for extra income is providing personal training and coaching to customers in your local area. Finally, if you are good with slogans, you could sell motivational T-shirts or other customized items.

ONLINE EXAMPLES

Total Body Fitness
http://www.tbfinc.com
A weight loss consultant for men and women based in Houston, Texas, who provides consulting for anyone through her Web site.

Herbal Life Independent Distributors
http://www.loseit.com
This site sells Herbalife weight loss pills.

101. Who's Who Directory

OVERVIEW OF BUSINESS

Prestige and honor are things everyone likes to have, no matter what walk of life they come from. You can start a Who's Who directory on the Internet to recognize those individuals who have accomplished much with their careers and in their community. There are many Who's Who directories already on the Internet. Some focus on individual communities; others focus on people who have high achievements in a particular industry.

How does this business generate revenue? It's simple. When individuals visit your Web site and see the prestige that others have received from being listed on your site, they will be willing to pay to be listed also. If you host an industry-specific Who's Who directory, you would be surprised how many industry professionals will contact you to be listed on your site. You obviously wouldn't charge an obscene price for a listing on your site. Most Who's Who directories charge anywhere from $10 to $100 for a listing.

Your Who's Who listings could include the individuals' names, their achievements, and where they are from. You could then charge an additional fee to list in-depth biographies on the individuals, photographs, links to personal or business Web sites, and previous awards and recognitions that the individuals have received.

SKILLS NEEDED

Since this type of business requires that your site receive a high number of Web site visitors, knowledge of online marketing techniques would be an asset. If you are targeting individuals in a particular industry, it would be an asset to possess knowledge of the industry and what is involved in being successful in that particular industry.

COST TO START THIS BUSINESS

Initially you will have to pay for the development, design, and hosting of your Web site, computer hardware, computer software, a scanner (to scan your clients' photographs if they don't have a digital copy), and a printer. If you currently have some of these items, your initial start-up costs will be considerably lower. If you plan to set up a mailing list for your Who's Who site, you will have to purchase mailing list software to help you organize and maintain it. Other costs that you will incur are related to the promotion of your Web site. Estimated cost is $3,000 to $10,000 to start.

NUMBER OF EMPLOYEES NEEDED TO START

This type of business requires approximately one part-time employee. This business is one that can be worked on in the evenings. You could fulfill all requests during the evenings and communicate with potential clients via e-mail; thus you don't have to worry about being in an office.

INTERNATIONAL POTENTIAL

This business has strong international potential, particularly if you target the Who's Who of a specific industry.

E-BUSINESS MODEL/PAYMENT PROCESSING METHOD

E-business level 1 would be most appropriate for this type of business. For more information on this, see Part 1.

IMPORTANT BUSINESS ISSUES TO BE ADDRESSED

If you are trying to keep your Who's Who directory extremely elite, make sure you don't let members pay to join who are not remotely qualified to be on the list. If you let just anyone pay to join your directory, your site will become saturated with people who are not worthy of being listed. This could discourage some industry professionals from purchasing listings on your site.

Since the success of your Who's Who directory relies heavily on the number of Web site visitors that you receive, you will have to dedicate a significant amount of time to the online promotion of your site. You should participate in as many different online marketing media as possible to promote your site.

ONLINE MARKETING TECHNIQUES

- Participating in newsgroups and discussion forums related to your target market would be a great way to generate traffic to your Web site. If you are targeting specific industries, you could participate in newsgroups related to those particular industries. For example, if you were targeting Internet Technology (IT) professionals, you would want to participate in newsgroups related to IT.

- You should develop a newsletter that can be distributed weekly or monthly that will update visitors about new additions to your Web site, specials, and news about your Who's Who directory.

- You can ask people if they would like to be notified via e-mail whenever a new listing is added to your site. This would be a great way to encourage repeat traffic to your Web site.

- You could have a Featured Listing section on your site, where you choose a particular person who you feel has excelled in his or her field. People will return to your site constantly to see who is the new featured listing. Again, you could ask people if they would like to be notified via e-mail when you make updates to your Featured Listings page. This will remind them to return to your site to see who is listed.

- Develop a sponsored listings campaign to bid on appropriate keyword phrases with the popular search engines.

- Develop as many links as possible from Web sites, directories, and meta-indexes related to your target market. There are hundreds of Who's Who directories and meta-indexes on the Internet that would be appropriate for your site. This would generate targeted exposure for your online business.

For a more detailed description of these techniques, along with many other effective online marketing methods, I recommend the companion book *101 Ways to Promote Your Web Site*. You can also find tons of free resources at *http://www.susansweeney.com/resources.html*.

ADDITIONAL INCOME

An additional way to generate revenue for your Who's Who site is to sell annual or quarterly publications of your Who's Who listings. This would be of interest to many industry professionals who are researching competitors or are simply interested in finding out more about what's happening in their industry.

ONLINE EXAMPLES

Marquis Who's Who on the Web
http://search.marquiswhoswho.com/executable/login.aspx
This is a dynamite Who's Who directory that includes over 1.3 million leaders and archives.

Who's Who on the Web
http://vl.fmnet.info/whos-who
An Internet directory featuring "The Best of the Web" of people involved in various catagories. Basic listings on this site are free.

About the Author

Susan Sweeney, CA, CSP

Susan Sweeney, CA, CSP, renowned industry expert, consultant, and speaker, tailors lively keynote speeches and full- and half-day seminars and workshops for companies, industries, and associations interested in improving their Internet presence and increasing their Web site traffic and sales.

Susan is a partner of Verb Interactive (*www.verbinteractive.com*), an international Internet marketing and consulting firm. She is also president of Connex Network Incorporated and SusanSweeney.com.

Susan holds both the Chartered Accountant and Certified Speaking Professional designations. She is an experienced Internet marketing professional with a background in computers, marketing, and the Internet.

Susan is the author of several books on Internet marketing and e-business: *101 Ways To Promote Your Web Site, Internet Marketing for Your Tourism Business, 3G Marketing on the Internet, Going for Gold, 101 Internet Businesses You Can Start from Home,* and *The e-Business Formula for Success.*

She is also the developer of a two-day intensive Internet Marketing Boot Camp. Susan offers many Web-based teleseminars, seminars on CD, and e-books related to Internet marketing.

Susan is a member of the Board of Directors of the Canadian Association of Professional Speakers, and is a member of the National Speakers Association and the International Federation for Professional Speakers. Susan holds her Certified Professional Speakers designation which is the only earned designation for professional speakers. Less than 10 percent of professional speakers hold this professional designation.

Verb Interactive is a marketing firm that provides Internet and international marketing consulting and training services to industry and government. Their clients range in size from single-person startup operations to multi-million-dollar international firms. Their primary services include Internet marketing workshops, Web site design and development, Internet marketing strategies, Web site report cards, Internet marketing consulting, market research, and competitive analysis.

SusanSweeney.com is Susan's speaking and training business. During her workshops and training sessions, she ensures that her clients have a complete understanding of the principles involved with developing a strong online presence.

The team of Internet marketing analysts at Verb Interactive is highly trained in the area of Internet marketing, and all stay up-to-date with the latest technological advancements and industry trends in the online marketing world. Every person on the team has extensive practical hands-on experience and the necessary skills to use proven tips, tools, and techniques to generate high volumes of traffic to your site.

As a result of technological change and global competitiveness, a strong Internet presence is essential. Susan instructs individuals with her enthusiastic personality combined with her vast hands-on international marketing experience, which keeps her listeners informed and captivated. Let Susan help you increase your traffic and make your business prosper!

Susan Sweeney, CA, CSP
75 Brentwood Drive
Bedford, Nova Scotia, Canada B4A 3S2
Phone: 902/468-2578; Fax: 902/468-0380
www.susansweeney.com
www.verbinteractive.com
susan@susansweeney.com

Index

Reader Feedback Sheet

Your comments and suggestions are very important in shaping future publications. Please e-mail us at *moreinfo@maxpress.com* or photocopy this page, jot down your thoughts, and fax it to (850) 934-9981 or mail it to:

Maximum Press
Attn: Jim Hoskins
605 Silverthorn Road
Gulf Breeze, FL 32561

_____
_____
_____
_____
_____
_____
_____
_____
_____
_____
_____
_____
_____
_____
_____
_____
_____
_____
_____

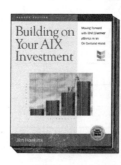

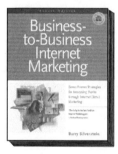